Lecture Notes in Information Systems and Organisation

Volume 4

Series Editors

Richard Baskerville
Marco De Marco
Nancy Pouloudi
Paolo Spagnoletti
Dov Te'eni
Jan vom Brocke
Robert Winter

For further volumes:
http://www.springer.com/series/11237

Felix Piazolo · Michael Felderer
Editors

Innovation and Future of Enterprise Information Systems

ERP Future 2012 Conference, Salzburg, Austria, November 2012, Revised Papers

 Springer

Editors
Felix Piazolo
Department of Strategic Management,
  Marketing and Tourism
University of Innsbruck
Innsbruck
Austria

Michael Felderer
Institute of Computer Science
University of Innsbruck
Innsbruck
Austria

ISSN 2195-4968
ISBN 978-3-642-37020-5
DOI 10.1007/978-3-642-37021-2
Springer Heidelberg New York Dordrecht London

ISSN 2195-4976 (electronic)
ISBN 978-3-642-37021-2 (eBook)

Library of Congress Control Number: 2013934274

© Springer-Verlag Berlin Heidelberg 2013

This work is subject to copyright. All rights are reserved by the Publisher, whether the whole or part of the material is concerned, specifically the rights of translation, reprinting, reuse of illustrations, recitation, broadcasting, reproduction on microfilms or in any other physical way, and transmission or information storage and retrieval, electronic adaptation, computer software, or by similar or dissimilar methodology now known or hereafter developed. Exempted from this legal reservation are brief excerpts in connection with reviews or scholarly analysis or material supplied specifically for the purpose of being entered and executed on a computer system, for exclusive use by the purchaser of the work. Duplication of this publication or parts thereof is permitted only under the provisions of the Copyright Law of the Publisher's location, in its current version, and permission for use must always be obtained from Springer. Permissions for use may be obtained through RightsLink at the Copyright Clearance Center. Violations are liable to prosecution under the respective Copyright Law.
The use of general descriptive names, registered names, trademarks, service marks, etc. in this publication does not imply, even in the absence of a specific statement, that such names are exempt from the relevant protective laws and regulations and therefore free for general use.
While the advice and information in this book are believed to be true and accurate at the date of publication, neither the authors nor the editors nor the publisher can accept any legal responsibility for any errors or omissions that may be made. The publisher makes no warranty, express or implied, with respect to the material contained herein.

Printed on acid-free paper

Springer is part of Springer Science+Business Media (www.springer.com)

Program Committee

Rogerio Atem de Carvalho	State University of Norte Fluminense Darcy Ribeiro
Josef Bernhart	European Academy of Bozen/Bolzano
Goetz Botterweck	University of Limerick–Lero
Ruth Breu	University of Innsbruck
Jörg Courant	HTW University of Applied Sciences Berlin
Michael Felderer	University of Innsbruck
Kerstin Fink	University of Applied Sciences Salzburg
Kai Fischbach	University of Bamberg
Hans H. Hinterhuber	University of Innsbruck
David Meyer	University of Applied Sciences Technikum Wien
Felix Piazolo	University of Innsbruck
Kurt Promberger	University of Innsbruck
Irene Barba Rodriguez	University of Seville
Friedrich Roithmayr	Johannes Kepler University of Linz
Stéphane S. Somé	University of Ottawa
Victoria Torres Bosch	Polytechnic University of Valencia
Alfred Taudes	Vienna University of Economics and Business

Sponsored by

COMARCH

Contents

ERP Future 2012 1
Felix Piazolo and Michael Felderer

Part I ERP Future

The Future of ERP: A Critical Outlook 9
Helmut Guembel

Lean ERP: How ERP Systems and Lean Management
Fit Together 13
Martin Adam, Johannes Keckeis, Peter Kostenzer and Heiner Klepzig

Social Content Management Systems: Challenges and Potential
for Organizations 19
Andrea Herbst and Jan vom Brocke

Part II ERP Planning Requirements

ERP-Planning Garbage: Realizing and Preventing 31
Karlheinz Haberlandt

Enterprise Resource Planning Requirements Process:
The Need for Semantic Verification 53
Peter Bollen

Part III Human Interaction with ERP Systems

ERP Clients: Browser-Based or Dedicated: Do We Need
Both?—An Evaluation Based on User Perceptions 71
Christian Leyh and Walter Heger

**Critical Success Factors of e-Learning Scenarios
for ERP End-User Training** 87
Lukas Paa and Nesrin Ates

Part IV ERP Implementation and Integration

**Does Predefined ERP Implementation Methodology Work
for Public Companies in Transitioning Country?** 103
Adnan Kraljić, Denis Delismajlović and Tarik Kraljić

**A Team-Oriented Investigation of ERP Post-Implementation
Integration Projects: How Cross-Functional Collaboration
Influences ERP Benefits**.. 115
Daphne Rich and Jens Dibbern

Part V ERP Landscape

**Analysis Pattern for the Transformation of ERP System
Landscapes by SaaS** 131
Kurt Porkert and Howard Sutton

Part VI ERP: Cost-Benefit Analysis

Automated Testing of ERP GUI: A Cost-Benefit Analysis.......... 143
Johannes Keckeis, Jan-Peter Eberle, Kurt Promberger and Pascal Erhart

**Utilizing Enterprise Resource Planning
in Decision-Making Processes** 153
Bahram Bahrami and Ernest Jordan

Part VII Critical Success Factors

**Flexibility and Improved Resource Utilization Through Cloud
Based ERP Systems: Critical Success Factors
of SaaS Solutions in SME** 171
Ariane Gerhardter and Wolfgang Ortner

**Analysis of the Critical Success Factors for ERP Systems
Implementation in U.S. Federal Offices** 183
Asmamaw A. Mengistie, Dennis P. Heaton and Maxwell Rainforth

Contents

Part VIII Business Process

Towards a Framework and Platform for Mobile, Distributed Workflow Enactment Services on a Possible Future of ERP Infrastructure 201
Dagmar Auer, Dirk Draheim, Verena Geist, Theodorich Kopetzky, Josef Küng and Christine Natschläger

Part IX Quality of ERP Systems

A Business View on Testing ERP Systems with Value-Based Requirements Coverage 219
Rudolf Ramler, Theodorich Kopetzky and Wolfgang Platz

A Quality Analysis Procedure for Request Data of ERP Systems 235
Michael Felderer, Emir Tanriverdi, Sarah Löw and Ruth Breu

Part X Implementation of Innovative Business Concepts

How to Consider Supply Uncertainty of Renewable Resources in the Basic Data Structures of ERP-Systems 253
Stefan Friedemann and Matthias Schumann

Towards Total Budgeting and the Interactive Budget Warehouse 271
Dirk Draheim

Part XI Selection and Customization

Customization of On-Demand ERP Software Using SAP Business ByDesign as an Example 289
Karl Kurbel and Dawid Nowak

Index 299

Contributors

Martin Adam University of Applied Sciences Kufstein, Kufstein, Austria, e-mail: martin.adam@fh-kufstein.ac.at

Nesrin Ates University of Innsbruck, Innsbruck, Austria, e-mail: nesrin.ates@uibk.ac.at

Dagmar Auer FAW University of Linz, Linz, Austria, e-mail: dagmar.auer@faw.uni-linz.ac.at

Bahram Bahrami Macquarie University, Sydney, Australia, e-mail: m.j.bahrami@gmail.com

Peter Bollen Maastricht University, Maastricht, Netherlands, e-mail: p.bollen@maastrichtuniversity.nl

Ruth Breu University of Innsbruck, Innsbruck, Austria, e-mail: ruth.breu@uibk.ac.at

Denis Delismajlović University of Zenica, Zenica, Bosnia and Herzegovina, e-mail: denisdelismalovic@gmail.com

Jens Dibbern University of Berne, Berne, Switzerland, e-mail: jens.dibbern@iwi.unibe.ch

Dirk Draheim University of Innsbruck, Innsbruck, Austria, e-mail: draheim@acm.org

Jan-Peter Eberle University of Innsbruck, Innsbruck, Austria, e-mail: jan-peter.eberle@uibk.ac.at

Pascal Erhart University of Innsbruck, Innsbruck, Austria, e-mail: pascal.erhart@uibk.ac.at

Michael Felderer University of Innsbruck, Innsbruck, Austria, e-mail: michael.felderer@uibk.ac.at

Stefan Friedemann University of Göttingen, Göttingen, Germany, e-mail: stefan.friedemann@wiwi.uni-goettingen.de

Verena Geist Software Competence Center Hagenberg, Hagenberg im Mühlkreis, Austria, e-mail: verena.geist@scch.at

Ariane Gerhardter FH Joanneum University of Applied Sciences, Graz, Austria, e-mail: ariane.gerhardter@gmx.at

Helmut Guembel Strategy Partners International, Scuol, Switzerland, e-mail: helmuth.guembel@strategypartners.com

Karlheinz Ludwig Haberlandt Heilbronn University, Heilbronn, Germany, e-mail: karlheinz.haberlandt@hs-heilbronn.de

Dennis Heaton Maharishi University of Management, Fairfield, USA, e-mail: dheaton@mum.edu

Walter Heger Dresden University of Technology, Dresden, Germany, e-mail: walter.heger@tu-dresden.de

Andrea Herbst University of Liechtenstein, Vaduz, Liechtenstein, e-mail: andrea.herbst@uni.li

Ernest Jordan Macquarie University, Sydney, Australia, e-mail: gpt@mq.edu.au

Johannes Keckeis University of Innsbruck, Innsbruck, Austria, e-mail: johannes.keckeis@uibk.ac.at

Heiner Klepzig University of Innsbruck, Innsbruck, Austria, e-mail: heiner.klepzig@uibk.ac.at

Theodorich Kopetzky Software Competence Center Hagenberg, Hagenberg im Mühlkreis, Austria, e-mail: theodorich.kopetzky@scch.at

Peter Kostenzer University of Applied Sciences Kufstein, Kufstein, Austria, e-mail: peter.kostenzer@fh-kufstein.ac.at

Adnan Kraljić International Burch University Sarajevo, Sarajevo, Bosnia and Herzegovina, e-mail: akralic@ibu.edu.ba

Tarik Kraljić International Burch University Sarajevo, Sarajevo, Bosnia and Herzegovina, e-mail: tkraljic@ibu.edu.ba

Karl Kurbel European University Viadrina Frankfurt, Frankfurt (Oder), Germany, e-mail: wi-sek@europa-uni.de

Josef Küng FAW University of Linz, Linz, Austria, e-mail: jkueng@faw.uni-linz.ac.at

Christian Leyh Dresden University of Technology, Dresden, Germany, e-mail: christian.leyh@tu-dresden.de

Sarah Löw University of Innsbruck, Innsbruck, Austria, e-mail: sarah.loew@uibk.ac.at

Contributors

Asmamaw A. Mengistie Maharishi University of Management, Fairfield, USA, e-mail: asmamawa@gmail.com

Christine Natschläger Software Competence Center Hagenberg, Hagenberg im Mühlkreis, Austria, e-mail: christine.natschlaeger@scch.at

Dawid Nowak European University Viadrina Frankfurt, Frankfurt (Oder), Germany, e-mail: wi-sek@europa-uni.de

Wolfgang Ortner FH Joanneum University of Applied Sciences, Graz, Austria, e-mail: wolfgang.ortner@fh-joanneum.at

Lukas Paa University of Innsbruck, Innsbruck, Austria, e-mail: lukas.paa@uibk.ac.at

Felix Piazolo University of Innsbruck, Innsbruck, Austria, e-mail: felix.piazolo@uibk.ac.at

Wolfgang Platz TRICENTIS Technology & Consulting GmbH, Vienna, Austria, e-mail: w.platz@tricentis.com

Kurt Porkert Pforzheim University of Applied Sciences Business School, Pforzheim, Germany, e-mail: kurt.porkert@hs-pforzheim.de

Kurt Promberger University of Innsbruck, Innsbruck, Austria, e-mail: kurt.promberger@uibk.ac.at

Maxwell Rainforth Maharishi University of Management, Fairfield, USA, e-mail: rainforth@mum.edu

Rudolf Ramler Software Cometence Center Hagenberg, Hagenberg im Mühlkreis, Austria, e-mail: rudolf.ramler@scch.at

Daphne Rich University of Berne, Berne, Switzerland, e-mail: daphne.rich@iwi.unibe.ch

Matthias Schumann University of Göttingen, Göttingen, Germany, e-mail: matthias.schumann@wiwi.uni-goettingen.de

Howard Sutton Pforzheim University of Applied Sciences Business School, Pforzheim, Germany, e-mail: howard.sutton@hs-pforzheim.de

Emir Tanriverdi University of Innsbruck, Innsbruck, Austria, e-mail: emir.tanriverdi@uibk.ac.at

Jan vom Brocke University of Liechtenstein, Vaduz, Liechtenstein, e-mail: jan.vom.brocke@uni.li

Editors Biography

Felix Piazolo is Postdoc Researcher at the Department of Strategic Management, Marketing and Tourism at the University of Innsbruck and lecturer at diverse universities in the areas of strategic management, enterprise information systems and innovation processes (including AAL projects). He has studied at the University of Innsbruck, University of St. Gallen and the University of Granada and holds a Ph.D. as well as a master's degree in Business Economics. Being responsible for several national and international research projects in these fields, he additionally provides business consulting services for companies.

Michael Felderer is a Research Associate at the Institute of Computer Science at the University of Innsbruck, Austria. He holds a Ph.D. and a master's degree in Computer Science. His research interests are software testing, software quality engineering, requirements engineering and ERP systems. Michael Felderer leads several research projects. Additionally, he transfers his research results into practice as consultant and speaker on industrial conferences.

ERP Future 2012

Felix Piazolo and Michael Felderer

Abstract This is the introduction of the ERP Future 2012 Research Conference proceedings. It provides a short motivation and an overview of the topics covered by the conference.

Todays distributed business processes cannot be managed efficiently without the use of information technology. In particular, enterprise resource planning (ERP) systems have significantly increased the profitability, productivity and competitiveness of corporations by removing the barriers to sharing information between functional areas and managing processes holistically. The key driver for this productivity and efficiency is the ability of modern ERP systems to manage business processes from beginning to end in an integrated, consistent and highly effective manner. But ERP systems are very complex information systems and the business as well as the technical environment is steadily evolving. Therefore innovations in business and IT resulting in suitable implementations have to be developed, adopted and evaluated to profit from the benefits of ERP systems permanently. According to the customer needs and influences of the rapidly changing business and technological environment the paradigm for ERP systems in general will change in the future.

Actual trends in ERP include without limitation software as a service (SaaS), cloud services in general, mobile solutions, ERP for small and medium sized enterprises (SME), open source and freeware solutions, e-learning support, social media integration, efficient and effective quality management and planning methods as well as techniques and criteria for the selection and evaluation process. The decision whether and how to take these trends into account has to be supported by scientifically evaluated studies. To provide a realistic result, such studies

---

F. Piazolo (✉) · M. Felderer
University of Innsbruck, Innsbruck, Austria
e-mail: felix.piazolo@uibk.ac.at

M. Felderer
e-mail: michael.felderer@uibk.ac.at

have to consider business and IT aspects. For instance, software as a service, i.e. on-demand software hosted on the cloud, comprises business challenges like total cost of ownership or ERP for SME as well as technical challenges like application integration or IT-security.

The ERP Future 2012 Research conference is a platform for research in ERP systems and closely related topics like business processes, business intelligence, and enterprise information systems in general. To master the challenges of ERP comprehensively, the ERP Future 2012 Research conference accepted contributions with a business as well as an IT focus to consider enterprise resource planning from various viewpoints. This combination of business and IT aspects is a unique characteristic of the conference that resulted in several valuable contributions with high practical impact. Revised versions of these conference contributions are collected in the present proceedings of the ERP Future 2012 Research conference entitled "Innovation and Future of Enterprise Information Systems".

A critical outlook regarding the future of ERP is given by the initial keynote speaker [1]. Two contribution related to keynotes discuss on how ERP systems and Lean Management methods fit together [2] and the challenges and potentials for organizations realized by Social Content Management Systems (SCMS) [3].

Understanding critical factors for successful implementation of ERP systems is essential for organizations. On the one hand, critical success factors of SaaS in SME are investigated [4]. On the other hand, critical success factors of implementation projects in U.S. federal offices are analyzed by a survey [5]. Additionally it is investigated, whether predefined ERP implementation methodology works for public companies in transitioning countries [6] and how cross-functional collaboration influences ERP benefits in ERP post-implementation integration projects [7].

Innovative business concepts require suitable implementations in ERP systems. In this context, the consideration of supply uncertainty of renewable resources in the basic data structures of ERP systems [8] as well as total budgeting and the interactive budget warehouse are presented [9].

ERP planning requirements are looked at by two contributions. One addresses the ERP planning garbage and how to prevent it in the manufacturing industry [10], and the other evaluates the need of semantic verification in planning requirements in general [11].

For taking the business perspective in testing ERP systems into account value-based requirements coverage [12] and a cost-benefit analysis for automated testing of ERP GUIs are proposed [13]. Additionally, one contribution presents a quality analysis procedure for request data of ERP systems that is applied in an industrial case study [14].

As SaaS is a major trend influencing the ERP market the analysis pattern for the transformation of ERP system landscapes by SaaS [15] and the customization of on-demand ERP software for SMEs [16] are discussed. To manage business processes, one contribution presents a platform for mobile, distributed workflow enactment services [17].

Looking at the human interaction with ERP systems, it is evaluated based on user perceptions whether a browser-based or a dedicated ERP client is needed [18] and what the critical success factors for e-learning as an end-user training method are [19].

Finally, to what extent ERP is utilized and suitable for decision making is also presented [20].

We thank all authors for their contributions. We hope that the contributions are interesting for the reader and valuable for the scientific community as well as for industrial application.

Special thanks go to Kerstin Fink, rector of the Salzburg University of Applied Sciences, and her team for their commitment and cooperativeness to host the ERP Future 2012 Research conference, Kurt Promberger and Christoph Weiss for initializing the ERP Future Business conferences in 2009, Ruth Breu for supporting the set-up of the first ERP Future Research conference, Comarch, Comarch Innovation Lab (CIL) and SIS Consulting as premium sponsors and last but not least all members of the ERP Future 2012 team who enabled us to organize such a very successful and valuable conference.

Thank you,

Felix Piazolo, Michael Felderer

References

1. Guembel, H.: The Future of ERP—a critical outlook. In: Piazolo, F., Felderer, M. (eds.) Innovation and Future of Enterprise Information Systems. ERP Future 2012 Research Conference Proceedings. Lecture Notes in Information Systems and Organisation, vol. 2, pp. 9–11. Springer, Berlin, Heidelberg (2013)
2. Adam, M., Keckeis, J., Klepzig, H.: Lean ERP—how ERP systems and lean management fit together. In: Piazolo, F., Felderer, M. (eds.) Innovation and Future of Enterprise Information Systems. ERP Future 2012 Research Conference Proceedings. Lecture Notes in Information Systems and Organisation, vol. 2, pp. 13–18. Springer, Berlin, Heidelberg, (2013)
3. Herbst, A., vom Brocke, J.: Social content management systems—challenges and potentials for organizations. In: Piazolo, F., Felderer, M. (eds.) Innovation and Future of Enterprise Information Systems. ERP Future 2012 Research Conference Proceedings. Lecture Notes in Information Systems and Organisation, vol. 2, pp. 19–28. Springer, Berlin, Heidelberg, (2013)
4. Gerharter, A., Ortner, W.: Flexibility and improved resource utilization through cloud based ERP systems – critical success factors of SaaS solutions in SME. In: Piazolo, F., Felderer, M. (eds.) Innovation and Future of Enterprise Information Systems. ERP Future 2012 Research Conference Proceedings. Lecture Notes in Information Systems and Organisation, vol. 2, pp. 31–51. Springer, Berlin, Heidelberg (2013)
5. Mengistie, A.A., Heaton, D.P., Rainforth, M.: Analysis of the critical success factors for ERP systems implementation in U.S. Federal Offices. In: Piazolo F, Felderer M (eds.) Innovation and Future of Enterprise Information Systems. ERP Future 2012 Research Conference Proceedings. Lecture Notes in Information Systems and Organisation, vol. 2, pp. 53–67. Springer, Berlin, Heidelberg (2013)
6. Kraljić, A., Delismajlović, D., Kraljić, T.: Does predefined ERP implementation methodology work for public companies in transitioning country? In: Piazolo, F., Felderer,

M. (eds.) Innovation and Future of Enterprise Information Systems. ERP Future 2012 Research Conference Proceedings. Lecture Notes in Information Systems and Organisation, vol. 2, pp. 71–86. Springer, Berlin, Heidelberg (2013)
7. Rich, D., Dibbern, J.: A team-oriented investigation of ERP post-implementation integration projects: how cross-functional collaboration influences ERP benefits. In: Piazolo, F., Felderer, M. (eds.) Innovation and Future of Enterprise Information Systems. ERP Future 2012 Research Conference Proceedings. Lecture Notes in Information Systems and Organisation, vol. 2, pp. 87–100. Springer, Berlin, Heidelberg (2013)
8. Friedemann, S., Schumann, M.: How to consider supply uncertainty of renewable resources in the basic data structures of ERP-systems. In: Piazolo, F., Felderer, M. (eds.) Innovation and Future of Enterprise Information Systems. ERP Future 2012 Research Conference Proceedings. Lecture Notes in Information Systems and Organisation, vol. 2, pp. 103–113. Springer, Berlin, Heidelberg (2013)
9. Draheim, D.: Towards total budgeting and the interactive budget warehouse. In: Piazolo, F., Felderer, M. (eds.) Innovation and Future of Enterprise Information Systems. ERP Future 2012 Research Conference Proceedings. Lecture Notes in Information Systems and Organisation, vol. 2, pp. 115–127. Springer, Berlin, Heidelberg (2013)
10. Haberlandt, K.: ERP-Planning garbage—realizing and preventing. In: Piazolo, F., Felderer, M. (eds.) Innovation and future of enterprise information systems. ERP Future 2012 Research Conference Proceedings. Lecture Notes in Information Systems and Organisation, vol. 2, pp. 131–139. Springer, Berlin, Heidelberg (2013)
11. Bollen P (2013) Enterprise Resource Planning Requirements Process: The need for Semantic Verification. In: Piazolo, F., Felderer, M. (eds.) Innovation and Future of Enterprise Information Systems. ERP Future 2012 Research Conference Proceedings. Lecture Notes in Information Systems and Organisation, vol. 2, pp. 143–151. Springer, Berlin, Heidelberg (2013)
12. Ramler, R., Kopetzky, T., Platz, W. A business view on testing ERP systems with value-based requirements coverage. In: Piazolo, F., Felderer, M. (eds.) Innovation and Future of Enterprise Information Systems. ERP Future 2012 Research Conference Proceedings. Lecture Notes in Information Systems and Organisation, vol. 2, pp. 153–168. Springer, Berlin, Heidelberg (2013)
13. Keckeis, J., et al.: Automated testing of ERP GUI—a cost-benefit analysis. In: Piazolo, F., Felderer, M. (eds.) Innovation and Future of Enterprise Information Systems. ERP Future 2012 Research Conference Proceedings. Lecture Notes in Information Systems and Organisation, vol. 2, pp. 171–182. Springer, Berlin, Heidelberg, (2013)
14. Felderer, M., et al.: A quality analysis procedure for request data of ERP systems. In: Piazolo, F., Felderer, M. (eds.) Innovation and Future of Enterprise Information Systems. ERP Future 2012 Research Conference Proceedings. Lecture Notes in Information Systems and Organisation, vol. 2, pp. 183–198. Springer, Berlin, Heidelberg (2013)
15. Porkert, K., Sutton, H.: Analysis pattern for the transformation of ERP system landscapes by SaaS. In: Piazolo, F., Felderer, M. (eds.) Innovation and Future of Enterprise Information Systems. ERP Future 2012 Research Conference Proceedings. Lecture Notes in Information Systems and Organisation, vol 2, pp. 201–215. Springer, Berlin, Heidelberg (2013)
16. Kurbel, K., Nowak, D.: Customization of On-demand ERP software using SAP business by design as an example. In: Piazolo, F., Felderer, M. (eds.) Innovation and Future of Enterprise Information Systems. ERP Future 2012 Research Conference Proceedings. Lecture Notes in Information Systems and Organisation, vol. 2, pp. 219–234. Springer, Berlin, Heidelberg (2013)
17. Auer, D., et al.: Towards a framework and platform for mobile, distributed workflow enactment services. In: Piazolo, F., Felderer, M. (eds.) Innovation and Future of Enterprise Information Systems. ERP Future 2012 Research Conference Proceedings. Lecture Notes in Information Systems and Organisation, vol. 2, pp. 235–249. Springer, Berlin, Heidelberg (2013)

18. Leyh, C., Heger, W.: ERP clients: browser-based or dedicated—do we need both?—an evaluation based on user perceptions. In: Piazolo, F., Felderer, M. (eds.) Innovation and Future of Enterprise Information Systems. ERP Future 2012 Research Conference Proceedings. Lecture Notes in Information Systems and Organisation, vol. 2, pp. 253–269. Springer, Berlin, Heidelberg (2013)
19. Paa, L., Ates, N.: Critical success factors of e-learning scenarios for ERP end-user training. In: Piazolo, F., Felderer, M. (eds.) Innovation and Future of Enterprise Information Systems. ERP Future 2012 Research Conference Proceedings. Lecture Notes in Information Systems and Organisation, vol. 2, pp. 271–286. Springer, Berlin, Heidelberg (2013)
20. Bahrami, B., Jordan, E.: Utilizing enterprise resource planning in decision-making Processes. In: Piazolo, F., Felderer, M. (eds.) Innovation and Future of Enterprise Information Systems. ERP Future 2012 Research Conference Proceedings. Lecture Notes in Information Systems and Organisation, vol. 2, pp. 289–297. Springer, Berlin, Heidelberg (2013)

Part I
ERP Future

The Future of ERP: A Critical Outlook

Helmut Guembel

Abstract This is a short and critical outlook regarding the future of ERP systems given by the keynote speaker of the ERP Future 2012 Research conference.

Enterprise Resource Planning software is the standard commercial software backbone in enterprises, many financial services companies and even in government agencies, including defense organizations. It has developed over decades and has been around since about 1990. Since then, it has expanded considerably in functionality. Today, organizations using ERP find themselves allocating an ever increasing portion of their IT-budget.

This is accompanied by a strong sense of disillusionment as most of the original expectations have not been met. The once so attractive integration has grown quite uneven in quality and plans to roll out all available functionality globally have been either curtailed or tacitly shelved. In particular, the leading ERP vendors have been very successful in achieving customer lock-in as the costs for switching to other solutions is prohibitively high. Due to the common practice of precluding partial cancellations of maintenance agreements, customers cannot easily migrate function-by-function to a better fitting solution. In some cases, customers are paying for thousands of users that once existed but are no longer required due to organizational changes. This has caused them to think harder when buying ERP software—but by no means hard enough. ERP vendors find new ways to sell additional and often unnecessary software and they really have become good at it.

Well protected by this situation, ERP vendors seek to leverage the situation. Under the pressure of their investors who pride themselves with having achieved maintenance income margins around or exceeding the 90 % level, they have grown into huge organizations with painfully low productivity levels. Huge development budgets have created dozens of mediocre extensions that permeated the installed base in a snail's pace. While the ERP customers were reluctant to

---

H. Guembel (✉)
Strategy Partners International, Scuol, Switzerland
e-mail: helmuth.guembel@strategypartners.com

spend millions migrating to newer versions without any positive effect to their own bottom line, the vendors found themselves having lost contact with their installed base. The newer products often required updating to the latest ERP base product version before a customer could install them.

Sustainability was and is not part of the vendors' agenda. With enormous creativity, they found new ways to make their customers buy add-ons regardless of their ability to install and use them productively. Products that sit on the shelf create maintenance revenue without burdening the vendor as products that are not installed will not break.

In the longer run, however, this is likely to harm both ERP customers and ERP vendors. The customers lose their ability to innovate for a number of reasons:

- Their budgets are increasingly confined to software that is not used.
- The architecture of the ERP products is both antiquated and hard to understand making extensions of any kind difficult.
- The ERP software, once viewed as a business enabler, causes enterprises to adapt to newer market scenarios slowly.

The ERP vendors, on the other hand, face new competition and are increasingly exposed to plans of line of business managers that do not primarily focus on ERP. They rather fancy pursuing their own route to what they believe is emancipation from the limitations imposed by the ERP behemoth. It is a clear repeat of what happened when mainframes started to vanish and departmental computing became a key trend. Cloud computing, mobile applications, and, in some cases, even Open Source offerings challenge the incumbent vendors. They find it difficult to leave their lucrative business models behind. This, however, is a key pre-requisite for their own transformation into a next generation vendor.

In the interim, they aim at achieving this transformation on a cosmetic level. Through acquisitions they increase both their functional footprint and market share. Cleverly working some impressive key performance indicators, they try to convey the impression that they have a leading position in every respect. In actual fact, it is the stable core ERP business that creates 80 % of their revenue with the new business contributing much less. It remains to be seen if the incumbent vendors will continue to prevail or if they will be replaced by new and more agile players who neither want to be in their footsteps nor believe in the once so promising tight integration from a single source—a paradigm that the big vendors themselves can no longer deliver on.

The current "sea of tranquility" may be challenged in the near future. The advent of machine to machine (M2M) communication capabilities can easily increase transaction volumes by orders of magnitude. Data volume will explode and transaction networks will emerge. Both Oracle and SAP have understood the impact on data management and preparing themselves to take advantage of "Big Data" even though there are still only a few projects. Financial analysts have bought the story and SAP's stock has climbed to new all-time record levels.

While this certainly will influence the whole ERP market in a great way, it will not unfold overnight. Nor will the effect reach all industries and market segments at the same time. It will, however, quite likely put up as many challenges for the incumbent vendors as it creates opportunities. It is hard to see the kind of dominance recurring that we have experienced in the ERP market as we know it for the very reason that these transaction networks cannot be dominated by a few vendors. They are much more volatile and we are heading towards increased requirements for openness and interconnectivity. There is no room for the lock-in that we see today.

There are a few requirements that have been stubbornly ignored by the ERP industry. They will become increasingly important in the dawning age of the Internet of things. One is the possibility to scale back maintenance agreements or to replace them altogether by maintenance on demand models. Another requirement is to provide management tools for distributed processes. New requirements in the governance area will cause users to install tools to manage these that are application independent. The user empowerment caused by a plethora of smart devices will create a new breed of ERP users. As the current philosophy of the leading ERP products has its roots in the pre-Internet era, we can sense the approach of a turning point. ERP will not survive as the holy grail of its protagonists hoping for an ERP^{III}. It rather may quite likely emerge in a quite different guise—this time a lot closer to a "best of breed" approach.

Haven't we made good progress with application integration recently?

Lean ERP: How ERP Systems and Lean Management Fit Together

Martin Adam, Johannes Keckeis, Peter Kostenzer and Heiner Klepzig

Abstract Lean Management and ERP systems are seen as contradicting each other. Lean Management goes for low cost automation, simplicity and high visibility of information flow whereas ERP systems might become complex and intransparent. This article outlines a research project that combines pros of both. This is called Lean ERP. First results of a study showed that it really is a niche market while a surprisingly high number of ERP providers already offer Lean support in their software.

1 Introduction

1.1 Lean Management and its Cons

Lean Management has its origin in the Toyota Production System (TPS). TPS is a management philosophy that includes the entire organization—people, culture, processes. Its first elements go back to the 1920's and were meant to fix cost problems when Toyota was still a loom company. Further elements were developed by Taiichi Ohno to cope with new challenges concerning flexibility in the

---

M. Adam (✉) · P. Kostenzer
University of Applied Sciences Kufstein, Kufstein, Austria
e-mail: martin.adam@fh-kufstein.ac.at

P. Kostenzer
e-mail: peter.kostenzer@fh-kufstein.ac.at

J. Keckeis · H. Klepzig
University of Innsbruck, Innsbruck, Austria
e-mail: johannes.keckeis@uibk.ac.at

H. Klepzig
e-mail: heiner.klepzig@uibk.ac.at

1950's. Low costs, high flexibility and quality lead to profitability which is the ultimate goal of TPS. Costs are reduced by eliminating waste, demand-driven planning and balanced processes. Small batch sizes reduce lead time and drive flexibility. Enabling employees and customer orientation helps to reach quality [1]. "Lean Management" as a term was introduced by Womack et al. [2] in the 1990's after having studied the TPS.

Lean Management nowadays is widely applied in the automotive industry. It also became popular in other industries, even in services. New terms like Lean Accounting, Lean Office or Lean IT demonstrate its popularity. Nevertheless, cons were expressed that will be discussed in the following [3]. As excessive inventory raises costs and huge batch sizes lowers flexibility, Lean Management goes for short planning horizons and produces only according to customer demand. By nature Lean is reaction-based as it does not consider forecast. Lean is more tactical and job-floor oriented than strategic. This might be a problem for companies with long production cycles or for companies that rely on high demand components with long order lead times.

Ideally, production is balanced and the product flows without interruption from one step to the other. If cycle times of the process steps vary too much, balancing is not possible and Kanban signals are used to pull from downstream. The most downstream process step triggers the entire production line. This simplifies planning a lot as only one step in the entire production lines needs to be scheduled. As Supply Chain Management becomes more integrated, critics argue that physical Kanban signals cannot move out of the plant to suppliers. This might also be a problem in case of multisite companies.

Data handling engenders criticism as well. A core element in Lean is Visual Management. Current performance data are displayed on the job floor to everybody. Employees and management see at a glance if the process is in or out of control. Correction actions can be taken immediately. Therefore current performance data are needed. Critics argue that without adequate IT support, data gathering, formatting and displaying might become exhaustive and lead to errors.

1.2 ERP Systems and its Cons

Similar to Lean Management, "Enterprise Resource Planning Systems" (ERP) also face its challenges. ERP started from simple Material Requirements Planning Systems (MRP) and moved into all aspects of a company including its relationship with suppliers and customers. Functionality steadily grows and with it ERP are getting complex. Visibility of processes gets lost.

ERP provide workflows for business processes that are often best practice. On the one hand, companies may reach a better level of process support by implementing ERP. On the other hand, this promotes inflexibility as the processes are primarily hard coded and modification is mostly limited by the companies to a minimum in order to avoid additional costs.

One big advantage of ERP is data handling. All relevant data are inside the ERP database. Decomposing bills of material, analyzing component order lead times, calculating tact, timing and sequencing orders is done automatically. On the other hand, data are often average and variation is not considered. Job floor scheduling ignores real demand and central steering does not react properly to unplanned incidents like broken die.

1.3 Lean Management Versus ERP Systems

Lean Management and high cost automation are often seen as contradictory [4]. This also applies to IT support. Lean advocates argue that IT leads to intransparency of the process flow as visibility is lost. Job floor employees no longer see the information flow. They cannot react immediately if something happens, like postponing material replenishment due to longer change over times, as everything is preplanned and steered centrally by computers in large scale. In that case, IT diminishes the problem solving ability of a single worker just where continuous improvement is essential to Lean. Companies often move towards Lean Management as a response to the complexities and intransparency brought in by IT. So, typically, the Lean advocates resist using IT until lean principles are implemented manually [5].

Nevertheless, IT systems are heavily used in most of the companies. So, whenever, a company moves toward Lean Management, and as we have noticed, a growing number of companies does this, there are always discussions of pros and cons of ERP. Sometimes they follow more the ideological path than the rational. Sometimes simple questions occur like, how much "pull" is needed? Do we still need our push signals from ERP or do we rely purely on paper based pull signals from downstream? Shall we skip forecasting and rely entirely on current demand? These are the kind of questions that laid the ground for the following research.

1.4 Lean Management and ERP Systems

Having highlighted some of the challenges that Lean Management and ERP face today, we argue that both complement each other well. As discussed before, Lean Management has its pros in demand driveness and its short comings in forecasting and coping with long ordering lead times. As far as ERP is concerned it is not able to handle unplanned situations on the job floor. Combining both ERP forecasting functions, including decompositions of complex bills of material with Lean pull job scheduling might help [6].

One main reason why ERP is implemented is accurate real time reporting. This is exactly what Lean needs for its continuous improvement principle: accurate data of current performance with high visibility to those who are concerned. Without a single database, dedicated data entry points and analyzing and displaying functions as it is offered by ERP and Business Intelligence systems this might become time consuming and error prone. ERP can make these processes less labor intensive and provide visibility to performance, error handling, job status and inventory more easily [7].

So this is what we call Lean ERP: ERP systems that support Lean principles.

2 Spread of Lean ERP

In a recent study conducted by the University of Applied Science in Kufstein/Tyrol 21 out of 35 ERP software producers reported that their systems offered some sort of Lean Management support. These functions have been developed in the last 2–4 years in most cases. Consequently, supporting Lean principles within ERP are quite a new phenomenon. Software producers that are new in business and those that are well-established offer more Lean support than others. The new and small companies often built their ERP on the base of Lean principles and found a new niche. Whereas the established ones, like SAP, Oracle or Infor, augmented their existing wide range of functionalities with Lean support.

Whether an ERP system has implemented Lean functions or not also depends on the industry, e.g. ERP for the construction branch have less Lean support. The more international the users of an ERP system are, the more they use ERP with Lean functionalities. ERP support Lean principles mainly in their material management, production and sales modules. This is not surprising, as this is where Lean comes from and where Lean is mostly applied. Interestingly most of the ERP producers do not plan to further develop into Lean as customer demand is low.

This leads us to the second part of the study. Although many software providers offer Lean functionalities in their systems only 4 out of 80 companies within our study are using them. This means that it is really a niche market. As stated above, Lean advocates are ambiguous about IT support, this has also be proven in the study: companies who go for Lean do not automatically use Lean ERP. They often modify functionalities in their classical ERP systems and they don't buy specific Lean ERP software. On the other hand, if an ERP system offers Lean support, companies are likely to use them. The use of Lean ERP systems depends of the size of the company, showing that mid-size companies are more ahead than small or large ones.

3 Areas of Research in Lean ERP

We found that Lean Management and ERP systems is not a question of one or the other but that they might fit together. We have identified fives areas of interest for further research (see Fig. 1).

Lean ERP: How ERP Systems and Lean Management Fit Together

II. Spread of Lean ERP (Customer demand, ERP software)	**III. Lean Principles in ERP** (Realization of Lean principles in ERP)	**IV. Modification of classical ERP** (Effort of changes)	**V. Roadmap Lean ERP** (Steps in implementation and transformation)

I. Concept
(Challenges in Lean Management and ERP, reasons for Lean ERP)

Fig. 1 Areas of research in Lean ERPLean ERP

A first comparison of the Toyota Production System and a modern ERP system showed the following differences (see Fig. 2).

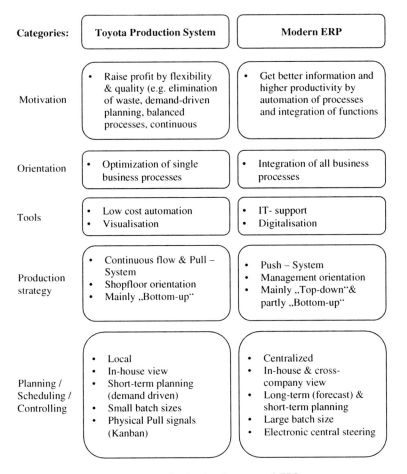

Fig. 2 Differences between the Toyota Production System and ERP systems

The comparison shows that modern ERP systems follow a philosophy that emphasizes on large-scale production and full load of machinery. This is contrary to the Lean principles.

4 Conclusion and Further Research

In this paper we have outlined that Lean Management and ERP systems are seen as contradicting each other. On the one hand, modern ERP systems implemented a production system that focuses more on equipment efficiency than on demand flexibility. On the other hand, Lean advocates have their doubts about the intransparency and complexity of fully IT-automated processes. Nevertheless, most of the companies have implemented ERP systems in order to overcome some of the cons of Lean Management. This is the motivation of a research project which looks for opportunities to combine both, Lean Management and ERP systems. This is called Lean ERP. First results of a study showed that Lean ERP is a niche market while a high number of ERP providers already offer Lean support in their software. Further areas of research were, besides the realization of Lean principles in ERP systems, the modification of classical ERP towards Lean and a roadmap for Lean ERP.

References

1. Ohno, T.: Toyota Production System: Beyond Large Scale Production. Productivity Press, Cambridge (1988)
2. Womack, J.P., Jones, D.T., Ross, D.: The Machine that Changed the World. Rawson Associates, New York (1990)
3. Gill, R.: Lean manufacturing and ERP systems: different by design. Ceram. Ind. 19–20 Aug (2007)
4. Takeda, H.: LCIA—Low Cost Intelligent Automation. mi-Fachverlag, München (2006)
5. Wheatly, M.: ERP is needed to sustain the gains of lean programs. Manuf. Bus. Technol. 30–32 June (2007)
6. Bell, S.: Lean Enterprise Systems—Using IT for Continuous Improvement. Wiley, New Jersey (2006)
7. Nakashima, B.: Lean and ERP: friend or foe? Adv. Manuf. Sept (2007)

Social Content Management Systems: Challenges and Potential for Organizations

Andrea Herbst and Jan vom Brocke

Abstract At around the time of the new millennium, Enterprise Content Management (ECM), a concept for the enterprise-wide management of information, emerged. However, the trend toward adapting social media technology brings a new situation for ECM, as organizations are challenged to manage diverse "social content" from social media in order to ensure quality and compliance. At the same time new opportunities arise from social content as a powerful asset for creating business value. Recognizing the importance of social content has led to the development of a new generation of information systems, Social Content Management Systems (SCMS). SCMS are ECM systems that focus on the management of social content. SCMS have yet to receive much attention in research, particularly in terms of their potential benefits and the challenges organizations may face in using them. This paper evaluates the importance, potential benefits, and challenges of SCMS for organizations through a survey of 89 professionals from several countries and industries. For the survey we draw on challenges and potential addressed in the existing literature of SCMS and social media use in organizations.

1 Introduction

Organizations are continuously challenged by the management of increasing amounts and varieties of digital information types and formats [24]. Particularly the management of unstructured information, such as emails, presentations, and Word documents, which constitutes around 80 % of an organization's information

---

A. Herbst (✉) · J. vom Brocke
University of Liechtenstein, Vaduz, Liechtenstein
e-mail: andrea.herbst@uni.li

J. vom Brocke
e-mail: jan.vom.brocke@uni.li

assets [13], presents major difficulties. Around the time of the new millennium, Enterprise Content Management (ECM) a concept for the enterprise-wide management of information, emerged [13, 14, 23]. ECM can be defined as "the strategies, tools, processes, and skills an organization needs to manage its information assets over their lifecycle" [20].

The emergence of social media in organizations has created a paradigm shift in how people interact and communicate [1, 16]. Organizations have come to recognize the benefits of using social media technology for internal purposes, such as improved collaboration and knowledge sharing [15]. However, the growing use of social media in organizations has also led to high volumes of social content [6] which are not managed by most organizations yet. Nevertheless, it has to be acknowledged that social content, such as expert answers, team chats, and blogs, can be powerful business assets for creating business value over time [1]. Managing and controlling social content may further play an important role for quality and compliance purposes [1]. Recognizing the importance of controlling social content over its entire lifecycle has led to the development of a new generation of information systems for the management of content that is created through using social media, Social Content Management Systems (SCMS).

SCMS are ECM systems that focus in particular on the management of social content [6, 8]. Vendors promise that, through SCMS, organizations can enhance information sharing, improve collaboration, and increase productivity (e.g., [3, 11]). However, research has yet to systematically investigate SCMS, particularly in terms of the organizational need for SCMS and its potential and challenges.

In order to address this gap, we draw potential benefits and challenges from existing literature on SCMS as well as organizational use of social media and conducted a survey with 89 professionals from eleven industries in seven countries. Our evaluation of the potential and challenges of SCMS is not meant to be exhaustive but to provide a starting point for discussions on the significance of the emerging concept of SCMS.

The paper is structured as follows: First, we provide general background about SCMS and its potential benefits and challenges, drawn from the existing literature. Next, we give an overview of the data collection process (Sect. 3) and present the results of the study (Sect. 4). Then Sect. 5 discusses selected results of the study, and Sect. 6 concludes the paper with a brief summary as well as the implications and limitations of the study.

2 Background

2.1 Social Content Management Systems

SCMS is a new generation of ECM systems. The term "social content management," coined by software vendors, refers to traditional ECM systems with built-in social media functionalities, such as commenting, chats, or blogs, that are designed to manage content in a social world [6]. SCMS create an environment for communication and collaboration with a business purpose that provides information and content for discussions and is able to capture the results of these discussions [8].

The use of social media in organizations can be distinguished in two ways: the internal perspective, which is the use of social media technology within the organization to make employees more productive [7], and the external perspective, which uses social media technology to connect with customers, business partners, suppliers, or other external parties [19]. These two perspectives can also be differentiated in terms of how the social content is managed: the internal perspective refers to the creation and management of social content through the use of social media within the organization, while the external perspective refers to the controlled generation and publication of content on external social media platforms like Facebook, Twitter, and Xing. Although some SCMS offer both functionalities, this article focuses on the internal perspective of managing social content.

The next section discusses some of the potential benefits associated with SCMS that have been presented in the literature

2.2 SCMS Potential

The literature has reported a number of potential benefits in the context of social media usage in organizations and SCMS. One major benefit of using social media in organizations is *transparency* [4, 27]. SCMS can support transparency by capturing social content, such as interactions and discussions between employees. This transparency supports organizations in complying with legal regulations but can also be used to generate business value.

Another potential benefit mentioned in the literature is that of *improving organizational knowledge management* [1, 18, 22] by capturing social content in SCMS and providing the content to other employees in the form of, for example, FAQs and wikis. This benefit is in line with *improving communication and interaction* in the organization [27], a potential benefit mentioned in the context of social media usage in organizations. SCMS support communication and interaction by providing tools needed for communication, such as chats or forums, and it supports interaction by making required content available to fellow employees.

Especially for teams that are geographically dispersed, such a virtual social environment can help to *overcome geographical barriers* [1, 12]. This environment provides easy-to-use virtual communication tools and ensures that all group members have the same level of knowledge by facilitating their ability to follow the activities in the environment independent of their location or time zone.

Another potential benefit of SCMS mentioned in the literature is *improvement of the team efficiency*, such that teams can achieve the same results in collaborative projects in shorter times [1] because of social media technology and the availability of required content. Finally, through a social environment that supports interaction and communication, organizations can realize *cost reductions* by minimizing the need for travel and reducing communication that uses more expensive, traditional communication tools, such as telephones and fax machines [2, 27].

The next section presents some of the challenges organizations may face when adopting SCMS.

2.3 SCMS Challenges

A common challenge reported in the context of social business systems in general is the *reluctance of the users to contribute* [2]. Differences in age, personal attitudes toward social media, and hierarchical positions in the organization are just a few of the factors that can influence willingness to use such a system. SCMS that no one uses are clearly no benefit for the organization.

The second challenge concerning the use of social media in organizations is the additional *cost of usage* in terms of time and effort [21]. For an employee, contributing to SCMS may mean the expenditure of additional effort or time that he or she may not be willing to make if it is faster and easier simply to call or meet with someone to solve a problem. Another issue that has been mentioned in the literature is the *system as a barrier* if willing users perceive using SCMS as difficult and cumbersome [9]. Especially for people who are minimally IT-adept, this might hold them back from contributing to virtual communication and interaction.

Another possible challenge is that presented by users who are just *not willing to share any information or knowledge* because they fear losing power by giving up their exclusive hold on information to an environment like SCMS [26]. In addition, while transparency created through SCMS can be an important benefit for organizations, for employees it might be perceived as a threat since *transparency* also allows organizations to monitor an employee's actions and interactions. For example, organizations might be able to identify the person responsible for errors or problems, leaving the employee fearful of consequences and sanctions [17].

Finally, a challenge reported in the context of using social media technology in organizations is the *codification of knowledge* [25], which refers to the transfer of knowledge into accessible and applicable formats [5]. Although people might have the skills and knowledge to contribute in a social environment, in some cases it might not be possible to transfer their knowledge into a format that can be communicated easily.

The next section begins our report on the empirical study we conducted in November 2012.

3 Study Overview

We conducted a survey to evaluate the potential benefits and challenges of SCMS, to measure its importance from the internal and external perspectives and to assess the use of social media in organizations. Most of the survey questions used a

5-point Likert scale (1 = "very unimportant" to 5 = "very important"), with the option to mark items as "I can't say". After conducting a pretest to ensure the questions' comprehensibility, we slightly rephrased some of the questions. Data from the pretest was not further considered. The survey was then distributed as a paper questionnaire at a practitioner conference in Austria and was in addition transferred in an electronic version via email to professionals in Switzerland, Austria, Liechtenstein, and Germany.

The survey returned 89 valid responses. The software IBM SPSS Statistics 20 was used for data analysis. The size of the organizations the respondents represented ranged from 1 to more than 10,000 employees. However, about half of the organizations had fewer than 500 employees. Forty-three percent of the organizations were from the manufacturing branch, 11 % were from the information and communication branch, and another 11 % were from the financial activities branch. While the turnover of the organizations ranged from less than 500,000 euros to more than 10 billion euros, most of the organizations (66 %) had a turnover between 1 million and 5 billion euros.

The next section presents the results of the study.

4 Study Results

Nearly 80 % of the respondents reported that their organizations are using social media. Comparing the size of the organization with the use of social media in organizations showed a significant ($p = 0.002$) positive correlation (contingency coefficient: $c = 0.4$).

More respondents who indicated that their companies were using social media agreed that it is used more for internal communication (3.2) than for external communication (3.0). When asked what type of social media technology is used in the organization, 60 % named messaging, 59 % wikis, 51 % project sites, and between 20 and 26 % for newsfeeds, forums and blogs. Although they played a secondary role, forums ($c = 0.404$) and blogs ($c = 0.423$) showed a significant ($p < 0.003$) positive correlation with the organization size.

Nearly 33 % of respondents from organizations that use social media for internal communication said that their organizations store content created in this way, while another nearly 23 % stated that they didn't know. Around 44 % reported that their organizations provide stored social content to other employees, so more people agreed that social content is provided to other employees than that the content is stored in the organization.

We asked the respondents to evaluate the importance of SCMS in their organizations' internal and external communications, and most confirmed that both perspectives were important for their organizations. However, the average value shows a slightly higher result for the internal (3.3) than for the external perspective (3.1). Comparing the organization size with these results showed a low but significant ($p = 0.002$) correlation (Kendall-tau b: $\tau = 0.248$) between the size of the

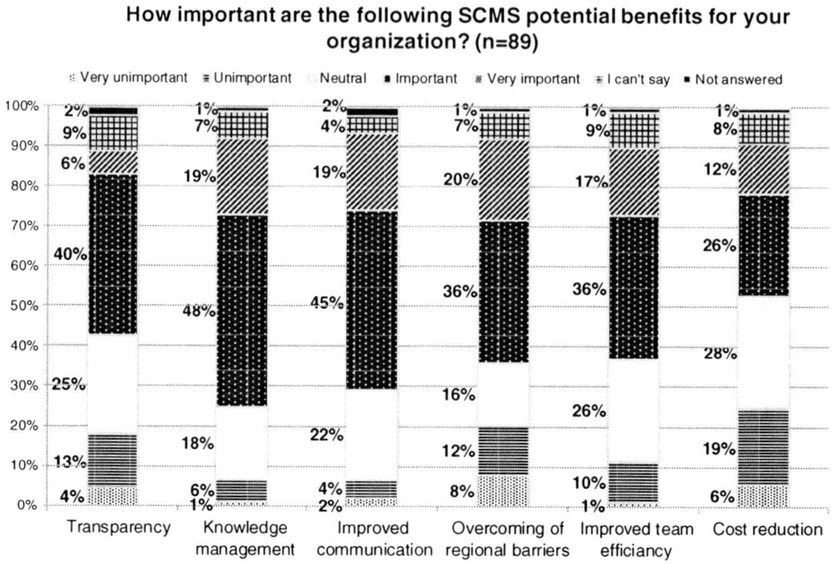

How important are the following SCMS potential benefits for your organization? (n=89)

Legend: Very unimportant · Unimportant · Neutral · Important · Very important · I can't say · Not answered

Category	Very unimp.	Unimp.	Neutral	Important	Very important	I can't say	Not answered
Transparency	4%	13%	25%	40%	6%	9%	2%
Knowledge management	1%	6%	18%	48%	19%	7%	1%
Improved communication	2%	4%	22%	45%	19%	4%	2%
Overcoming of regional barriers	8%	12%	16%	36%	20%	7%	1%
Improved team efficiency	1%	10%	26%	36%	17%	9%	1%
Cost reduction	6%	19%	28%	26%	12%	8%	1%

Fig. 1 SCMS potential

organization and the importance of SCMS for the internal perspective. However, no relationship was identified for the external perspective.

Finally, we asked for the respondents' assessment of the identified SCMS potential benefits for their organizations. All SCMS potential benefits had a value above 3, so all were rated as important.

The two highest-rated SCMS potential benefits were knowledge management (3.9) and improved communication (3.8), whereas cost reduction (3.2) had the lowest value (Fig. 1). The average number of people who couldn't evaluate the importance of the SCMS potential benefits was only 7 %. With one exception, we found no relationships between SCMS potential benefits and demographic data like organization size, branch, or turnover: there is a low but significant ($p = 0.003$) correlation ($\tau = 0.241$) between the potential of costs savings and turnover.

The respondents rated the challenges of SCMS lower than the benefits (see Fig. 2). All challenges had an average value around 3, with problems with knowledge codification (3.4) and reluctance of the user (3.3) the two highest-rated challenges, and cost of usage (2.9) the lowest-rated. The average number of people who couldn't rate the challenges was again relatively low, at 7 %. We tested for correlations between demographic data and the challenges and found no significant relationships.

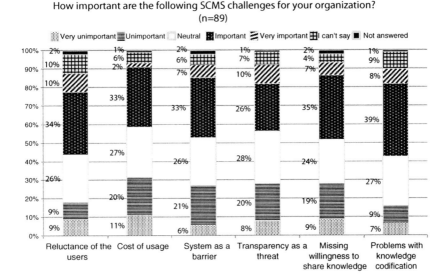

Fig. 2 SCMS challenges

5 Discussion of Selected Results

This section focuses on a few selected results from the survey that concern mainly the SCMS potential benefits and challenges. The results suggest that organizations in general recognize the importance of SCMS, especially for the internal perspective, and that the SCMS potential benefits tend to be rated in average higher (3.6) than the challenges (3.2), although the difference is moderate.

Interesting is also the fact that the reduction of costs has the lowest value of the SCMS potential benefits, although it still has a value above 3. This indicates that for organizations improving their practices by enhancing their knowledge management, communication, and team efficiency has a higher importance than reducing costs.

Another finding worth review is that improving knowledge management was suggested as the biggest potential benefit of SCMS (3.9), while problems with knowledge codification was rated as the biggest challenge (3.4). The two items are moderately but significantly correlated (Pearson's R: $r = 0.508$; $p < 0.001$). Previous research has shown that the conversion of tacit knowledge to explicit knowledge is often problematic and time-consuming (e.g., [5]), and the present research shows that organizations also see knowledge codification as a problem in the context of SCMS.

It is also interesting that the costs of usage had the lowest rating among the SCMS challenges. A qualitative study we conducted in the area of ECM showed that users are often not willing to spend additional time and effort using systems, including ECM systems, to store and search for information and content [10], even though doing so would benefit the organization. The study also showed that users would rather use faster and easier ways to get their work done, such as calling a colleague [10]. Nevertheless, it seems that the participants in the SCMS survey did not perceive this challenge as highly problematic.

Finally, we find that neither the SCMS potential benefits nor the challenges are related to any particular organization size, branch, or level of turnover, suggesting that these potential benefits and challenges are likely to be of concern to any organization.

6 Conclusion

The present paper reports on an emerging concept of SCMS through a survey fielded to evaluate the relevance of the SCMS' potential benefits and challenges drawn from existing literature. The survey, which was conducted with 89 professionals from several countries and industries, also assessed the importance of SCMS for organizations and the organizational adoption of social media. The study is not meant to be exhaustive but should be seen as a first attempt to understand the relevance of SCMS for organizations.

The results indicate that organizations have recognized the importance of SCMS, especially for their internal communications. Further, there were above-average ratings for all of the potential benefits of SCMS, particularly improving knowledge management and enhancing internal communication. The challenges of SCMS were rated somewhat lower, but the results still indicate that the challenges are relevant for organizations, particularly the challenge related to knowledge codification.

For research this study is an initial step in investigating the emerging concept of SCMS and its relevance for organizations. Practitioners can gain an understanding of what organizations could gain through SCMS but also what challenges they might face when using SCMS.

The study's limitations include the comparatively small number of survey participants, which cannot be considered representative. In addition, the survey addresses only a few selected SCMS potential benefits and challenges and cannot be seen as exhaustive. However, the study should be understood as a good starting point from which to begin to understand SCMS and its relevance to organizations. We will address this study's limitations through further research.

References

1. AIIM: Managing social content—to maximize value and minimize risk. http://www.aiim.org/pdfdocuments/MIWP_Manage-Social-Content_2011.pdf (2011). Accessed 20 Oct 2012
2. AIIM: The social business system—connecting people and content. http://www.aiim.org/pdfdocuments/MIWP_SocialBus-PeopleContent_2012.pdf (2012). Accessed 19 Oct 2012

3. Alfresco: Alfresco's new cloud connected content platform enables enterprise tablet productivity. http://www.alfresco.com/news/press-releases/alfrescos-new-cloud-connected-content-platform-enables-enterprise-tablet (2012). Accessed 20 Oct 2012
4. Buhse, W., Stamer, S.: Enterprise 2.0—The Art of Letting Go. iUniverse, New York (2008)
5. Davenport, T.H., Prusak, L.: Working Knowledge: How Organizations Manage What They Know. Harvard Business Press, Boston (2000)
6. Entertainment Close Up: Alfresco provides critical foundation for social content management with new enterprise release. http://search.proquest.com/docview/847911633?accountid=143123 (2012). Accessed 20 Oct 2012
7. Fraser, M., Dutta, S.: Throwing Sheep in the Boardroom: How Online Social Networking will Transform Your Life, Work and World. Wiley, Chichester (2008)
8. Gartner: Magic quadrant for enterprise content management. http://www.adobe.com/content/dam/Adobe/en/enterprise/pdfs/magic-quadrant-for-enterprise-content-management.pdf (2013). Accessed 02 Jan 2013
9. Hatala, J.P., Lutta, G.J.: Managing information sharing within an organizational setting: a social network perspective. Perform. Improv. Q. **21**, 5–33 (2009)
10. Herbst, A., Brocke, J.: Information seeking strategies in organizational information architecture. In: Rahman, H., Mesquita, A., Ramos, I., Pernici, B. (eds.) Knowledge and Technologies in Innovative Information Systems, vol. 129, pp. 36–50. Springer, Berlin (2012)
11. IBM: Social content management. http://www-01.ibm.com/software/ecm/social-content-management/ (2012). Accessed 20 Oct 2012
12. Lai, L.L., Turban, E.: Groups formation and operations in the Web 2.0 environment and social networks. Group Decis. Negot. **17**, 387–402 (2008)
13. O'Callaghan, R., Smits, M.: A strategy development process for enterprise content management. In: 13th European Conference on Information Systems (ECIS 2005) (2005)
14. Päivärinta, T., Munkvold, B.E.: Enterprise content management: an integrated perspective on information management. In: 38th Annual Hawaii International Conference on System Sciences (HICSS '05) (2005)
15. Postman, J.: SocialCorp: Social Media Goes Corporate. New Riders Publishing, Berkeley (2009)
16. Richter, D., Riemer, K., vom Brocke, J.: Internet social networking. Bus. Inf. Syst. Eng. **3**, 89–101 (2011)
17. Schmiedel, T., vom Brocke, J.: Cultural values matter: the role of organizational culture in ECM. In: vom Brocke, J., Simons, A. (eds.) Enterprise Content Management in Information Systems Research: Foundations and Cases. Springer, Berlin (in print)
18. Schneckenberg, D.: Web 2.0 and the empowerment of the knowledge worker. J. Knowl. Manag. **13**, 509–520 (2009)
19. Schneckenberg, D.: Web 2.0 and the shift in corporate governance from control to democracy. Knowl. Manag. Res. Pract. **7**, 234–248 (2009)
20. Smith, H.A., McKeen, J.D.: Developments in practice VIII: enterprise content management. Commun. Assoc. Inf. Syst. **11**, 647–659 (2003)
21. Thackeray, R., Neiger, B.L., Hanson, C.L., McKenzie, J.F.: Enhancing promotional strategies within social marketing programs: use of Web 2.0 social media. Health Promot. Pract. **9**, 338–343 (2008)
22. Velev, D., Zlateva, P.: Enterprise 2.0 knowledge management development trends. In: International Conference on Economics, Business Innovation (ICEBI '12) (2012)
23. vom Brocke, J., Simons, A.: Enterprise Content Management in Information Systems Research: Foundations and Cases. Springer, Berlin (in print)
24. vom Brocke, J., Simons, A., Cleven, A.: Towards a business process-oriented approach to enterprise content management: the ECM-blueprinting framework. Inf. Syst. e-Bus. Manag. **9**, 475–496 (2011)

25. Wahlroos, J.K.: Social media as a form of organizational knowledge sharing. https://helda.helsinki.fi/bitstream/handle/10138/24624/Thesis.Johanna.Wahlroos.pdf?sequence=1 (2012). Accessed 20 Dec 2012
26. Wang, S., Noe, R.A.: Knowledge sharing: a review and directions for future research. Hum. Resour. Manag. Rev. **20**, 115–131 (2010)
27. Wilkins, J., Baker, A.: Social business roadmap. http://www.aiim.org/~/media/Files/AIIM%20White%20Papers/Social-Business-Roadmap/Social-Business-Roadmap-Paper.ashx (2013). Accessed 02 Jan 2013

Part II
ERP Planning Requirements

ERP-Planning Garbage: Realizing and Preventing

Karlheinz Haberlandt

Abstract MRP II is still the planning core of most ERP-software systems and practically usage with well known but often ignored weaknesses. These weaknesses and their reasons are described in detail. Most APS are concentrated only on partial planning aspects with insufficient results. Until now all well known OR methods prove as unsuitable to solve the high complex planning ERP tasks for practical use. Rolling Detail Planning (RDP) is an approach, which changes fundamentally ERP-MRP II philosophy. TPS is an innovative alternative software system based on simulation techniques and fuzzy logic by realizing RDP. It claims to avoid the faults of MRP II based software systems and to get over the weaknesses in calculation, concepts, transparency, and cost of OR based APS.

1 MRP II is Still the ERP Planning Core

In ancient times the powerful King Agram reigned a large empire. His people were living in peace, freedom and wealth. One day Agram fell off his horse and broke both of his legs. The doctors were unable to heal his legs so that he could not walk again without crutches. He lost his will to live and neglected his royal duties. An assembly of the elders therefore decided to force all the people also to walk on crutches as a sign of solidarity. With time walking with crutches became normal and identified the people. Only a few could image life without crutches. These few began to realize that only those can be happy who throw away their crutches and walk on two legs [1].

For over than 40 years Manufacturing Resource Planning (MRP II) has been the planning core of the most of Enterprise Resource Planning Systems (ERP) with

---

K. Haberlandt (✉)
Heilbronn University, Heilbronn, Germany
e-mail: karlheinz.haberlandt@hs-heilbronn.de

all its well known but often also hidden and forgotten weaknesses. Nevertheless most ERP users are well satisfied with their ERP software, as is shown by the 9th worldwide satisfaction study (Zufriedenheitsstudie) in 2012, containing 1923 companies in 17 countries. But only 69 % of them still define functionality as the primary software selection criteria. Focus is shifting to internationalizing, adaptability, and ergonomics of the systems [2]. In addition to the development of many specialized ERP software solutions countless so called advanced planning systems (APS) appeared and much of them also disappeared again during the last 30 years. That's the fate of weak systems, that they are depending on "the basic law of systems: poor systems breed more systems" [3]. For many software companies' life is not too bad by only partly curing ERP weaknesses (they are recycling the planning garbage by serving golden crutches) and most users and many of their employees are well accustomed to live with those weaknesses and all their lovely crutches they have. Often they are defending violently those crutches, fearing changes or fearing to lose their job when the crutches are taken away from them.

Most ERP-solutions and other IT-applications in usage today are based on MRP II. Precursors are the Bill of Material Processor (BOMB), early in the 1960 pleaded by Josef Orlicky, and Material Requirement Planning (MRP) already early in 1972 pleaded by Oliver Wright [4]. The impetuous IT-development made it possible to expand MRP by including capacity planning, shop floor control, and purchasing at least theoretically to "Closed Loop MRP", and by including the important financial functions to Manufacturing Resource Planning (MRP II) [5]. Oliver Wright stated in 1981 that MRP II "is not a new 'theory' on industrial behaviour, it is all fact. MRP II is what's happening today in a number of companies" [6] and he mentioned Black & Decker, Cameron Iron Works, Corning Glass, Hewlett Packard, Steelcase, Tennant, Xerox [6]. The extension of MRP II to ERP (Enterprise Resource Planning) includes all pre- and post-manufacturing activities from order acquisition up to the after sales services. This also will include SCM and CRM, whereas MRP II still remains as operating planning core. In effect, ERP could be thought of as a customer-to-customer cycle [7].

Figure 1 shows Wight's MRP II Standard Diagram. At a first glance it appears relatively simple. But also it is very comprehensive. It could include the total planning system of every manufacturing company. All steps also include financial activities and constraints and scheduling. It is applicable to all production systems—discrete, process, line—, and to all marketing strategies—make to stock (MTS), assemble to order (ATO), make to order (MTO), and engineering to order (ETO). In 1980 increased computer capacity already made it possible, to break down the time phase of ordering into monthly and weekly time periods [8]. But the main attention has to be directed to the closed loop idea and its requirements. The numerous arrows within the diagram should clarify this. Rescheduling on all levels has to ensure, that all production, procurements, financial activities, policies, and regulations are to be synchronized within the total company.

Already in 1980 Wight emphasized, that modern computers and the knowledge that had been developed in the application of this knowhow over the last 30 years, made it possible, to provide the techniques for the company game plan. "How

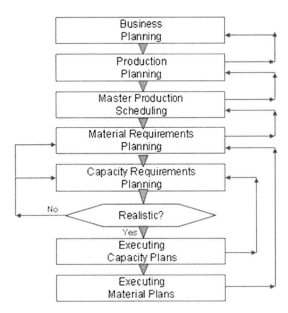

Fig. 1 MRP II standard diagram

effectively these techniques are put to work is up to the people who run a manufacturing business" [9]. However the question at present is how IT-companies 30 years later have carried out this origin MRPII vision by developing adequate software solutions as well as how the users are handling the planning of their manufacturing business.

2 ERP Planning Software Weaknesses

In order to be correct, the original MRP II vision of Oliver Wight, as shown in Fig. 1 contains no statement about any planning method. The idea is just a sequential planning in several steps, with an overall synchronisation of all activities in order to fulfill customers' requirements by means of companies' production. ERP Planning weaknesses therefore are weaknesses of software systems and its usage.

2.1 Demarcation of ERP Software Planning Solutions

Over the last 30 years ERP software solutions have developed dramatically in functionality, but today still don't include the first two stages of business planning and production planning. Both are planning activities with a strategic dimension. They not are involved with operational activities. Fact is that in reality business and production planning are still and often pretty miserable. The business plan should deal with policies that among others aim at market position and manufacturing shape. The production plan contains in more detail organisational strategies and development of marketing strategies as well as production systems. So far ERP software solutions mostly deal exclusively with operational planning carrying out manufacturing to fulfill the market demand. In the 80s those systems were called Production Planning Systems (PPS). In 2011 the ERP-systems of some well known IT-vendors (APplus; Canias ERP; EPICOR 9; M3; Microsoft Dynamics; SAP ERP; Semiramis/Comarch ERP) where tested by GPSmbH and all were awarded with "ERP Excellence". All had to undergo eight different test scenarios, but again typically no test referred to planning or planning methodologies [10, 11]. For many years this has actually been no subject of a discussion. Only partial planning and its methodologies are mentioned in context with manufacturing execution systems (MES) and APS.

Most of ERP-vendors nowadays are not only selling solutions imbedded with simple MRP II functionality. All above mentioned ERP-solutions provide an Advanced Planning System (APS), but without describing the planning methodologies that are applied and the interface to the planning functionality of the main MRP II system. Nevertheless it seems convenient at first to explain the weaknesses of ERP-systems without APS. This also makes sense because many users still are using older ERP or PPS systems without APS. As a typical application of a MRP II based ERP software solution the well known SAP R/3 will be used as an example. In addition and on the contrary to other ERP-vendors' systems a huge series of publications are describing SAP R/3, SAP ERP, SAP SCM inclusive enhanced Advanced Planner & Optimizer (APO), and many additional ERP modules; for details see:[12]. Gronau reports, that in 1998 SAP had installed about 20.000 R/3 systems [13] and 14 years later, in 2012, SAP informs having about 183.000 costumers [14].

2.2 ERP-MRP II Weaknesses

Weaknesses of a manufacturing scheduling system have to been judged by their ability to calculate and maintain valid due dates of requirements and availability of resources. Those dates are start- and end dates of any manufacturing activities, of any type of orders, of resource availability, promising, delivering, and ordering. Wrong, rough-cut, or inaccurate dates will cause delays, bottlenecks, inadequate availability of resources, additional costs, and simply many not assessable problems. Inadequate time periods such as weeks, months, or determined by dates, also have a big influence on the calculated quantities of all sorts of inventories and backlogs. This will influence availability of resources and of course the cost of manufacturing.

Without a doubt, weaknesses of an ERP-IT-Solution are causing errors in the manufacturing process which results in financial losses. Consequently the manufacturing activities meet the company's' customer requirements insufficiently. Dealing with those problems, we have to distinguish software construction faults, inadequate handling by users, and inflexibility of both to cope with the continuous environmental changes in the market requirements, technique and business.

Another point of view is the tremendous interdependence of a fault or defect caused by a weakness e.g. customer order backward scheduling of a deeply structured product without attention to constraint capacities; look at Fig. 4. This causes a long chain reaction:—false purchase and manufacturing start dates—insufficient inventory of parts—higher costs—waiting periods in the shop floor—higher work in process and higher costs—additional production bottlenecks—longer lead times—delays of delivery—annoyed customers—and so forth, and so on. Such a functional system weakness is causing every day with each customer order results in hundreds and more mistakes and defects. Perhaps some of them will neutralize one another on another level within planning or production. More of such weak planning points, caused by software functions are multiplying defects in the manufacturing process. All three MRP II operating stages show together some quite serious and coherent weaknesses. The most important are false start- and end dates of orders and of most manufacturing processes, caused by scheduling ignoring limited capacities, backward scheduling, and rough cut planning [15]. The following numerical and graphical examples should clarify these statements and support the understanding of the serious reproachful claims regarding the present ERP planning solutions.

Table 1 Comparison scheduling with unlimited and limited capacity

Orders	Requirements			Income day	Unlimited start day	Capacity end day	Limited start day	Capacity end day
	1	2	3					
Order 1	1500	1000	1500	1	1	3	1	5
Order 2	1300	400	500	1	1	3	2	5
Order 3	1500	600	2000	2	2	4	3	7
Order 4	2000	1500	1000	3	3	5	4	9
Order 5	2500	1200	2000	4	4	6	6	11
Order 6	2000	300	1750	5	5	7	8	12
Total	10500	5000	8750					
Max.capacity per day/shift	1200	1000	1500					
Assumptions								
3 capacity units				1 shift per day				
Wanted delivery day = 8				Leadtime = 3 days + 1 day savety				
handling over next day				handling over time : 4 h				
				(quality control,transport)				

2.3 Scheduling Examples

Table 1 shows a simple scheduling example with 6 orders to produce on 3 different working places (e.g. machines) with different time requirements.

Further assumptions are: one shift per day with different time capacities per manufacturing unit, order income from day 1 to day 5, due date for all 6 orders is day 8; handing over from one machine to the following one needs 4 h (e.g. quality control, transport, set up); planning rule unlimited is handing over next day; calculated lead time therefore is 3 days plus one safety day.

Table 1 shows the different start and end dates between scheduling with unlimited capacities and limited capacities. In case unlimited all is o.k., in case limited only the first 3 orders can be delivered in time. Figure 2 and 3 clarify the problem in detail.

The ignorance of capacity constraints in Fig. 2 leads to quite false results, no start and end date reflects the real possibilities. Figure 3 shows workplace 1 obviously as a bottleneck unit with the consequence of underemployment of the two following workstations. Both units show typical gaps, which normally occur in scheduling process. Most ERP-vendors and numerous IT- and OR specialists often futile try to stop or to avoid these gaps in a convenient way. Looking at six orders one can recognize the gaps, its causes and development. But on scheduling some hundreds of orders already in a midrange manufacturing company gaps are often covert by evasive orders or jobs. Fact is that early recognition and avoidance of bottlenecks and gaps in manufacturing processes need a scheduling in view of restraints of all necessary recourses.

In this context backward scheduling with unlimited capacities as shown in Fig. 4 appear as an absolutely incomprehensible and really ridiculous planning method.

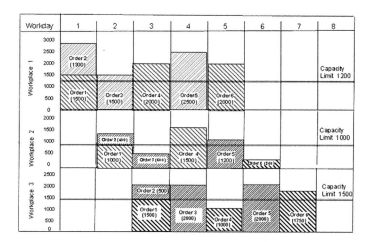

Fig. 2 Forward scheduling with unlimited capacity (1 shift per day, handling over next day)

ERP-Planning Garbage: Realizing and Preventing

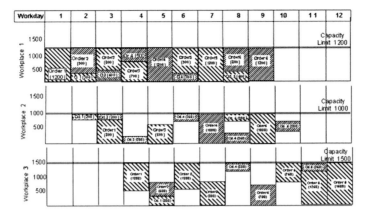

Fig. 3 Forward scheduling with limited capacity (1 shift per day, handling over next day)

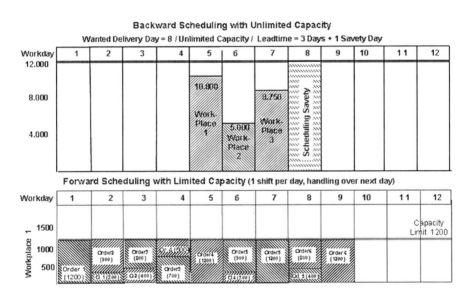

Fig. 4 Comparision unlimited backward schedudling with real forward scheduling

In Fig. 4 using backward scheduling the start date of all 6 jobs for workplace 1 are concentrated upon the 5th day with 10.800 time units and an available capacity of 1.200 units per day. We know that already starting at the 1st day is necessary to deliver at least the half of orders in time on day 8. Also as far as unlimited backward scheduling it used only as rough cut planning the date for provision of all sort of recourses always is false with all negative consequences.

And in general backward scheduling without or with limited capacities is a futile attempt also some ERP vendors are advertising with these method. Often

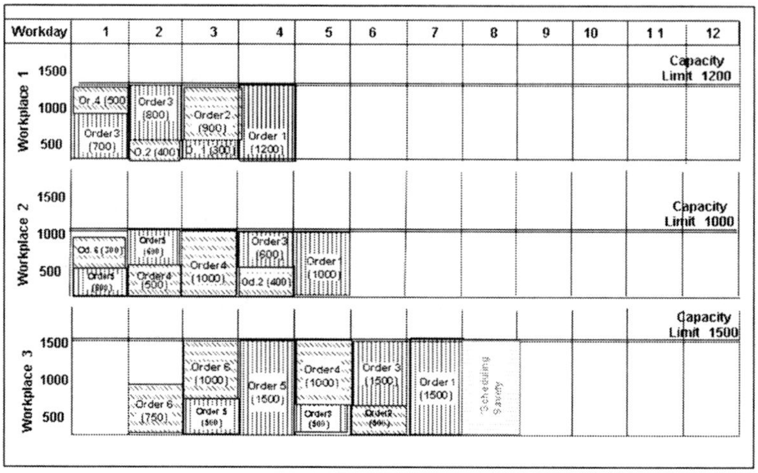

Fig. 5 Futile attemept at backward scheduling with limited capacity

backward scheduling is ending in the past as shown in Fig. 5. Only three orders can be produced, obviously starting with order 4 instead of order 1. That's why a start at actual date with all orders forward scheduling is to be done. An other crucial point is the question in what sequence or with what priorities backward scheduling has to start. Starting with the highest priority results, that orders with lower priorities are earlier finished. Starting with the lowest normally ends in the past.

We can conclude that scheduling without regard to limited recourses results in false start and end dates and that backward scheduling in this context is an inappropriate planning method.

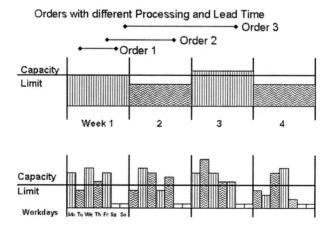

Fig. 6 Rough cut planning versus detailed planning

Figure 6 shows the problems of rough cut planning versus detailed operating planning. Planning with time buckets (weeks or months) with available due dates within the buckets make plans as basis for decisions unnecessary misty and spongy. Limited IT capacity and missing planning know how only could be an argument 30 years ago.

Rough cut planning make day precise Available to Promise impossible, discernible bottlenecks unknown and countermeasures in time impossible. Always rescheduling and troubleshooting within actual time buckets is necessary. Orders with lead time longer than a time bucket (see Fig 6, order 2 and 3) or across time buckets are causing daily many manufacturing challenges or troubles. To provide material and capacities in time needs detailed scheduling for the total operating planning period.

Details and explanations of these serious reproachful claims will be treated with regard to the three MRP II stages that ERP-software solutions normally contain.

2.4 Master Production Scheduling (Master Plan)

Figure 7 shows the rendering of the MRP II idea to the software system SAP R/3. It contains the operational part of MRP II with master production scheduling,

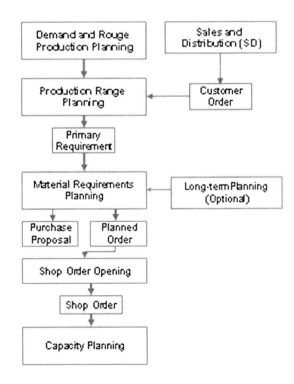

Fig. 7 SAP R/3 production planning (PP)

material requirements planning, and capacity requirements scheduling. In contrary to the MRPII standard diagram (Fig. 1) Fig. 7 contains no recurring arrows. This means, the software itself is running without the necessary closed loops. Regarding this planning approach, it's a poor hierarchal sequential system and an insufficient reflection of MRP II regarding the planning part; details refer to publications [12].

Demand and Rough-Cut Production Planning and Production Range Planning correspond to MRP II Master Production Scheduling. It has two functions: demand or sales planning (sales plan and forecast) and production planning. The sales planning horizon is usually 1 year divided into 12 months and should be organized with monthly reviews rolling 1 month forward. In real life many small and mid-range companies are not planning monthly sales in product units, but if they are, than only as monetary amounts of sales income. In this case the total manufacturing planning depends on sales order backlog and new incoming orders. Occasionally the material management indirectly assumes the necessary forecasts by anticipated purchasing. This situation could be adequate in some business environments (e.g. long range projects, machinery). But otherwise it represents a severe management inability which is causing many uncertainties and fluctuations in all the following planning and operating processes.

In order to reduce calculation time demand planning and forecasting is done in product groups or only for the critical units (lead units—Leitteile), in cases were a company has very many items [16]. Production planning is a rough-cut capacity planning. Also resources (e.g. workplaces) are aggregated to capacity production groups. Comparison between demand and relevant capacity within the different planning time periods—normally month or weeks—shows capacity overloads. These overloads have to be balanced interactively, that means manually to the rough-cut production plan. In the next module, production range planning, the output of the rough-cut production plan is matched with the backlog of customer orders. Monthly output of the production plan has to be distributed to the days of the period, while the integrated customer orders from the beginning are scheduled for the delivery days. All delivery dates are assumed to be requirements which could be fulfilled without checking resource availability. The output is a plan containing sales, production, and inventories of planned products distributed within the time periods of the planning horizon.

This output of the master plan contains a series of weaknesses regarding the further planning process. Planning with product groups and only critical parts as requirements against group resources using big time buckets is absolutely not satisfactory to ensure the proper identification of temporary overloads on production resources. Planned delivery dates don't correspond with the required start date and work period of required resources. Further on the daily required availability of a single resource within a single time period is very uncertain. Bottlenecks within and during the planed time periods can not be discovered. As a result dates and quantities of the primary requirements submitted to material requirements planning are not only uncertain but show inaccurate and therefore incorrect dates, due to the rough cut master planning. But master schedules are the basis for scheduling material requirements and accepting new incoming demands by the process called available to promise (ATP).

2.5 Material Requirements Planning

MRP corresponds to SAP module MM. In general it comprises the coordination of customer demand and requirements of material within the limits of an unsatisfactory master plans' output. This involves promising customer demands (ATP Available to Promise), managing all material inventories, planning purchase and production of material, and releasing shop floor orders.

A planning run of MPS (Material Planning Schedule) starts by comparison and reservation of the primary requirements,—these are customer and plan orders—, with available stocks of products to be sold. If not available the products and it parts have to be purchased and/or produced. The remaining orders have to be exploded down through their product structures. Start- and end dates are calculated for every part of the product in view of its individual lead time. In SAP R/3 and most other ERP systems order scheduling is done backwards from demanded delivery date as due date. The start date is calculated by subtracting the lead time from due date, whereas lead time often is increased by the planner for safety reasons. Only if the start date lies in past, forward scheduling is executed. First output is the required quantity of the different parts, with individual start- and end dates, called gross requirements. Debiting the available stocks, actual purchase orders and actual shop orders, the net requirements remain. Every part of the net requirements has quantities and an individual start and an end date. Wrong dates are normally already applied by using an incorrect lead time and additional safety time on top. The total calculation, however, is not taking the required capacity constraints into consideration. As a result often start- and/or end dates of many orders and their parts of ordered products are assigned to the same planned manufacturing time period without sufficient production capacity. Another crucial point is represented by the sequence of the orders to be processed. Most ERP solutions have no functionality to handle customer and shop floor order priorities in the required or in a satisfying way.

Net change methodologies are used for new incoming customer orders, in order to avoid a time consuming new planning run. This software module is generally called Available to Promise (ATP). It works after a MRS run is already completed only for a single order, but only the uncommitted amount of the inventory and of planned purchase- and shop orders within the MM module (Material Requirement Planning) will be applied as available. Wrong times are like the MPS faults, but orders with a later delivery date, scheduled earlier or in last MPS run, often are blocking later urgently required material. Those blocked new orders either imminently "get lost" because of promising insufficient delivery dates or become urgent orders with all consequences of trouble shooting within the manufacturing process.

A great deal of other planning weaknesses originates from inaccurate inventory, purchase management and lot sizing. One main issue is planning with high safety stock. At the end inappropriate stocks are caused by false or missing due dates as a result of the inaccurate scheduling and often missing customer order planning. The result is unforeseeable high deviation between planned and actual requirements. Often some material is required earlier and other material later. Stock replenishment therefore is often uncoupled from MPS (Master Plan Scheduling) through stochastic inventory planning by the material management. For this R/3 delivers more than 30 different methodologies in the system. Another source of weaknesses is lot sizing. No order determined inventory planning and the pooling of common components necessary for different customer orders uncouple purchasing and manufacturing from the customer orders. Lot sizes in purchase and manufacturing often are higher as really required in respect to cost savings. This will increase inventories, block production capacities and extend lead times.

SAP R/3 offers optionally the module Long-term Planning. This is a tool to simulate alternative demand forecasts. Scheduling works like material requirement planning. Therefore it is not really able to measurably reduce or change the above mentioned weaknesses.

The results of Material requirements planning are purchase proposals and so called planned orders for parts to be manufactured. The material availability for these orders is monitored in module Shop Order Opening. Those orders with start dates within the next time bucket, mostly a week, are released into shop floor to be executed and controlled either automatically but more often interactively by the workforce.

2.6 Capacity Requirements Planning

Capacity planning of most ERP-software is defined as detailed short-term execution and control module of the shop floor orders. The shop floor is the last link of the continuous requirements planning chain. Looking at the shop floor input one can see best the consequences of the on-going planning weaknesses. Short-term time periods normally are days. Machine capacity is planned in detail for work days or shifts taking into consideration the planned availability of manpower and partially the availability of required tools in the production process. This is absolutely insufficient for execution and control for the production on the shop floor. During a shift every workplace needs a detailed schedule normally based on minutes and the information of the sequence in which to manufacture the job orders. In addition the dates of released job orders are results of predetermined rough lead times which inherently are inaccurate. Scheduling of orders and the corresponding jobs on different production capacities again is usually done by scheduling backwards. By scheduling backward as well as by scheduling forward unavoidable there will occur time leaks of available capacities and job orders with too long processing times to fit into these leaks. Normally one tries to solve these planning problems interactively e.g. manually. Outstanding tools therefore are 'electronic control stations (Leitstände)' with user-friendly graphical displays based upon the classic Gantt chart format.

Altogether planning data input on shop floor result in "planned garbage", which has to be recycled in order to be at least able to reach a sufficiently accurate planning result. A detailed fine tuning is necessary which aligns all the requirements within the boundaries of the finite capacity that is available.

The weaknesses of applying the origin MRP II goals into sufficiently effective software systems is demonstrated by the ever increasing development of external Manufacturing Execution Systems (MES) [17–19] and countless Advanced Planning and Scheduling (APS) systems. MES solutions have multiple functions relating to the control the production process in very different environments. But in respect to planning they are recycling planning garbage of the previously executed master planning and material resource planning. This can cure only a partial portion of the total weaknesses thus causing financial losses and insufficient achievement of the other goals of the company.

2.7 APS Contraints

One major ERP planning weakness generally was accepted by IT- and OR scientists, as well and imperatively by IT companies: scheduling against infinite resources has to be changed by finite or constraint planning. This is the main source and objective of the development of most Advanced Planning Systems. The term Advanced Planning System (APS) might seem to imply that such a system is beyond and better than a system based on MRP II. But some doubt is required because of two reasons. First a system containing the entire production functionality as described in Fig. 2 will fail because of its complexity and the restrictions of applied OR methods like Linear Programming (LP); Mixed Integer Programming (MIP) [20], Genetic Algorithms (AG) [21], and Constraint Programming (CP) [22]. Secondly for this reason most APS deal only with one MRP II module or with a hierarchy of modules corresponding to MRP II structure [23]. And obviously the same planning approaches as in MRP II are used, with rough cut planning in Master Plan, with backward scheduling in Material Requirement Planning [24]. One has to assume, that the same weaknesses and faults are arising, which are existing in ERP-MRP II solutions.

The SAP APO system corresponds far, with the R/3 solutions [25]. In this regard one can assume that at least similar faults will occur as described in MRP II. Apparently again generally a multi level approach, at least a two level approach is implemented and obviously necessary. The first level (APO-SNP), optional to use, works as a rough cut scheduling system. The restricted usefulness of such an output was described above. The second level "Production Planning/Detailed Scheduling (APO-PP/DS)" again has two levels: Material Requirements Planning and Capacity Planning, the latter with detailed scheduling based on minutes or even seconds. But scheduling works only within a time period of 1 day to 1 week. As an alternative the planning input for detailed scheduling can be taken from ERP base system. Many functions have to work interactively, that means by many different planning specialists at the same time. The applied mathematic methods and the calculation steps are unknown to the user. The system is like a black box. Although the APO DS delivers many interesting features, especially with regards to Online Transaction Processing (OLTP) it appears that it gets planning garbage again as data input. With very great efforts regarding constructing models, using highly sophisticated LP software, huge input of manpower, of computer capacity, and of capital, the output appears to be only recycled planning garbage in regard to an effective smart operational production planning system. Generally one can agree to the opinion of Hartmut Stadtler and Christoph Kilger, that it will be a long way until we will reach satisfying and efficient APS [26].

2.8 Conclusion

On every of the three operating production planning stages ERP solutions show a multitude of planning weaknesses. The most important are:

- no clear priorities of customer and shop floor orders;
- only rough-cut planning in master production scheduling
- insufficient consideration of capacity constraints;
- often loss of contact between the customer order and shop floor order and relevant priorities.

Crucial results are false start- and end dates of orders and of most manufacturing processes. This causes many unforeseeable and often incomprehensible faults and leaks on every planning stage. Many of this must and will be cured by interactions between software system and the manual work of many different planning specialists. Others insufficiencies are handled from case to case or will be simply ignored. On this track MRP II, from Oliver W. Wight described as a formal, optimizing system, is shifting to a fragile informal system. Or, the system was all the time a weak, delicate, informal system, and software vendors are arguing, that any faults using their systems always are depending on inadequate or incomplete usage by the end users.

Mostly companies and their employees have gotten used to those defective planning-, information-, and manufacturing- processes and activities. Results are: they have forgotten about the potentials of a smart, cost saving, formal total manufacturing solution and also to think about and claim a lean, simple and cheap solution. Every day the upcoming mistakes and defects have to be cured by additional manual work, by experts, conferences, troubleshooting teams, "date chasers". The companies and their employees are using crutches like king Agrams' people.

3 Rolling Detail Planning the Planning Paradigm Change

Paradigm change in connection to ERP means a fundamental alternation of the total operating planning process, its objectives, methods, and applied information techniques. Instead of separating into long range and short range planning only detailed short range planning on minute- or second base is used for the entire operating planning period. No backward only foreword scheduling is done, all in consideration to finite capacities. Because principally most work on orders can only be done sequentially, prime attention has to be directed towards the sequence of processing customer orders, in order to fulfil customer demand in time. Therefore order priorities are essential elements of the total planning process. Its data volume is too huge and process structures are too complex in order to solve the whole detailed finite scheduling with mathematical method as LP, MIP, or CP. By applying heuristic simulation combined with fuzzy logic the exercise can be settled relatively easily and that with low computing capacity. In contrast Bella and Layer are mentioning that LiveCaches of SAP APO not seldom have a dimension of some dozens of gigabytes [27]. Breakthrough to avoid most weaknesses and faults caused by MRP II based software is realised by changing and simplifying planning process and planning method.

Rolling planning means that daily planning or planning in shorter time periods is necessary for the execution of a total planning cycle, taking in consideration all countless changes from order receipt up to recent events on the shop floor. Results are up to date and flexibly respond to every day's changes.

RDP uses all available planning information (facts and plans) of the basic ERP system, and executes an overall capacity plan on a minute base. This will guarantee precise start- and end dates on every planning stage.

In order to support and improve forecasts RDP works with flexible planning horizons for every product. Horizons are determined by lead time of purchase and production. Using rolling planning it is not necessary to work with longer planning periods and more planned orders than required.

Although RDP is a sequential planning system it includes in every planning run all relevant functions with all data relevant to the planning process, thus integrating sales, material, and capacity simultaneously. RDP works with clear priorities, some simple rules, and some optimization criteria. It minimizes the requirement for interactions by presenting reliable planning information. RDP looks at company and it operation planning as an open and learning cybernetics system. It supplies through daily total planning runs all necessary plan corrections and further adjustments as well as all information to control order promising, purchasing, inventories and manufacturing.

4 TPS: Planning and Simulation with Fuzzy Logic

Total Planning System (TPS) is the ERP-APS, which completely incorporates objectives and methods as used by RDP. Figure 8 shows the planning structure of TPS. The first stages of Fig. 8 contain the demand planning, which has to be done by the basic ERP system. It starts with the long range sales plan, the demand output of the strategic planning and framework for the midrange operating plan. The operating plan normally has a planning horizon of 1 year and should be reviewed and performed monthly. The planning horizon also can be shorter as 1 year with regard to shorter lead time of material and production. Only with regard to the potential availability of a product it is necessary to predict a possible order receipt. Normally, the shorter the period, the better could be the forecast. In addition, the planning horizon can be different for the different products. Demand requirements in a shorter planning horizon cause no difficulties. The planning horizon of TPS reaches automatically to the latest order delivery date. Output of

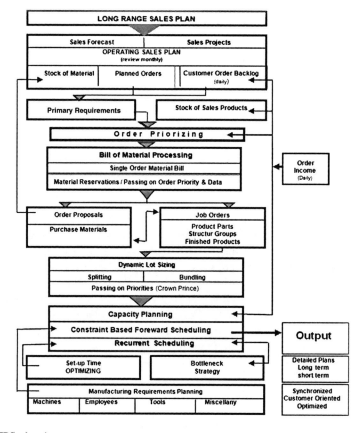

Fig. 8 TPS planning structure

ERP-Planning Garbage: Realizing and Preventing 47

the operating sales plan is the primary requirements. It consists of planned orders, customer orders in backlog, and daily order receipt. Planned orders are the sum of sales forecast and sales projects output, not grouped in any way but for every single sales product. Due dates have to be fixed to a day within the different time periods, normally towards the middle. The customer order backlog contains all actual orders, also those already in work in process, those with overdue delivery date or dates in the past, others beyond the planning horizon, and others with a fixed and promised delivery date. The status of an order is important for organizing further planning and manufacturing, and thus to prioritizing. Daily order receipt changes the stock of primary requirements every day. It contains all different sorts of delivery request, also very urgent ones. All the new orders coming in will be promised first after a completed TPS run. Thus all urgent orders are integrated in the sequence of manufacturing in consideration of availability and urgency. Set off of new customer orders against planned orders can be worked on before prioritization or within bill of material processing in an automatically or interactive mode.

The real TPS run starts with the time dynamically prioritizing of all orders contained in the actual stock of primary requirements. Priorities are calculated by the user's individual criteria. This can be different kinds of promising (fixed, precisely, within a period, and so on), actual dates or planned overdue dates, and orders for special customers, for stock of sales products, for plan orders. In practice the desired delivery date often plays a dominating role. Time dynamic prioritization means, that a promised delivery date gets more urgent every day and will get a higher priority. The priorities are newly calculated with every TPS-run regarding the actual status and are passed through to material resource planning, lot sizing, shop floor orders on all manufacturing levels as the main key to controlling work order sequence, resources availability and fulfilment of promises to customers.

In next step, bill of material processing, demand and customer orders are exactly processed successive to the calculated order priorities. All material reservations will be released, in order to save new reservations again and only for one day for the new calculated urgency of orders. The orders will be debited from available stock, regular purchase and job orders, and reserved orders until the next TPS run. The part structures of products consisting of several or many parts will be exploded down to the lowest level. All parts will be assigned correspondingly with the priorities of the planned- and customer orders. In case of unavailable purchase materials, the proposed material availability is calculated under consideration of individual purchase lead times. Output is proposals of purchase orders and all work orders, which differ between planned orders and customer orders. Decisive for a cost saving inventory policy and recommendation for the usage of TPS is, that all material requirements planning should be bases on this planning process, minimizing all other stochastic planning.

In order to retain work orders, which are meant for use on the shop floor, TPS contains a module for a dynamic lot sizing optimization. For all material to be produced minimal and maximal lot sizes and available ranges are calculated using fuzzy logic. The available ranges determine a number of planning time periods, which can be different for every part. The job orders are sorted into the planed different time periods in accordance with their delivery date. Smaller orders are bundled to manufacturing orders and large ones are split by requirement and spread to the next planning time period. Bundling means, that different orders with different priorities are combined together. In this case the bundled factory order gets the priority of the order with the highest priority. This is called crown prince principal and will cause, that parts, designed for other customer orders are earlier produced as needed in regard to a cost saving lot size. Parts for one customer order can be spread over manufacturing orders with different time periods. But capacity planning in sequence to priorities fits the right manufacturing sequence. The total lot sizing program will change every day because of new customer orders, new priorities, and events on the shop floor. What counts is the work to be done today or during the actual shift. Tomorrow the sun rises with a new actual plan to be executed.

Capacity planning is done sequential accordingly to the order priorities for every single customer order, mostly with its parts spread over different manufacturing orders. Scheduling is executed straight forward and straight against constraint capacities, bases on 1,440 min a day. Scheduling starts with the part of the lowest level, which passes on its end date plus transportation lead time as possible start date to the orders with parts in the following level. Thus product orders with multi levelled structure are correctly scheduled. In scheduling inevitably leaks of available capacity will occur and in addition orders with too long processing time for currently available resources. For these cases TPS has a comfortable tricky solution based on fuzzy logic. The planning of available manufacturing capacity has to take in account the availability of combined resources as machines, employees, tools, and miscellaneous other resources. These different availabilities are also planned and optimized by TPS. A special aspect and solution refers to set-up optimization. The described scheduling method shows every bottleneck at each capacity unit for every day and for every minute during the entire operating period. These are the waiting queues of orders in front of capacity units to be calculated, analysed, and visualized at every minute of the total planning period. TPS serves in time the necessary transparency to avoid bottlenecks, which have to be handled interactively by TPS simulations. In addition TPS contains a series of program modules to solve special requirements for instance:

– Alternative working sequences on various capacity units with scheduling and optimization;
– overlapped production with constraint based scheduling and time optimization;
– tool scheduling under consideration of combined multi tools;
– usage of flexible production lines;
– manpower orientated capacity planning.

TPS output is a detailed production plan, detailed on minute base over the entire planning horizon, combined with a BI (OLAP-) reporting system. Output can be sent to every ERP host system. The run time with thousands of factory orders takes less than 10 min. TPS is no black box. Every calculation step of every TPS run is recorded and is understandable in detail by the user.

A big advantage of TPS is its usability for strategic simulations. TPS can be considered to be the total simulation model of the company's production. It is impossible to optimize all the concurring production objectives on every level all the time. Solutions only can be satisfying in total. Strategies with the emphasis to individual objectives can easily be executed by changing or adding some TPS parameters. Thus strategies to be simulated for example could be: increase or reduce capacity availability by a multiple of different activities; consequences of any alteration of a product program; absolute emphasis on delivery on time for every customer order; reducing production costs by alternative lot sizes and/or extremely set up decisions; reducing lead time through overlapping production.

The author is convinced that applying Rolling Detail Planning in combination with TPS is able to avoid or at least to minimize the above described weaknesses of ERP solutions and of all APS, which are based on OR methods. But he also is convinced that the ERP vendors, the scientific OR community, and most ERP users and their specialists will defend their crutches violently, some of them are even gold plated.

5 Conclusion

Oliver W. Wright's vision in 1981 of MRP II (closed loop and company game plan) up to now is absolutely insufficient fulfilled by ERP-IT-solutions.

Due to limited IT-capacities in the 1980s production planning process was divided into two levels—rough cut planning and short-time fine tuning. This causes some severe planning weaknesses, which actually are ignored, or forgotten, or hidden, but until now not solved by ERP-solutions.

Main reasons for ERP planning weaknesses and faults are:

- insufficient consideration of capacity constraints
- backward scheduling
- rough cut planning
- missing of applicable manufacturing priorities
- uncoupling job orders from customer orders

They can be considered as planning knock-out criteria.

Results of ERP planning weaknesses are systematically false calculated due dates (start dates and end dates) for every type of order and each production activity. Answer: numerous partial temporary planning solutions (mainly human interactions).

Until now Advanced Planning Systems only deal with subsets of total PPS. Applied mathematical methods (OR) already are unable to manage the large scale and complexity of data of a midrange manufacturing company.

Since 1981 economical circumstances have changed fundamentally and require a planning paradigm change.

Answer: a holistic production planning system based on Rolling Detail Planning (RDP).

Total Planning System (TPS) is able to fulfil RDP requirements. It is based on heuristic simulation techniques with fuzzy logic. During the last 20 years it was successively developed to an effective and comprehensive ERP-Planning tool, to prevent ERP-planning weaknesses.

References

1. Berger, W.: Business Reframing, p. 11. Gabler, Wiesbaden (1996)
2. Naujoks, F.: (2012). Anwender geben ihrer ERP-Systeme gute Noten. http://www.computerwoche.de/software/erp/2494915/ (2012-07-23)
3. Wight, O.W.: Manufacturing Resource Planning: MRP II. Unlocking America's Productivity Potential, p. 51. Oliver WightTM Limited Publications, Essex Junction, Revised Edition (1984)
4. Sheikh, K.: Manufacturing Resource Planning (MRP II) with introduction to ERP, SCM, and CRM, p. 89. McGraw Hill, New York (2003)
5. Wight, O.W.: Manufacturing Resource Planning: MRP II. Unlocking America's Productivity Potential, p. 53. Oliver WightTM Limited Publications, Essex Junction, Revised Edition (1984)
6. Wight, O.W.: Manufacturing Resource Planning: MRP II. Unlocking America's Productivity Potential, p. xv. Oliver WightTM Limited Publications, Essex Junction, Revised Edition (1984)
7. Higgins, P., Le Roy, P., Tierney, L.: Manufacturing Planning and Control. Beyond MRPII, p. 45. Chapman & Hall, London (1996)
8. Wight, O.W.: Manufacturing Resource Planning: MRP II. Unlocking America's Productivity Potential, p. 44. Oliver WightTM Limited Publications, Essex Junction, Revised Edition (1984)
9. Wight, O.W.: (1984). Manufacturing Resource Planning: MRP II. Unlocking America's Productivity Potential, p. 55. Oliver WightTM Limited Publications, Essex Junction, Revised Edition (1984)
10. Gesellschaft zur Prüfung von Software mbH: ERP Testbericht 2011, http://www.gps-ulmde/98.0.html. (2012-09-07) (2011)
11. Schmid, W.: Sieben ERP-Produkte im Vergleich. http:www.computerwoche.de/mittelstand/2501372/ (2012-08-24)
12. Dickersbach, J.T., Keller, G., Weihrauch, K.: Produktionsplanung und -steuerung mit SAP. Galileo Press, Bonn (2006)
13. Gronau, N.: Management von Produktion und Logistik mit SAP R/3, p. 19. R.Oldenbourg Verlag, München (1999)
14. SAP: Our company. http://www.sap.com/corporate-de/ourcompany/index.epx (2012-09-07) (2012)
15. Haberlandt, K.: PPS-Anforderungen bei Werkstattfertigung. In: PPS Management 4, GITO Verlag, pp. 47–52 (1999)
16. Dickersbach, J.T., Keller, G., Weihrauch, K.: Produktionsplanung und -steuerung mit SAP, p. 241. Galileo Press, Bonn (2006)
17. Kletti, J. (ed.): MES Manufacturing Execution System. Springer, Berlin (2006)
18. Kletti, J.: Konzeption und Einführung von MES-Systemen. Springer, Berlin (2007)

19. Kletti, J., Schumacher, J.: Die perfekte Produktion. Springer, Berlin (2011)
20. Stadtler, H.: Lineare und Gemischt-Ganzzahlige Optimierung. In: Stadtler, J., Kilger, C., Meyr, H. (eds.) Supply Chain Management und Advanced Planning, pp. 427–439. Springer, Berlin (2010)
21. Klein, R., Faust, O.: Genetische Algorithmen. In: Stadtler, J., Kilger, C., Meyr, H. (eds.) Supply Chain Management und Advanced Planning, pp. 441–449. Springer, Berlin (2010)
22. Klein, R., Faust, O.: Constraint Programming. In: Stadtler, J., Kilger, C., Meyr, H.: (eds.) Supply Chain Management und Advanced Planning, pp. 451–459. Springer, Berlin (2010)
23. Knolmayer, G.: Advanced Planning and Scheduling Systems: Optimierungsmethoden als Entscheidungskriterium für die Beschaffung von Software-Paketen? In: Wagner, U. (ed.) Zum Erkenntnisstand der Betriebswirtschaftslehre am Beginn des 21. Jahrhunderts, Festschrift für Erich Loitlsberger zum 80. Geburtstag, Duncker & Humblot, Berlin, pp. 135–155 (2001)
24. Stadtler, J., Kilger, C., Meyr, H. (eds.): Supply Chain Management und Advanced Planning. Springer, Berlin (2010)
25. Knolmayer, G., Mertens, P., Zeier, A.: Supply Chain Management Based on SAP Systems (R/3 4.6; APO 3.0). Springer, Berlin (2002)
26. Stadtler, H., Kilger, C.: Zusammenfassung und Ausblick. In: Stadtler, J., Kilger, C., Meyr, H. (eds.) Supply Chain Management und Advanced Planning, pp. 403–409. Springer, Berlin (2010)
27. Balla, J., Layer, F.: Produktionsplanung mit SAP APO, vol. 2, p. 21. Galileo Press, Bonn (2010)

Enterprise Resource Planning Requirements Process: The Need for Semantic Verification

Peter Bollen

Abstract This paper reviews the relevance of requirements determination in the commercial-off-the-shelf (COTS) enterprise software era. State-of-the-art requirements determination methods must contain, facilities for allowing semantic verification. We will introduce a conceptual modelling approach that fulfills this requirement and that can be used in the process of ERP configuration and requirements determination in general. The fact-based conceptual modelling approach that we will use in this paper is CogNIAM.

1 Introduction

The London Stock exchange automated trading system Taurus, had to be withdrawn before it ever was used [38]. The failure of National Insurance Recording System in England lead to tax overpayments by 800,000 people [40]. These are examples of organizations that have become victims of an unsatisfactory user requirements determination process. Unsatisfactory user requirements determination is one of the most prevalent reasons for faulty information systems or information systems that turn out to be overdue and too costly. Requirements determination is the least well-defined phase in the systems development process [17] and: "has been widely recognized as the most difficult activity of information systems development." ([10], p. 224). Failures in the requirements determination process represent one of the leading causes of system failure: "Given an appropriate design, most information systems departments can successfully implement a system. The big problem is correctly determining information requirements and designing the right system." ([45], p. 52). Many IS failures can be attributed to a

---

P. Bollen (✉)
Maastricht University, Maastricht, Netherlands
e-mail: p.bollen@maastrichtuniversity.nl

lack of clear and specific information requirements." ([11], p. 118). "The major reason that IS does not meet user expectation is a failure to obtain the correct and complete set of user requirements." ([47], p. 412) "Often, much of post-delivery maintenance work can be traced to requirements which had been poorly or falsely described in the system requirements specification (SRS), or were missed altogether." ([22], p. 161). Errors in the requirements specification caused by a faulty requirements determination process can remain latent until the later stages in the IS development process ([43], p. 666) and will cost a manifold to fix in these later stages [3, 4].

The information systems development market place changed in the early nineties of the last century when the *product software*-suppliers, e.g. MFG/PRO, IFS, ORACLE, SAP, BAAN, Marshal, Peoplesoft ([1], p. 369, [34], p. 387–389) started to sell their enterprise solutions on the waves of the Business Process Reengineering (BPR) sea [15, 20]. These product software solutions, promised to solve many problems that were caused by the software crisis and were considered to be an attractive investment option in ICT for the large (Fortune 500) companies. The implementation of, for example, ERP systems in a company, however, in most cases meant that the business process had to be reengineered or redesigned to fit the 'reference-model' that underlies the ERP package. This reengineering process turned out to be feasible for standard application functionality, for example, accounting, payroll, human resource management, inventory control. However, company-specific, functionality remained a problem in the first generation ERP-solutions. The second generation ERP-solutions, however, tried to redefine the concept of company-specific functionality, by developing 'standardized' software solutions for specific 'branches', for example, health-care, utilities, retail and so forth [8]. An example is Customer–Relationship Management (CRM) by Siebel [26]. The development of the additional functionality in these second generation ERP systems, implied, in many cases, additional reengineering efforts on these specific application domains before an implementation could take place. In spite of the availability of the second –generation ERP solutions, many companies needed customized modules and interfaces that allows them to support the specific parts of their business [37]. In the last decade firms have added modules that address inter-firm activities [25] and cross-organizational coordination [13]. We will call these ERP-implementations third generation ERP systems.

2 Roles in Requirements Determination

The improvement of the requirements determination processes for enterprise applications is still a relevant research subject within the field of business information systems because improving the state of the art in requirements determination methods to be applied in these requirements determination processes will have the following impact on organizations:

- It will enable them to express their (information) requirements using less (human) resources (more efficient).
- It will enable them to express their (information) requirements in a more precise, consistent and complete way.

If we now look back at the development in the development of (business) information systems over the past 60 years we can distinguish a number of roles in the requirements determination process:

1. The role of *user* or (business *domain expert*), these roles involve the knowledge of the business domain as it exist with the knowledge workers in the enterprise, for example the knowledge on how to process an invoice or how to approve a loan.
2. The role of the *analyst*, this role involves the knowledge on how to elicit the knowledge of a knowledge worker in the focal enterprise in a format that can be used by a developer to develop an application system. The result of the work of the analyst we will call a requirements specification.
3. The role of the systems *developer*, this role involves the knowledge on how to transform an information systems specification into a working information system that complies with the *functional requirements* as embedded in the *requirements specification*.

In Fig. 1 we have illustrated the general relationships between the aforementioned roles.

The extent in which the role of an analyst can be played perfectly in the requirements determination process depends upon the availability of 'a way of working', 'a way of modeling' and 'a way of controlling' ([46], p. 14). A *way of modeling* refers to the model types that are required: "A way of modeling structures the models which can be used in information systems development. Several models are usually required for problem specification and solution in the application area" ([46], p. 15).

A *way of working* or a *prescriptive process model* [32]: "is a description of processes at the type level. It defines how to use the concepts defined within a product Model. A prescriptive Process Model is used to describe 'how things must/should/could be done." ([32], p. 62). The way of working refers to the process-oriented view of information system development, whereas the way of modeling refers to the product-oriented view of information system development.

Fig. 1 The roles in the requirements determination process in general

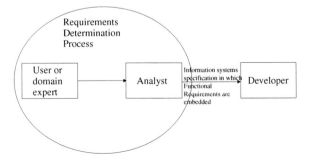

2.1 Sub-Steps in Requirements Determination

The general requirements determination process from Sect. 2.1 is generally viewed as consisting of three steps [10, 21]:

1. Information gathering (or requirements elicitation), during which an analyst elicitates requirements from (a) user (s) or domain expert(s),
2. Representation (or requirements specification), in which those requirements are specified in some modeling language by the analyst,
3. Verification (or requirements validation) in which the analyst verifies the correctness of these requirements with the user.

If we consider the aforementioned steps in the requirements determination process, then we can state that the scientific research on these steps has not exclusively taken place in the fields of Fig. 1. For example, with respect to the step information gathering or requirements elicitation, substantial research has taken place within the field of Knowledge Engineering [2] leading to knowledge acquisition methods like KADS [9]. These approaches are primarily directed at 'knowledge' green fields, i.e. those application domains that were generally considered to contain predominantly 'tacit' knowledge and these approaches were not developed for business application domains in which available knowledge has to be categorized and at most be made explicit.

With respect to the second step in the general requirements determination process: representation or requirements specification we can conclude that the definition of requirements specification languages has been a major research stream within the conceptual modeling and IS fields of study that deal with requirements determination. A Major data-oriented 'language family' in this respect is the (extended) ER language [12, 40]. As an example of a 'process-oriented' specification language we can consider Data Flow Diagrams (DFD's) [39] or Activity Diagrams (A-schemas) in ISAC [24].

With respect to the third step: requirements validation (or verification) we must make a distinction into *semantic verification* and *syntactic verification*. Semantic verification is the type of validation that is concerned with the capturing of the 'right' domain requirements in terms of the extent in which what the analyst records is what the domain user intends to express. Dullea et al. ([16], p. 171–172) define the concept semantic validity as follows: "An entity-relationship diagram is semantically valid only when each and every relationship exactly represents the modeler's concept of the problem domain". We will generalize this concept to every requirements determination method and more importantly, we will extend this concept beyond the modeler's interpretation of the application domain to the user's interpretation for the application domain, into our definition of a semantic correct specification. The outcome of a requirements determination process expressed in some specification language, therefore, should always be a semantically correct specification.

Syntactic verification, merely deals with the compliance of a specific application specification to the modeling rules that are contained in the meta-model of the specification language. We must be aware of the possibility that a semantic incorrect specification can be syntactically correct in any given situation.

The steps in the requirements determination process that cover the semantic verification are missing in the existing requirements determination methods for management information systems or business information systems ([18], p. 376). In this paper we will introduce a requirements determination method in which the semantic verification is incorporated in an explicit way.

2.2 Eras in Requirements Determination

In the 1970s a clear separation took place between the functional requirements and the way in which these functional requirements were coded in a specific implementation technology [42]. The distinction between an *information analyst* and *systems developer* emerged. The application of information systems development methodologies was aimed at the creation of 'tailor-made' information systems in which the needs of the domain users served as input.

In the ERP era (1990 and onwards) the roles of the user (or domain expert), analyst and developer were becoming more iterative instead of the linear sequence in which those roles were performed in the 1970 and 1980s. Because the implementation of ERP-systems usually is linked to business process redesign [14, 33] or a business process reengineering exercise ([35], p. 72), the role of the user or domain expert becomes more complex. In cooperation with the ERP-analyst the domain expert has to evaluate a number of proposed ways of working that will be supported by the specific ERP system in the company ([36], p. 183).

The roles that we have depicted in Fig. 1 have deliberately different names in Fig. 2, because an ERP analyst is not only modeling the user requirement of a proposed (or 'to-be') business process but in addition has to confront the user or domain expert with the different possible (or 'to-be') business logics or best practices that are available in the chosen ERP system. The business, therefore, is expected to select and adapt a reference model, based on available solutions with minimal changes and leaving no record of the enterprise's original requirements ([36], p. 183). On the other hand, even when they decide to implement an ERP system some organizations (for example Reebok) still choose to customize ([23], p. 417) and enhance the standard functionality of the ERP system [37]. We remark, that the focus of the requirements determination in this article is on the conceptualization of the information and decision rules that must be contained in an (ERP) application. The available functionality in the templates of an ERP product, however determines the 'boundaries of practice' for the organization that wants to implement an ERP system [44].

3 A Method for ERP Requirements Determination and Semantic Verification

In this section we will introduce a conceptual modeling approach that has proven successfully for the creation of (IS)-specifications that require a built-in semantic verification process. This approach is called the fact-based conceptual modeling approach and has evolved over 35 years from an architecture for databases [27] towards a versatile methodology for specifying knowledge bases, business rules and business processes [28]. Currently the fact-based approach is embedded in two main methods : Object Role Modeling (ORM-2) [19] and CogNIAM [28, 29]. Both methods take a single fact encoding modeling construct as a starting point. Both methods also apply a rigid 'way of working' for creating a conceptual schema for the data perspective. These methods, differ, however in terms of focus. In ORM-(2) a very large selection of constraints to model business rules in the data perspective has been introduced. In CogNIAM the focus is on a generic knowledge architecture that also covers the process and behavioural perspectives in conceptual modeling. In this article we will illustrate the application of the fact-based approach by using CogNIAM's knowledge architecture and notational convention for fact type diagrams. A theoretical foundation for CogNIAM can be found in [5–7].

In fact-based modeling we will use tangible documents or 'data-use cases' as a starting point for the modeling process. In most, if not all cases, a verbalizable knowledge source is a document that often is incomplete, informal, ambiguous, possibly redundant and possibly inconsistent. As a result of applying the fact-oriented knowledge extracting procedure (KEP), we will yield a document that only contains structured knowledge or a knowledge grammar which structures verbalizable knowledge into the following elements (*knowledge reference model(KRM)*) ([29], p. 766):

1. Knowledge domain sentences.
2. Definitions and naming conventions for concepts used in domain sentences.
3. Knowledge domain fact types including sentence group templates.

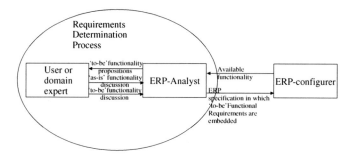

Fig. 2 The roles in the ERP requirements determination process

4. Population state (transition) constraints or validation rules for the knowledge domain.
5. Derivation rules that specify *how* specific domain sentences can be derived from other domain sentences.
6. Rules that specify *what* fact instances can be inserted, updated or deleted.
7. Event rules that specify *when* a fact is derived from other facts or when a fact must be inserted, updated or deleted.

A KRM of a complete organization would contain hundreds, possibly thousands of concept definitions, naming conventions, fact types, population constraints, derivation rules and event rules. In [30] a successful application of fact-based modeling using the NIAM2007 method (a predecessor to CogNIAM) for requirements analysis is documented. In this project 125 fact types were derived, 1260 concept definitions were created, 704 (business rule) constraints were modeled and 20 derivation rules were derived.

The fact-based knowledge extracting procedure (KEP) specifies *how* we can transform a possibly informal, mostly incomplete, mostly undetermined, possibly redundant and possibly inconsistent description of business domain knowledge into the following classes: *informal comment, non-verbalizable knowledge* and *verbalizable knowledge* to be classified into types 1 through 7 of the KRM. We note that the knowledge extraction procedure that is needed to instantiate the elements 1 through 5 (of the KRM) is an extension of ORM's conceptual schema design procedure (CSDP) [19]. In business domains, furthermore, we can capture the dynamic aspects by defining the exchange rules (element 6 of the KRM) and the event rules (element 7 of the KRM).

3.1 Knowledge Domain Sentences

The first element in the KRM is the group of sentences that represent an elementary fact (ground fact) in the domain. In our EOQ determination domain we encounter following example elementary sentences (that represent elementary (ground) facts):

```
The quantity of 1500 is the annual demand for the item ab3456
The quantity of 2500 is the annual demand for the item ab9876
The item ab3456 has an ordering cost of 25 euros
The item ab9876 has an ordering cost of 55 euros
The item ab3456 has a unit holding cost of 0,5 euros
The item ab9876 has a unit holding cost of 0,6 euros
The Item ab3456 has an economic order quantity 387
The Item df4567 has an economic order quantity 677
```

These sentences have a meaning for the people working in the logistics department. However, as soon as people communicate with people outside of this department, additional semantics have to be captured. For example, it should be agreed upon to what time-frame the amount of holding costs for a product refers: a day, a week, a month, a year ?. These agreements should be part of a list of concept definitions in which it will be recorded that the term *unit holding cost* always refers to the *unit holding costs per year*. Another semantic issue that has to be defined in a list of concept definitions is the naming conventions for domain concepts. For example of what name class is 'ab3456' an instance? In practice when there is inter-organizational communication it must be crystal-clear which name classes can be used in communication. In case more two or more alternative name classes exist in the domain, it must be agreed upon to explicitly qualify the names used in the communication with the name classes:

```
The item with item code ab3456 has an ordering cost of 25
euros
The item with EAN bar code 8734576287465 has an ordering cost
of 55 euros
```

3.2 Concept Definitions and Naming Conventions for Concepts Used in Domain Sentences

In order to be able to grasp the meaning of sentences in the business domain it was argued that when two or more actors are involved in a communication process, semantic consistency can only be achieved if the different actors have the same understanding of concepts and naming conventions. This will be established in CogNIAM by creating (and maintaining) a list of concept definitions. An instance of such a list of concept definitions for our running example is given in Table 1.

3.3 Knowledge Domain Fact Types

The next step in CogNIAM is the generalization of the ground facts into fact type forms. The example ground facts from Sect. 3.1 will lead to the following fact type forms by replacing the variable parts in those sentence by 'placeholders' (<..>):

```
The quantity <Quantity> is the annual demand for the item
<Item>
The item <Item> has an ordering cost <Cost>
The item <Item> has a unit holding cost <Cost>
```

Next to the difference in naming conventions, inter-organizational and even intra-organizational communication might necessitate the existence of two or more

Enterprise Resource Planning Requirements Process

Table 1 The list of concept definitions fort he EOQ

List of definitions for economic order quantity business process	
Item	An individual product that has an identifying item code and is held in inventory somewhere along the value chain.synonym: stock keeping unit
Item code	An {Item code} is a unique signification for an [item] that enables us to identify a specific [Item] within the set of all [Item]s within the context of a business organization
EAN bar code	An {EAN bar code} is a unique signification for an [Item] that enables us to identify a specific [Item]within the set of all [Item]s within the context of a business organization in Europe
Lot	A {lot} is a quantity of [Item]s that are processed together
Cost	A sacrifice or expenditure
Ordering cost	The [Cost] of preparing a purchase order for a supplier or a production order for shop
Inventory holding cost	The sum of the [Cost] of capital and the variable [Cost]s of keeping [Item]s on hand, such as storage and handling, taxes, insurance and shrinking, for a time period of a year
Cycle inventory cost	The portion of [Inventory Holding Cost] that varies directly with [Lot] size
Economic order quantity	An {Economic Order Quantity} is the quantity of a [Lot] that minimizes total annual [Cycle Inventory Cost] and [Ordering Cost] for a given [item]
Annual demand	The yearly total demand for a given [Item]
Natural number	A unique signification for an [Economic Order Quantity] or [Annual Demand] that enables us to identify a specific quantity within the set of all [Economic Order Quantity]s or [Annual Demand]s
Unit holding costs	The costs for holding one unit of an [Item] in inventory for a year
Dollar amount	A unique signification for a [Cost] that enables us to identify a specific [Cost] within the set of all [Cost]s

fact type forms to communicate instances of the same fact type in a *target group* specific way. For example for the fact type *Annual Demand Quantity* the following two fact type forms might exist together, each serving a different target group within or outside) the organization:

```
1: The quantity <Quantity> is the annual demand for the item
<Item>
2: Item <Item> has an annual demand of quantity <Quantity>
```

In Fig. 3 we have graphically shown the fact type *Annual Demand Quantity* together with the defining fact types for the object types that play the 'variable' roles in the fact type: *Item* and *Quantity*.

We note that we can define as many fact type forms for a fact type as are needed by the domain(s), e.g. we might add fact type forms in German, Russian, French and Spanish if a company's international business contacts require this. The black rectangles in the low-right corner of a 'variable' denote that a value must exist in order to get a correct sentence.

3.4 State (Transition) Constraints or Validation Rules

In Fig. 3 we have shown the model for the fact type *Annual Demand Quantity*. The next element of the KRM is the detection of those business rules that can be expressed as constraints or validation rules on the possible populations of the fact type(s), e.g. business rules that specify which actual sentence combinations are allowed to exist at any point in time, and which transitions between sentence combinations are permitted. In fact based modeling a large number of constraint types exist: uniqueness- mandatory role-, value, set-comparison-, ring constraints [19]. In this section we will give an illustration of uniqueness constraints and referential constraints.

Uniqueness Constraints

As an example of the application of a semantic verification process we will illustrate how we can meticulously derive all uniqueness constraints for a given fact type, by starting with sentence instances that represent ground facts:

```
The quantity of 1500 is the annual demand for the item ab3456
(sentence 1)
```

We will now create a second example sentence in which the value of the 1st variable or placeholder has changed:

```
The quantity of 1200 is the annual demand for the item ab3456
(sentence 2)
```

We confront the domain expert with these two example sentences and ask him/her whether these sentences can exist in combination at any point in time. The answer of the domain expert is: No, these sentences can not exist in combination, because at a given point in time there exists (at most) one specific value for the annual demand for a given item. This finding now has lead us to the detection of uniqueness constraint *C1* defined as an arrow covering the variable *Item* of fact type *AnnualDemandQuantity* in Fig. 4. We will now create a third example sentence by changing the value of the 2nd variable (of sentence 1):

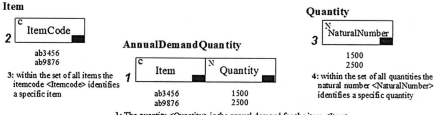

Fig. 3 Domain model for fact type annual demand quantity including object types

The quantity of 1500 is the annual demand for the item cd6457
(sentence 3)

In this case the domain expert will confirm that it is possible that sentences 1 and 3 coexist at any point in time. This means that there does not exist an uniqueness constraint that is defined on the role *Quantity* of the fact type *AnnualDemandQuantity* (see Fig. 4). Uniqueness constraints *C2* and *C3* on the object defining fact types *Item* and *Quantity* are implied because these fact types are unary, i.e. they contain exactly one variable.

Referential Constraints

A second group of constraints or validation rules is concerned with the issue of which object type is referenced by a variable in a fact type. The variable *Quantity* in fact type *Annual Demand Quantity* is played by the object type *Quantity*, hence the subset constraint *c5* departing from the variable role quantity in fact type *Annual Demand Quantity* and ending in the variable role *NaturalNumber* from the object defining fact type *Quantity* (see Fig. 4). Implying that at any point in time the set of annual demand quantities has to be a subset of all quantities.

We note that the referential constraint for the variable item from the fact type *Annual Demand Quantity* to the object type item is the equality constraint *C4* (see Fig. 4). This means that for every item that exists an annual demand quantity must be known. Similar reasoning for constraints *C7* and *C11*: for every item a holding cost and ordering cost must be recorded.

3.5 Derivation Rules

In Fig. 5 we have given a complete domain specific fact type model for the EOQ domain area in which we have added all uniqueness and referential constraints.

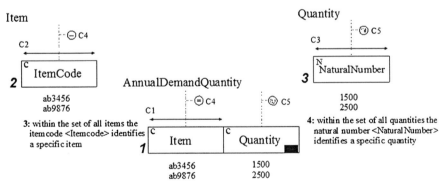

Fig. 4 Fact type annual demand quality including object types and uniqueness- and referential constraints

Furthermore, it can be noticed from the referential constraints that we do not record an Economic Order Quantity for every item. But what we do know is that for those items that fulfill the EOQ assumptions we will calculate the economic order quantity using the EOQ formula and rounding it to the next integer number. We will model this in fact-based modeling using derivation rules. In CogNIAM a derivation rule is signified by an 'f' box connected to the variables in the fact type that will be derived using the logic from the derivation rule (see Fig. 5).

To specify the logic of the derivation rule we use the notational convention (definition style) from ORM-2 ([19], p. 99) in Fig. 6.

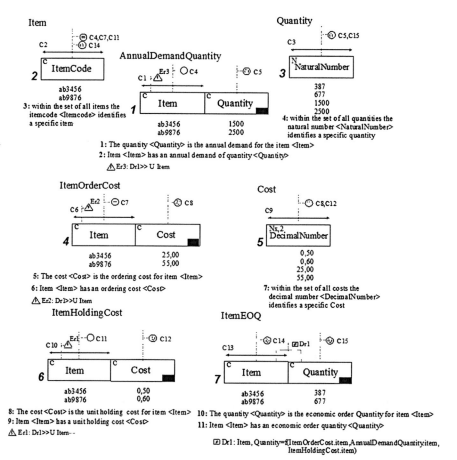

Fig. 5 Complete domain specific model for economic order quantity

```
{EOQ = ROUND(SQRT((2*annual demand*ordering cost)/unit holding cost))}
define  item has EOQ(units)
   as   item has annual demand    and
        item has ordering cost    and
        item has unit holding cost and
        EOQ= ROUND(SQRT((2*annual demand*ordering cost)/unit holding cost))
```

Fig. 6 Derivation rule logic for derivation rule Dr 1

3.6 Exchange Rules

In the former section we explained how instances of a derived fact type can be 'calculated' by using a derivation rule. For those fact types that are non-derivable or asserted we need to specify how, instances can be added, updated or deleted from the information base. Basically we distinguish between an insert (I), an update (U) and a delete (D) exchange rule.

3.7 Event Rules

The final element in the knowledge reference model (KRM) are the event rules. An event rule basically determines when (an) exchange rule(s) and/or derivation rules(s) must be executed. In the domain model from Fig. 5 three event rules are contained. Event rule *Er1* (Dr1 ≫ U Item) tells us that whenever an update (U) takes place on the holding cost for a specific item, derivation rule *Dr1* must be executed. In semantic terms this means that a new EOQ is calculated as soon as the holding cost of an item change. A similar reasoning applies to event rules *Er2* and *Er3* for a change in *order costs* and *annual demand quantity*.

4 Conclusion

What we can conclude is that in spite of the trends in information systems development from 'tailor-made' towards 'commercial-off-the-shelf' (COTS) software implementations, the *requirement determination process* still is a significant process in the development life cycle of information systems. Moreover, the increase in complexity of the requirements determination process due to the use of 'pre-fabricated' software with its numerous implementation options (see the discussion on *configuration tables* in [14]) has basically increased the need for *requirements determination methods* that have a way of modeling that can capture the complete set of user requirements and which way of working will guide the analyst in extracting all relevant business entities and business rules for a specific application domain. The steps in the requirements determination process that cover the semantic verification are missing in the existing requirements determination methods for management information systems or business information systems ([18], p. 376). We have shown that there exists generic RE models [31], i.e. CogNIAM [28] that fill this void in semantic-oriented coordination [13] and that can deliver a semantically verified requirements specification by guiding ERP-analysts and ERP-configurers in their task.

References

1. Bansal, V., Negi, T.: A metric for ERP complexity. LNBIP **7**, 369–379 (2008)
2. Barrett, A., Edwards, J.: Knowledge elicitation and knowledge representation in a large domain with multiple experts. Exp. Syst. Appl. **8**(1), 169–176 (1995)
3. Boehm, B.: Software Engineering Economics. Prentice-Hall, Englewood Cliffs (1981)
4. Boehm, B: Software Risk Management. IEEE computer society press, Los Alamitos (1989)
5. Bollen, P.: The Natural Language Modeling Procedure'. In: Halevy, A., Gal, A. (eds.) Proceedings Fifth Workshop on Next Generation Information Technologies and Systems (NGITS'2002), Lecture Notes in Computer Science 2382, pp. 123–146. Springer, Berlin (2002)
6. Bollen, P.: On the applicability of requirements determination methods. Ph.D thesis. Faculty of Management and Organization. Rijksuniversiteit Groningen (2004)
7. Bollen, P.: Natural language modeling for business application semantics. J. Inf. Sci. Technol. **2**(3), 18–48 (2005)
8. Boudreau, M. ERP Implementation and Forms of Organizational Change. Working paper Georgia State University (1999)
9. Breuker, J., Wielinga, B.: Knowledge acquisition as modeling expertise; The KADS methodology. Paper presented at the 1st European workshop on knowledge acquisition for knowledge based systems. Reading University (1987)
10. Browne, G., Rogich, M.: An empirical investigation of user requirements elicitation: comparing the effectiveness of prompting techniques. J. Manag. Inf. Syst. **17**(4), 223–249 (2001)
11. Byrd, T., Cossick, K., Zmud, R.: A synthesis of research on requirements analysis and knowledge acquisition techniques. MIS Q. **16**(1), 117–138 (1992)
12. Chen, P.: The entity-relationship model: towards a unified view of data. ACM TODS **1**(1), 9–36 (1976)
13. Daneva, M., Wieringa, R.: A coordination complexity model to support requirements engineering for cross-organizational ERP. Requirements Engineering, 14th IEEE International Conference, pp. 311–314 (2006)
14. Davenport, T.: Putting the enterprise into the enterprise system. Harvard Bus. Rev. **76**(4), 121–131 (1998)
15. Davenport, T., Short, J.: The new industrial engineering: information technology and business process redesign. Sloan Manag. Rev. **31**(4), 11–27 (1990)
16. Dullea, J., Song, I.-Y., Lamprou, I.: An analysis of structural validity in entity-relationship modeling. Data Knowl. Eng. **47**, 167–205 (2003)
17. Flynn, D.: Information Systems Requirements: Determination and Analysis. McGraw-Hill, London (1992)
18. Goldin, L., Berry, D.: Abstfinder, a prototype natural language text abstraction finder for use in requirements elicitation. Aut. Softw. Eng. **4**, 375–412 (1997)
19. Halpin, T., Morgan, T.: Information Modeling and Relational Databases 2nd edn. Morgan Kaufmann Publishers, San Francisco (2008)
20. Hammer, M.: Reengineering work: don't automate, obliterate. Harvard Bus. Rev. **68** (4), 104–112 (1990)

21. Lalioti, V., Loucopoulos, P.: Visualisation of conceptual specifications. Inf. Syst. **19**(3), 291–309 (1994)
22. Lang, M., Duggan, J.: A tool to support collaborative software requirements management. Requir. Eng. **6**, 161–172 (2001)
23. Light, B.: The maintenance implications of the customization of ERP software. J. Softw. Maint. Evol. Res. Pract. **13**, 415–429 (2001)
24. Lundeberg, M., Goldkuhl, G., Nilsson, G.: A systematic approach to information systems development. Inf. Syst. **4**, 1–12, 93–118 (1979)
25. Madapusi, A., D'Souza, D.: The influence of ERP system implementation on the operational performance of an organization. Int. J. Inf. Manag. **32**, 24–34 (2012)
26. Molenaar, T.: Siebel zet in op personeelsbeheer. Computable 43: 26 oktober: p. 11 (2001)
27. Nijssen, G.M.: On the gross architecture for the next generation database management systems. In: Gilchrist, B., (ed.) Information Processing'77, pp. 327–335 (1977)
28. Nijssen, G.M., Le Cat, A.: Kennis Gebaseerd Werken: de manier om kennis productief te Maken. PNA Publishing, Heerlen (2009)
29. Nijssen, M., Lemmens, I.: Verbalization for business rules and two flavors of verbalization for fact examples. LNCS **5333**, 760–769 (2008)
30. Nijssen, M., Lemmens, I., Mak, R.: Fact-orientation applied to develop a flexible employment benefits system. LNCS **5872**, 745–756 (2009)
31. Niu, N., Easterbrook, S.: Exploiting COTS-based RE methods: an experience report. LNCS **5030**, 212–216 (2008)
32. Nurcan, S., Rolland, C.: A multi-method for defining the organizational change. Inf. Softw. Technol. **45**, 61–82 (2003)
33. Rolland, C., Prakash, N.: Bridging the gap between organisational needs and ERP functionality. Requir. Eng. **5**, 180–193 (2000)
34. Siriginidi, S.: Enterprise resource planning in reengineering business. Bus. Process Manag. **6**(5), 376–391 (2000)
35. Skok, W., Legge, M.: Evaluating enterprise resource planning (ERP) systems using an interpretive approach. Knowl. Process Manag. **9**(2), 72–82 (2002)
36. Soffer, P., Golany, B., Dori, D., Wand, Y.: Modelling off-the-shelf. Information systems requirements: an ontological approach. Require. Eng. **6**, 183–199 (2001)
37. Soffer, P., Golany, B., Dori, D.: ERP modeling: a comprehensive approach. Inf. Syst. **28**(6), 673–690 (2003)
38. Stock exchange kills projects to focus on Taurus. (1989). Editorial
39. Computing NoSystem problems leave Inland revenue with £ 20 of taxpayers' cash (2002). Computer Weekly. February 14
40. Theory, T., Yang, D., Fry, J.: A logical design methodology for relational databases using the extended E-R model. ACM Comput. Surv. **18**(2), 197–222 (1986)
41. Tsichritzis, D., Klug, A.: The ANSI/X3/SPARC DBMS framework. Info. Syst. **3**, 173–191 (1978)
42. Viller, S., Bowers, J., Rodden, T.: Human factors in requirements engineering: a survey of human sciences literature relevant to the improvement of dependable systems development processes. Interact. Comput. **11**(6), 665–698 (1999)
43. Wagner, E., Scott, S.V., Galliers, R.: The creation of 'best practice' software: myth, reality and ethics. Inf. Organ. **16**, 251–275 (2006)
44. Wetherbe, J.: Executive information requirements: getting it right. MIS Q. **15**(1), 51–65 (1991)
45. Wijers, G.: Modelling support in information systems development. Doctoral thesis. Technical University Delft (1991)
46. Wu, I.-L., Shen, Y.-C.: A model for exploring the impact of purchasing strategies on user requirements determination of e-SRM. Inf. Manag. **43**, 411–422 (2006)
47. Yourdon, E., Constantine, L.: Structured Design. Prentice Hall, (1979)

Part III
Human Interaction with ERP Systems

ERP Clients: Browser-Based or Dedicated: Do We Need Both?—An Evaluation Based on User Perceptions

Christian Leyh and Walter Heger

Abstract Due to recent technological developments, enabling mobility to users becomes more and more important for ERP manufacturers. With mobile devices employees can use their ERP applications on the road to take advantage of business capabilities. Here, "putting everything into the browser" is a challenge for ERP manufacturers. Additionally, the question arises whether to provide only one client—a browser-based one—or to still provide additionally a dedicated client? To gain first insight for answering this question, we measured the workload of selected ERP users by using NASA's Task Load Index (TLX) while fulfilling tasks of a limited business scenario within a dedicated client and within a browser-based client. According to our results the workload for the dedicated client is lower whereas usability is rated higher with the browser-based client. Therefore, a browser-based client could be a good enhancement for ERP systems, but dedicated clients are still necessary.

1 Introduction

Today's enterprises are faced with the globalization of markets and fast changes in the economy. In order to be able to cope with these conditions, the use of information and communication systems as well as technology is almost mandatory. Specifically, the adoption of enterprise resource planning (ERP) systems as standardized systems that encompass the actions of whole enterprises has become an important factor in today's business [1]. Therefore, during the last few decades, ERP system

---

C. Leyh (✉) · W. Heger
Dresden University of Technology, Dresden, Germany
e-mail: christian.leyh@tu-dresden.de

W. Heger
e-mail: walter.heger@tu-dresden.de

software represented one of the fastest growing segments in the software market; indeed, these systems are one of the most important recent developments within information technology. Due to the saturation of ERP markets targeting large-scaled enterprises, current ERP system manufacturers are also now concentrating on the growing market of small and medium-sized enterprises (SMEs) [2, 3]. This has resulted in a highly fragmented ERP market and a great diffusion of ERP systems throughout enterprises of nearly every industry and every size [4, 5]. Thereby, ERP systems claim to combine best business practices that replace separate functional systems. A properly selected and implemented ERP system offers several benefits such as considerable reductions in inventory costs, raw material costs, lead time for customers, production time, and production costs [6, 7]. Therefore, current standardized ERP systems are used in a majority of enterprises around the world. For example, according to a survey conducted in Germany in 2009, ERP systems are used in more than 92 % of all German industrial enterprises [8].

Due to technological revolution and developments, enabling mobility to users becomes increasingly important [9]. With mobile devices such as laptops, PDAs, and tablets, employees can use their ERP applications on the road to take advantage of business capabilities. They can access mobile information from home or any other location as a place of work [10]. Therefore, the business world is beginning to adopt mobile capabilities in their evaluation, selection, and implementation or upgrades of enterprise software systems. Studies from IFS indicate that 47 % of employees access information on the move once or twice a week. With remote access, 63 % would even reason to work outside of normal business hours [11].

However, "putting everything into the browser" is a challenge for software and IT system vendors and manufacturers. For example, it is mandatory for web-based application not only to provide web-access to all necessary functionalities but also to ensure clarity and good usability of their user interfaces [12], since much time is lost by users who encounter frustrating experiences with information systems, for example, caused by inappropriate usability of user interfaces or missing functionality [13].

Here, ERP systems, as information systems with complex structure and functions, were designed with dedicated clients during the last decades. And even today, most systems are still using dedicated clients. However, some ERP manufacturers have already shifted towards browser-based clients and are only providing this type of access for the newer versions of their systems; whereas other manufacturers provide both—a dedicated client and a browser-based client. Therefore, the question arises whether to provide only one client—a browser-based one—or to still provide additionally a dedicated client?

To gain first insight for answering the above question, we focus on user and expert perceptions. Therefore, we created a scenario that builds upon delimited business processes that had to be completed by selected experts who had to fulfill the tasks of the scenario and to evaluate the scenario within a dedicated client and within a web browser.

As an ERP system, we selected Microsoft Dynamics NAV due to our background and since the upcoming release of NAV will provide a browser-based client parallel to its dedicated one. However, this integration functionality was not fully provided within the NAV version (NAV 2009) that was available for our study. Therefore, to test and to evaluate the browser integration we provided a web-access using Microsoft Office Sharepoint. Selected results of this evaluation will be presented within this paper.

Therefore, the paper is structured as follows. Next to the introduction we describe shortly our methodology. We will explain the scenario itself as well as the evaluation methodology. Afterwards, Sect. 3 will be the main part of this paper. Here, selected results of the expert evaluation considering the NAV dedicated client versus the browser-based application will be given. Finally, the paper ends with the conclusion, limitations, and future work.

2 Data Collection Methodology

2.1 Microsoft Dynamics NAV: Browser Integration

Microsoft Dynamics NAV is an ERP system from Microsoft for medium sized businesses. It is part of the product group Microsoft Dynamics such as Microsoft Dynamics AX, Microsoft Dynamics GP, and Microsoft Dynamics SL.

The release used in our study is Microsoft Dynamics NAV 2009 R2. A new version, Microsoft Dynamics NAV 7, is already under development where browser integration will be embedded.

Microsoft Dynamics NAV provides two clients to work with, currently. The Classic Client is the original user interface for working and customizing business logic. To increase the customizability and flexibility, Microsoft Dynamics NAV 2009 offers the Role-Tailored Client (RTC) based on .NET. With the upcoming release of Microsoft Dynamics NAV 7, Microsoft provides a third client for Microsoft Office SharePoint [14]. The user interface of the Classic Client is very similar to the one of Microsoft Office. The RTC inherits its appearance from a web browser. Unlike the Classic Client, pages are displayed in independent new windows and not as inner-framed windows. With Microsoft Dynamics NAV 7 (the upcoming release), an integration of pages in Microsoft Office SharePoint is planned. It will include web browser capability to access data in the cloud or on premises. Integration into a browser application such as Microsoft Office SharePoint would bring out quite some benefits. Of ERP users, 29 % see the SharePoint as an alternative to hard-to-use enterprise software. Therefore, they outsource missing functionality of the ERP system. Even more, 72 % use Microsoft Office Excel to store data [11]. Since Microsoft Office SharePoint is directly linked to Microsoft Office products, browser integration could merge functionality of both systems and allow the user to work with his files more easily.

2.2 Business Process Scenario

To evaluate the usability of such a browser-based client, we created a scenario with integration of selected business processes connected to NAV 2009.

According to Holtstiege et al. [14], the major business processes of Microsoft Dynamics NAV are purchase, warehouse, sales, and finance. Due to a high complexity of finance, a mainly setting-character of warehouse and a high customer need of time reporting, the selection for our study differs. Magal and Word [15] define the procurement, production, and fulfillment as general key business processes of an organization. To evaluate possible browser integration we focused on routine tasks that need a high system support (see [16]). Those tasks are for example purchase and sales order processing as well as time reporting. The tasks of the scenario are, therefore, as follows: (1) To create an item; (2) To create a purchase query; (3) To convert the purchase query into an order; (4) To create a sales query; (5) To convert the sales query into an order; (6) To report times.

Those business processes have to be done in both systems to be compared. The complexity of the scenario is orientated on a lower level of understanding ERP systems. Therefore, the tasks are designed simple with the result that the most important processes, which need a high system support, are covered. Every process can be done without completing the previous one. This was necessary to enable continuous progression even after failing in one of the tasks. The detailed scenario will not be part of this paper but can be provided upon request.

2.3 Evaluation and Data Collection Methodology

Interacting with an ERP system requires among others a certain amount of concentration and time. The Human Performance Group at NASA Ames Research Center developed a procedure for collecting workload ratings between human and machines. Asking people to describe the feelings they experienced is one way to learn about workload. Therefore, the so-called Task Load Index (TLX) uses the dimensions Mental, Physical and Temporal Demands to the demands imposed on the subject and Effort, Frustration and Performance to the interaction of a subject with the task [17]. The TLX represents the workload necessary to fulfill the completion of a task. To calculate the TLX, all participants had to answer questions about the mentioned factors directly after accomplishing the scenario tasks. Therefore, for the TLX the participants had to answer a survey both after performing the scenario tasks with the RTC of Microsoft Dynamics NAV and also after using the browser-based client. Each factor was rated in a 20-point Likert scale and mapped on a value between 0 and 100. Comparisons of the workload according to TLX and additional questions like the needed time and handling of the tasks give an overview about which system is preferred to fulfill and solve the task of the scenario and which one is more convenient.

Besides the workload, we aimed additionally for a "general" evaluation of the user interfaces of both clients. Therefore, for evaluating ERP user interfaces the five criteria, Navigation, Presentation, Task Support, Learnability, and Customization, can be identified to verify usability problems [18]. Navigation is a design issue that aims to identify how effectively an end-user can access appropriate information, options, reports, elements, and menus. The Presentation of Screen and Output defines the suitability of the layout of menus, controls, dialog boxes and information on the screen, meaning the complexity of the screen display. The Task Support aims to ensure task completion by identifying accurate alignments between the real world and the execution of the system. Learnability is used to assess the effort required to understand and learn the usage. Customization describes the ability of the system to be suited to specific needs of the enterprise's processes [18]. Since our scenario contains only selected and limited business processes, Learnability and Customization cannot be determined, sufficiently. Therefore, those two criteria were discarded and were not part of the data collection.

For understanding what makes socio-technical systems successful, multi-method approaches involving, e.g., case studies, observations, interviews, or other longitudinal techniques, may be appropriate [19]. Therefore, we used a combination of a survey-based data collection and a simple time diary. For our study the whole evaluation is divided into two main parts (see Fig. 1). The first part is about the questions necessary for the TLX. Therefore, two nearly equal questionnaires had to be filled out for this part—one after the completion of the scenario in each

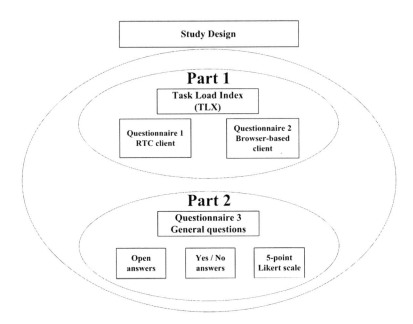

Fig. 1 Study design

of the systems. These questionnaires contained the workload questions and the weight of all six factors (Mental, Physical and Temporal Demands as well as Effort, Frustration and Performance) necessary for the calculation of the TLX. The second part consisted of a third questionnaire containing general questions involving both systems. The answer possibilities for the general questions reach from given options where the user had to select none, one, or multiple possibilities, to open text fields where the respondents could write their own words and opinions.

Due to our background, as participants, we focused on a range of experts to perform and to evaluate the scenario in the RTC and the browser-based client. For our study, experts are people who have to work frequently with an ERP system and run parts of business processes. The experts were supposed to be employees of a German consulting company focusing on Microsoft Business Solution products. For identifying properties [20] the experts can be separated by their jobs in the company (e.g., employees of the sales & marketing department, software engineers, software consultants, and trainees). Further separations can be the knowledge and interaction level with Microsoft Dynamics NAV and Microsoft Office SharePoint as well as the intensity of customer contact. In total the sample had a size of 20 employees who had to complete the scenario in both systems. After the completion of the scenario in each system they had to fill out surveys according to their experience within the systems.

As a pretest (according to [20, 21]), a small group of respondents (experts with high Microsoft Dynamics NAV knowledge and some people who never had contact with an ERP system) tested the questionnaires and reviewed the scenario. After the pretest, only one question was seen as unsure by two respondents and, therefore, was reviewed and reworded. Additionally, the structure of the TLX questions was changed from a big block into separate items.

3 Selected Results of the Client's Evaluation

The processing of data is achieved by using statistical analysis as well as graphical presentations. The statistical analysis can therefore be distinguished in a descriptive statistic, meaning the description of data based on measured parameters, and an inferential statistic. In this paper we focus on descriptive statistics to present the results. The differentiation of property values that display the data happens by determining categories to delimit and group the information. The standard deviation is used to describe the variation of the average. It has the same measuring unit and means based on the arithmetic average that the data deviate around this value [21].

Each participant completed the scenarios on his own computer without any additional help besides the accompanying documents. In total, they had 2 weeks, January 2, 2012 to January 16, 2012, to fulfill the tasks and answer all questions. Not a single person had problems that led to aborting the study. Therefore, all

Table 1 Response rate by occupation

Job description	Sample	Usable responses	Response rate (%)
Software engineer	10	8	80
Software consultant	5	5	100
Trainee	3	1	33.3
Sales & marketing	2	1	50
Total	20	15	75

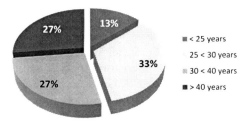

Fig. 2 Respondent's age

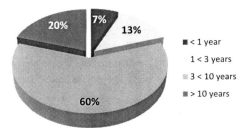

Fig. 3 Respondent's ERP experience

participants who decided to fulfill the scenario completed all tasks and answered all questions of the questionnaires. One reminder email after the first week helped to gather additional results. Table 1 shows the response rate of 75 %, itemized by the occupation. Except the trainees, more than 50 % of each group participated in the study.

An age analysis (see Fig. 2) shows that the respondents are spread pretty much even among younger and older employees. 54 % are 30 years or older; 33 % are between 25 and 30 years; and 13 % are younger than 25 years. The experience with ERP systems (see Fig. 3) is high with 80 % who has worked 3 years or longer in the business. The sample represents thereby experienced participants with excellent knowledge to judge both systems. About 87 % do actually have a deeper contact with customers and can partially estimate their business processes.

3.1 Results of Working with the RTC of Microsoft Dynamics NAV

Figure 4 shows the results of the rating for each factor and each respondent. Flat bars point to low demands or a positive satisfaction (performance). The high values represent negative characteristics because major effort was necessary to complete the task.

The results reveal that some factors, especially performance, are rated very different (see Fig. 4). Some respondents see their accomplishing of the goals as very good and some see it as very bad. Since everybody successfully finished the scenario, this could be caused by misunderstanding the question or accidentally interchanging the scale. Some factors such as effort and physical demand have a lower variance in answers. A full list of the average values and the variance is illustrated in Table 2. Since the maximum possible value is 100 and all factors are less than 30, the tasks seem to be minor demanding. In comparison against each other, with average values of 25–28, the mental demand, the temporal demand, and the frustration are assessed highest. In other words, the most stressful were the thinking, time pressure, and insecurity. The general effort is with about 18.25 a bit less behind and a value of 7.02 for the physical demand indicates nearly no need in physical activity at all.

The rating of all factors is subjective and can vary much among different people (see Fig. 5). Therefore, the TLX procedure weights the items to differ the importance of each factor for each person. The respondents answered thereby

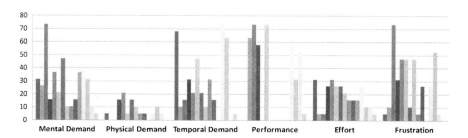

Fig. 4 TLX factors for the RTC (rectified scale)

Table 2 Average and variance of TLX factors for the RTC

Factors	Average	Variance	Standard deviation
Mental demand	27.37	321.28	17.92
Physical demand	7.02	42.22	6.5
Temporal demand	27.72	603.22	24.56
Performance	27.72	987.12	31.42
Effort	18.25	90.52	9.51
Frustration	25.97	536.07	23.15

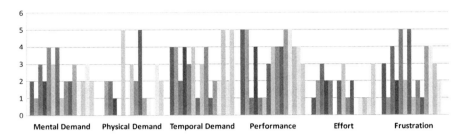

Fig. 5 TLX weighting (points) for the RTC

another 15 contractive questions about the factors. Two characteristics are compared and one point could be assigned for the more important one. The number of favors (points) for each factor is divided by 15 (total number of questions). Figure 5 shows the results (points) for all answers.

The results of the weighting are numbers that yield totalized in 1 (100 %). On average, the most important factors, having thereby a high weighting, are the performance (23.56 %) and the temporal demand (20.4 %). The frustration (17.33 %) and mental demand (16 %) are slightly behind and followed by the less important factors of physical demand (12 %) and effort (10.67 %).

All factors are multiplied with their weighting for each participant and summarized in a total workload. This number represents the TLX. The TLX is a value between 0 and 100. Zero means no effort at all and 100 is an exhausting task demanding everything from the respondent. The final TLX values for the case study are illustrated in Fig. 6. The average is 24.44 and the standard deviation is 13.64. This confirms the previous assumption of the single factor's analysis, which already indicated minor demands to fulfill the first part of the scenario. This value does not show any details. It classifies the full workload that was necessary to complete the tasks while working with the RTC.

A glimpse on the time diaries shows, except for a few aberrations, an obviously more balanced result than the TLX. The average time needed is 21.8 min with a standard deviation of 9.79. The variation can result for example from a different knowledge about the system or a varying of reading speed. Since one participant noted 23 min just for the first stage of the first part, he might have added the time for reading the case study introduction.

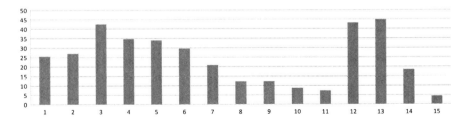

Fig. 6 TLX (per participant) for the RTC

3.2 Results of Working with the Browser-Based Client

All participants had to rate again the six factors for the TLX after completing the scenario using the browser integration. The results (see Fig. 7) are more unequivocal among the participants and have in most cases lower variances compared to the RTC (see Table 3).

Again, the big variance of the factor performance might be caused by misunderstanding the question or scale. The differences of the average values are bigger. The performance is with 42.26 of maximum 100 the highest factor and represents a mediocre satisfaction of task-completion. The frustration (30.53) is also pretty high compared to the others. The mental demand, temporal demand, and effort are among each other similar and in the lower quarter of the scale. Once more, the physical demand is the lowest factor with a value of 6.32.

The results of the TLX for the browser-based client are displayed in Fig. 8. With an average value of 26.9 the workload is again rather low. The standard deviation of 14.95 is slightly higher compared to the RTC. Therefore, the values are a bit more ambiguous.

The total time needed is, with an average value of 14.67 min, low. A standard deviation of 2.44 reveals equal times for all participants. Again, the same participant as in the RTC part needed again the most time to complete the task.

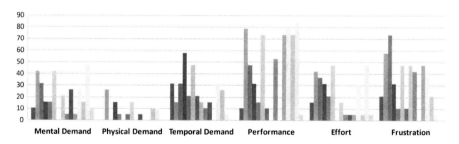

Fig. 7 TLX factors for browser-based client (rectified scale)

Table 3 Average and variance of TLX factors for browser-based client

Factors	Average	Standard deviation browser integration	Standard deviation RTC
Mental demand	21.05	14.62	17.92
Physical demand	6.32	8.01	6.5
Temporal demand	22.11	16.31	24.56
Performance	42.46	33.08	31.42
Effort	21.05	17.0	9.51
Frustration	30.53	22.7	23.15

ERP Clients: Browser-Based or Dedicated

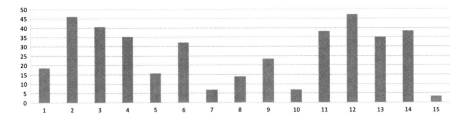

Fig. 8 TLX (per participant) for browser-based client

3.3 Comparison of Both Clients

Way more important than just an analysis of each system is the analysis about the changes from RTC to browser integration and thereby a comparison of both systems as user interfaces.

The average TLX value from the RTC (24.44) is less than the one from the browser integration (26.9). That implies a 9 % lower workload for the tasks of the scenario with the Microsoft Dynamics NAV internal client. In total, 47 % of the participants had a lower TLX value for the browser integration, averagely 30.97 %. The other 53 % of the participants who had an increased workload rated the index on average 90.47 % higher. This shows that the percentages of each side are even, but especially those who had a higher workload, had a particularly higher one. Some of them, such as participant number 11 and 14, show an enormous difference in their TLX. But this does not apply to all participants, as Fig. 9 illustrates.

Analyzing the TLX by each occupation of the experts leads to the values shown in Fig. 10. Because the number of participants for the group trainee and sales is only one each, their results are more ambiguous. Anyhow, they still reflect the increasing value of the TLX from RTC to browser integration. Thereby the trainee had a 107.55 % increased workload, whereas the sales person only had a 2.02 % higher value. The software developers (53 % of the participants) are the only employees who had a lower TLX value for the browser-based client. With a decrease of 3.44 % it is still less than the 17.34 % increase of the software

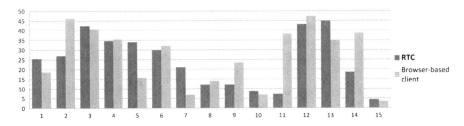

Fig. 9 TLX comparison (per participant) for RTC and browser-based client

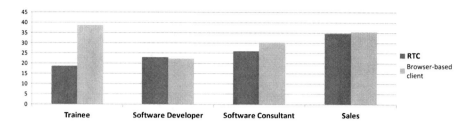

Fig. 10 TLX comparison by occupation

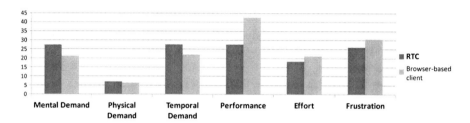

Fig. 11 Average TLX factors for both clients

consultants (33 % of the participants). Since three of four groups have an increased TLX value, a higher workload for the browser-based client is reasonable.

The same goes for the analysis of the TLX values grouped by the respondent's ERP experience. Only one group has a decreased workload, whereas the other three showed with 9.8 % for the rookies (less than 1 year experience with ERP systems), 29.4 % for the beginners (1–3 years), and 24.9 % for the experienced (3–10 years), a nearly constant increase of four to six TLX points. The distribution of the respondents is more regular, since each of the groups consists of two or more participants. The analysis reveals that the TLX is higher for the participants with less experience. Therefore, a higher contact with ERP systems implies a lower workload for both systems.

Comparing the averages of each of the several factors (see Fig. 11) reveals that the three demands are conceived as less stressful with the browser-based client, whereas the accomplishing of the tasks, the degree of work, and the frustration are assessed higher. Especially, the performance shows a 53.2 % increased value, whereas the average difference of all other factors is only 14.38 %.

To sum up, NASA's analysis procedure makes the RTC the better user client to work with Microsoft Dynamics NAV. The workload is assumed higher with the browser-based client. A more detailed view clarifies a lower TLX with both systems for more experienced users. Especially the browser integration profits from more knowledge.

Beside the TLX values we posed some general questions to evaluate both clients. Some of those evaluated attributes can be seen in Fig. 12. Noticeable is

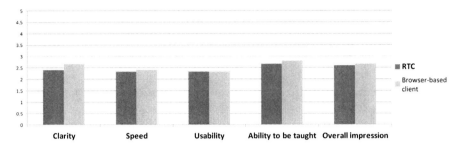

Fig. 12 General evaluation of RTC and browser-based client (rectified scale)

that every attribute is either rated better with the browser integration, or is equivalent. All participants prefer averagely the browser integration.

The clarity has the highest difference with an increase of 11.1 %. The browser-based client does only contain a fractional amount of the functionality. Therefore, the participants conceive the client in Microsoft Office SharePoint 2010 less confusing. A further investigation of the reasons is not possible due to a lack of particularly measurement results. A standard deviation of only 0.737 for the RTC and 0.9 for the browser integration shows a coherent representation of the results.

The speed (2.86 %), ability to be taught (5 %), and overall impression (2.56 %) differ only in a small value. However, they are still rated better with the browser-based client. Interesting is that the participants felt an increase of speed with the browser-based client and simultaneously the total time needed decreased, too. This shows compliance in the perception and the actual reality.

The usability is the only value that has the same average rating with both systems. With an average value of 2.67 of 5 it is only slightly above the half and additionally the worst rated attribute.

4 Conclusion, Limitations and Future Work

Through mobile devices and an expansion of the Internet, mobility of ERP systems is getting more important. So, system access via the Internet and web browser becomes necessary. Therefore, the aim of our study was to gain first insight and first answer for the question whether ERP systems still need both—a dedicated client and a browser-based client.

Therefore, we set up a study and a scenario to evaluate one possible realization of a browser-based client by integrating some selected business processes of Microsoft Dynamics NAV in Microsoft Sharepoint. Delimited and simplified modifications of the business processes warehouse, procurement, sales, and time reporting have been implemented and have been evaluated by 15 experts. They completed therefore the same scenario in two different client types, the Role-Tailored Client (RTC), the dedicated client of Microsoft Dynamics NAV, and a browser-based client. After fulfilling the tasks of the scenario, the participants had to answer a questionnaire after each part, as well as a general questionnaire at the end of the study. Whereas the first two surveys were directed towards a technique developed by the NASA to measure the workload of a Human Computer Interaction, the so called Task Load Index [17], the last questionnaire was used to collect time diaries, general opinions about characteristics such as the usability, and personal notifications.

Overall, the results of the evaluation are balanced. Minor differences can often only be seen by having a detailed look. According to NASA's analysis procedure, the RTC is the better user client to work with Microsoft Dynamics NAV according to the selected processes. The average workload is with 24.44 of 100 assumed 9 % lower than the TLX value 26.9 of the browser-based client. An analysis of the TLX based on the ERP experience reveals that the index decreases with an increasing knowledge. Thereby, especially the browser-based client benefits with a 71.8 % lower average value for participants who work more than 10 years with ERP systems, whereas the RTC still showed a 28.4 % enhancement. A glimpse on the TLX factors showed that the demands are slightly lower with the browser-based client, while the frustration, effort and performance (dissatisfaction) were obviously higher. This could be caused among others by the familiarity of the RTC for most of the experts.

However, the general survey favors the browser integration. The clarity, ability to be taught, and overall impression were rated averagely 4.8 % higher than using the RTC. Still, with values between 2.6 and 3.1 out of 5, all characteristics were rated with mediocre satisfaction.

In summary, it can be stated that the RTC has a lower workload to complete the scenario, but the participants needed less time with the browser-based client. The participants preferred the browser-based client and rated thereby among others the usability and overall impression higher. The integration into the browser still has weaknesses but wins in a direct comparison three out of four evaluation approaches for the business processes treated in this research's scenario.

So, as a first answer towards the question whether a dedicated and a browser-based client are both necessary or not, it can be stated that at the moment both clients should be provided by ERP manufacturers that are offering systems that provided dedicated clients in the past. According to our results the workload for those dedicated clients would be lower whereas usability may be higher with a browser-based client. Therefore, a browser-based client could be a good enhancement for ERP systems with dedicated clients since an integration of ERP systems into a browser-based application is thereby a frequently claimed demand by many customers. However, some ERP systems may be to complex to put all their functions and functionalities into a browser-based application. So, the system's complexity could be another reason to provide both clients—a dedicated one for the full functionality and a browser-based one for selected functions and services.

As limitations for our study we have to mention that we only focused on a specific ERP system and used only selected business processes. Additionally the used ERP system's version did not provide a browser-based client; so, we therefore integrated the selected functions into Microsoft Sharepoint to provide web access which is per definition not a classic web client. Another limitation is the composition and the range of our sample. Here, we focused on 15 ERP experts due to our background. Also, we applied only the TLX as measurement instrument. We are aware that other evaluation tools and instrument can be used as well. We will deal with this in future steps.

As for further future work and to cope with those limitations, we seek to extend the range of our sample as well as the extent of the scenario within the upcoming release of Microsoft Dynamics NAV. Another step will be to shift towards other ERP systems, to deepen and widen our insight on the question of the clients.

References

1. Gronau, N.: Industrielle Standardsoftware: Auswahl und Einführung. Oldenbourg Publishing, München (2001)
2. Deep, A., Guttridge, P., Dani, S., Burns, N.: Investigating factors affecting ERP selection in made-to-order SME sector. J. Manufact. Technol. Manage. **19**, 430–446 (2008)
3. Koh, S.C.L., Simpson, M.: Change and uncertainty in SME manufacturing environments using ERP. J. Manufact. Technol. Manage. **16**, 629–653 (2005)
4. Winkelmann, A., Klose, K.: Experiences while selecting, adapting and implementing ERP systems in SMEs: a case study. In: Proceedings of the 14th Americas Conference on Information Systems (AMCIS 2008), Paper 257 (2008)
5. Winkelmann, A., Leyh, C.: Teaching ERP systems: a multi-perspective view on the ERP system market. J. Inf. Syst. Educ. **21**, 233–240 (2010)
6. Hawking, P., McCarthy, B.: Industry collaboration: a practical approach for ERP education. In: Proceedings of the Australasian Conference on Computing Education (ACSE'00), pp. 129–133 (2000)
7. Somers, T.M., Nelson, K.: The impact of critical success factors across the stages of enterprise resource planning implementations. In: Proceedings of the 34th Annual Hawaii International Conference on System Sciences (HICSS-34) (2001)
8. Konradin: Konradin ERP-Studie 2009: Einsatz von ERP-Lösungen in der Industrie. Konradin Mediengruppe, Leinfelden-Echterdingen (2009)
9. Dospinescu, O., Fotache, D., Munteanu, B.A., Hurbean, L.: Mobile enterprise resource planning: new technology horizons. Commun. IBIMA. **1**, 91–97 (2008)
10. Satyanarayanan, M.: Mobile information access: accessing information on demand at any location. IEEE Pers. Commun. **3**, 26–33 (1996)
11. IFS: IFS ERP Mobility Survey Report (2011)
12. Bias, R.G., Mayhew, D.J.: Cost-justifying usability: an update for the internet age. Morgan Kaufmann Publishers, Amsterdam (2005)
13. Ceaparu, I., Lazar, J., Bessiere, K., Robinson, J., Shneiderman, B.: Determining causes and severity of end-user frustration. Int. J. Hum Comput Interact. **17**, 333–357 (2004)
14. Holtstiege, J., Köster, C., Ribbert, M., Ridder, T.: Microsoft dynamics NAV 2009— Geschäftsprozesse richtig abbilden: Ein praxisorientierter Compliance-Leitfaden. Microsoft Press, Unterschleißheim (2009)
15. Magal, S.R., Word, J.: Essentials of business processes and information systems. Wiley Publishing, Hoboken (2009)
16. Gadatsch, A.: Grundkurs Geschäftsprozess-Management: Methoden und Werkzeuge für die IT-Praxis: Eine Einführung für Studenten und Praktiker. Vieweg + Teubner Publishing, Wiesbaden (2010)

17. Human Performance Research Group: NASA Task Load Index. NASA Ames Research Center, Moffet Field (1986)
18. Scholtz, B., Cilliers, C., Calitz, A.: Qualitative techniques for evaluating enterprise resource planning (ERP) user interfaces. In: Proceedings of the 2010 Annual Research Conference of the South African Institute of Computer Scientists and Information Technologists (SAICSIT'10), pp. 284–293. ACM Press, New York (2010)
19. Lazar, J., Feng, J.H., Hochheiser, H.: Research methods in human-computer interaction. Wiley Publishing, Chichester (2009)
20. Möhring, W., Schlütz, D.: Die Befragung in der Medien- und Kommunikationswissenschaft: eine praxisorientierte Einführung. VS Publishing, Wiesbaden (2010)
21. Wosnitza, M., Jäger, R.S.: Daten erfassen, auswerten und präsentieren - aber wie?: Eine elementare Einführung in sozialwissenschaftliche Forschungsmethoden, Statistik, computerunterstützte Datenanalyse und Ergebnispräsentation. Empirische Pädagogik Publishing, Landau (2006)

Critical Success Factors of e-Learning Scenarios for ERP End-User Training

Lukas Paa and Nesrin Ates

Abstract Based on the updated DeLone and McLean information system success model (ISSM) this study examines the determinants for successful use of e-learning to teach theoretical knowledge and skills concerning an ERP system. A blended learning scenario applied at an undergraduate course at the University of Innsbruck served as the object of investigation. Particular attention was paid to the impact of a reduction in the duration of instructor led lectures on the six dimensions of the ISSM and the effects among each dimension. The results show that information quality and service quality have significant influence on the learners' satisfaction and success, especially when face-to-face session duration is reduced. With high quality content on the learn management system and good support during e-learning periods however, no significant loss in learning success, perceived by learners as well as measured in test results, could be detected.

1 Targets

The rising number of implementations of enterprise resource planning (ERP) systems in companies around the world increases the demand for ERP end user trainings (EUT) as well as the demand for graduates with know how in the field of ERP [1, 2]. In order to provide sufficiently skilled graduates, the necessity arises for universities to transfer the demanded knowledge and skills to students and graduates [3]. The possibilities and advantages of teaching those skills by using live ERP systems are frequently discussed in literature [4–7]. ERP end user trainings are most efficient in regard to learning outcome when taught on a live

---

L. Paa (✉) · N. Ates
University of Innsbruck, Innsbruck, Austria
e-mail: lukas.paa@uibk.ac.at

N. Ates
e-mail: nesrin.ates@uibk.ac.at

ERP-system (hands-on) as mentioned by Noguera and Watson [8]. Especially in the area of software training there is a vast diversity of previous knowledge, skills, affinity towards technology and pace of learning. Therefore, e-learning fits perfectly for the teaching of basic knowledge as it is learner-centered, self-paced and cost-effective even for learners as there is no need to travel and pay for printing [9, 10]. For complex and comprehension issues however, a personal and synchronic meeting of trainer and trainee is hardly avoidable without accepting a major loss in perceived learning quality [11]. End-user training (EUT), not only in the area of ERP systems, is one of the most pervasive methods for enhancing the productivity of individuals. EUT deals with teaching skills to effectively use software and applications. Today most EUT is done through computer-based training or e-learning [12]. We believe in a combination of e-learning and a traditional instructor led lectures approach for the most efficient learning success. This combination is usually referred to as blended learning (BL). As lectures led by an instructor are a major cost driver [13, 14], the aim of this study is to understand how the duration of face-to-face sessions, as part of a blended learning course, affects learning outcome and satisfaction of learners. [12].

Finally we would like to state if and under which circumstances a reduction of face-to-face sessions by identical course content is possible in a BL scenario and which features are most efficient as compensation in perception of end users.

1.1 Object of Investigation

A mandatory course for students of the bachelor of business administration degree at the University of Innsbruck served as the object of investigation. During one semester students of this course get taught basic knowledge and skills concerning an ERP system like *purchase, sales, warehousing* and *production* through a learn management system (LMS) and a web-based live ERP system. The students are studying the mentioned units via the LMS by themselves prior to face-to-face lessons with an instructor (Fig. 1).

The knowledge transfer happens mere via e-learning [15]. The e-learning consists of theoretical input via text, illustrations and video screenings of the ERP-system which show relevant actions and relations in the ERP system. Additionally a support forum via which students can communicate with other students and tutors is provided. For the completion of every single e-learning session, in the frequency of two weeks, students have to solve a working package (WP), in which they have to reproduce a process in the live ERP system. For example create a contractor and order a certain amount of an item. Learners can practice those tasks as often as they want during a two week period. At the end of each e-learning session students have to hand in their solutions for the working package through an upload feature on the LMS. After every e-learning session an attendance session with 25–30 students per class takes place in which the lecturer explains solutions to frequent mistakes and problems and answers questions concerning the topic of

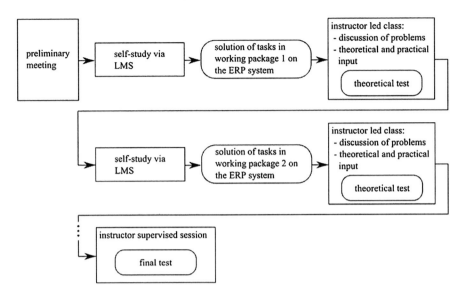

Fig. 1 Cycle of the course

the prior e-learning session. At the end of each instructor led session, a multiple choice test (MC) in form of an online assessment is conducted on the LMS which controls theoretical knowledge of learners. This cycle is repeated four times. At the last attendance session a final test has to be passed in class in which students have to solve a task similar to one of the working packages.

1.2 Methodology

We researched this course over four consecutive terms, beginning with the summer term 2010 (ST) and ending with the winter term 2011 (WT). The learning content concerning the ERP system remained nearly unchanged, except for minor adaptions and reorganizations. The only parameter that changed considerably is the duration of instructor led classes. In the first two terms of the research (ST2010 and WT 2010), in the following referred to as "*group 1*", each attendance session had a duration of 90 min. In the last two terms (ST2011 and WT2011), in the following referred to as "*group 2*", the duration was shortened to 45 min for each face-to-face session due to restructuring of the course design. We gathered all data concerning test results in working packages and multiple choice tests, drop outs and the information from an online survey conducted at the end of each term concerning the satisfaction of the participants with the LMS during the four researched terms. In this study we compared those measures between both groups to gain insight into the relevance of face-to-face session duration in a blended learning scenario for ERP end-user training.

Table 1 Test results and dropout rates

	Group 1		Group 2	
	ST2010	WT2010	ST2011	WT2011
Students enrolled	184	268	239	302
Instructor led class	90 min	90 min	45 min	45 min
No line up	12/6.9 %	5/1.9 %	9/3.8 %	7/2.3 %
Dropout at 1st test	4/2.3 %	–/–	2/0.8 %	3/1.0 %
Results MC/WP 1	2.89/14.15	2.99/14.59	2.46/14.60	2.67/14.52
Dropout at 2nd test	4/2.3 %	4/1.5 %	7/2.9 %	4/1.3 %
Results MC/WP 2	2.39/14.37	2.84/14.52	2.28/13.54	2.53/13.65
Dropout at 3rd test	2/1.2 %	2/0.8 %	4/1.7 %	4/1.3 %
Results MC/WP 3	2.43/14.18	2.71/14.39	2.61/14.22	2.53/14.21
Dropout at 4th test	2/1.2 %	6/2.2 %	–/–	–/–
Results MC/WP 4	3.02/13.45	2.82/13.95	2.38/14.78	2.44/14.79
Dropout at final test	7/4.1 %	19/7.3 %	10/4.2 %	20/6.6 %
Total dropout[a]	19/11 %	31/12 %	23/10 %	31/11 %
Participants survey	142	150	182	65

[a] Excluding students who never showed up

2 Examinations of Test Results and Dropout Rates

At the first stage we studied the success of participants by their achieved results in the working packages, the corresponding theoretical tests and the final test. Thereby we also analyzed drop outs, whereat we did not differentiate between students who did not hand in a solution and the ones who did not achieve the required score.

2.1 Sample

Over the four terms of the study 993 students were enrolled in the examined course, of which 854 successfully finished it. Students participating in the course were in their fifth (5.3) term on average. 570 participated in the online survey of which 271 were female and 286 male with age reaching from 20 to 39 years and an average age of 23.3 years at the end of the term. 144 of those already had experience in e-learning courses through other lectures. 112 already had experience with an ERP system. The sample, consisting merely of young students, estimated themselves as ones with a high affinity towards the web, 3.9 measured on a seven-point Likert scale compared to other students. They estimate their knowledge concerning computers and software as high (Table 1).

2.2 Findings

The following graph shows the test results in working packages, theoretical tests and the final test summarized for both groups. In each of the four tests learners could reach a maximum of 20 points, 15 in the working package and five in the theoretical test. In the final test 20 points where achievable, without a theoretical test. Achieved points are measured on the left axis. On the right axis dropout rates are shown in percent of the number of students enrolled in the course at the beginning of the term, without students who never handed in a solution to the first test.

It can be seen that the dropout rates during the term was relatively low and no significant difference could be found between the two groups. Drop outs were calculated by participants who did not hand in a solution or did not achieve the required score of 60 % of the reachable points, in relation to students enrolled in the course without the ones who never handed in any test. In the final test, which is also conducted on the ERP system, there was no relevant negative influence trough the reduced attendance class duration. Dropout rates were even lower in the second period of the study when observed in relation to enrolled students. The overall performance of students in the first two terms concerning the theoretical tests, conducted as online multiple choice tests, was slightly better than of the ones in the last two terms. This leads to the conclusion that the more time is spent in attendance classes and the possibility to explain and discuss some topics helps learners to gain a slightly better theoretical understanding of ERP systems and their functionalities. Concerning the skills in the ERP system, which were tested as working packages on the live system, no significant difference can be seen. So far we can state that the reduction of face-to-face teaching time has no relevant influence on dropout rates and learning outcome measured in tests. In the next step we studied the self-estimation of students with their learning success, measured in an online survey conducted at the end of each term (Fig. 2).

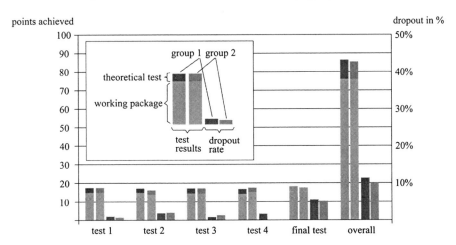

Fig. 2 Test results and dropout rates compared

3 Study of the Perceived Benefit of Learners through the ISSM

The Information System Success Model (ISSM) of DeLone and McLean is one of the widely recognized models which originated out of a systematic review of 180 studies. The first ISSM presented in 1992 was used by nearly 300 studies. In 2003 DeLone and McLean reviewed another 100 articles regarding information system success and presented the updated ISSM [16]. A meta-study by Petter et al. [17] has shown that the updated version of the model has received great appreciation in the IS community. A relevant aspect for the use of the ISSM in the background of education at a University is that the ISSM has been empirically tested in a quasi-voluntary use context as well as in a mandatory one [18]. Those facts led to our decision to use the ISSM as basis for our study in which we examined the influence of various parameters (*information quality, system quality, service quality* and the relation of face-to-face sessions to e-learning units) on *user satisfaction, use* and *net benefit*. [19].

3.1 Measures of the ISSM

In order to operationalize the constructs of the conceptual model, we have followed the recommendation of various authors [20–23] to use tested and proven measures in order to enhance validity. We have adapted items identified in previous studies and modified them for use in the e-learning context. However where we saw the necessity to add items in order to measure the intended dimensions, we did so but paid particular attention to suggested writing principles [24].

The analysis examines the influence of the five dimensions of the ISSM on *net benefit* as well as the impact of the reduction of the duration of face-to-face sessions on learners' success and satisfaction. Furthermore changes in the perceived relevance of certain components of the LMS in dependence of the abbreviated face-to-face sessions were analyzed.

The dimensions for measuring the LMS success consist of the following items:

- *Information Quality* measures the perceived quality of the information itself, its multimedia preparation and its relevance for the aim of the course. Additionally the arrangement, comprehensibility and the fact that they are unambiguous were taken into account. Information quality is a prominent success factor when investigating user satisfaction, especially when face-to-face time gets reduced.
- *System quality* considers characteristics of the performance like usability, accessibility, functionality and response time of the LMS.
- *Service quality* summarizes measures of the support provided by the operator of the LMS. Distributions of user accounts are as well a criterion as the speed, helpfulness and kindness of answers on any support inquiry.

- *Use* is influenced by the three first mentioned dimensions and covers the perceived use of the LMS by learners in terms of frequency and duration of logins as well as the intensity of the time spent on the LMS. It is also recommended to evaluate the use of different content types and functionalities of the LMS.
- *User satisfaction* captures the affective attitude of learners to the LMS and can be considered as a very important dimension when investigating the benefit of a LMS.
- *Net benefit* measures several aspects of perceived individual benefits experienced by learners through the use of the LMS. Aspects like efficiency, task performance and overall usefulness are covered by this dimension.

3.2 Analysis and Results of the Survey

Following Gebering and Anderson [25], we conducted a confirmatory factor analysis to assess the reliability and validity of the multi-item scales. We included all constructs of the structural equation model as well as the moderators within this analysis to ensure convergent and discriminant validity. Any observation that had missing values among the observed variables were dropped from the analysis. Global fit measures are provided as follows: comparative fit index (CFI) = 0.72, Tucker-Lewis index (TLI) = 0.69, root mean square error of approximation (RMSEA) = 0.089. The results of the confirmatory factor analysis are shown in Table 2. With little exceptions we can see high factor loadings in all dimensions and high levels of explained variance by the model.

As all factor loadings for the dimensions are statistically significant this shows that all indicators are effectively measuring the same construct and have high convergent validity [25]. Correlations between latent variables are reported in Table 3.

We conducted a simultaneous equation model, as some equations contain endogenous variables among the explanatory ones, on the dimensions as shown in Fig. 3. The coefficients and their significance are shown in the graph. We calculated the exact same model for each of the two groups of the study separately. Values above connecting vectors apply to students who had 90 min instructor led classes (group 1) the lower ones to students who had 45 min (group 2).

---

[2] We measured the items using seven-point Likert scales anchored by "strongly agree" (7) and "strongly disagree" (1), unless otherwise noted.

Notes: CFI = comparative fit index, TLI = Tucker–Lewis index, RMSEA = root mean square error of approximation, and SRMR = standardized root mean square residual.

[3] CFI = comparative fit index, TLI = Tucker–Lewis index, RMSEA = root mean square error of approximation, and RMSR = standardized root mean square residual.

Table 2 Results of the confirmatory factor analysis

Item[2]	Loadings	R^2
Information quality (IQ)		
The LMS provides high quality content.	1.000	0.500
... easy comprehensible information.	0.989	0.490
... high quality multimedia preparation of the information.	0.994	0.491
System quality (SYQ)		
The LMS is always accessible.	0.777	0.366
... is easy to use.	0.828	0.527
... runs error free.	1.000	0.926
Service quality (SEQ)		
The operator of the LMS provides an easy log in.	0.877	0.423
... provides competent support concerning the learning content.	0.960	0.526
... has the necessary knowledge to attend the system.	1.000	0.564
... provides an appropriate level of support and explanation online.	0.905	0.396
... reacts in a cooperative manner on suggestions for improvement.	0.831	0.367
... responds comprehensibly to my enquires.	0.850	0.385
... responds helpfully to my enquires.	0.853	0.384
... responds pleasantly to my enquires.	0.861	0.359
Use (USE)		
The overall duration of time spent on the LMS adds up to: (hours)	0.464	0.440
The quantity of logins to the LMS adds up to: (quantity)	0.855	0.272
When using the LMS I concentrate exclusively on the LMS.	0.959	0.251
I use the provided possibilities for communication on the LMS frequently.	1.000	0.239
User satisfaction (SAT)		
All in all I think the LMS is very good.	0.616	0.584
I would perceive a similar LMS a reasonable supplement for other courses.	0.822	0.395
My personal learning success is very high.	0.811	0.531
I am very satisfied with the LMS.	0.923	0.648
I like the e-learning experience.	1.000	0.673
I can unreservedly recommend the LMS.	1.000	0.676
I imagine that others would be very satisfied with this LMS.	0.829	0.570
Net benefit (NET)		
All in all I see a large benefit in the LMS.	0.288	0.689
The LMS is a good basis for the work with an ERP system.	0.891	0.493
... good insight in various processes covered by an ERP system.	0.897	0.441
... provides a good summary of the functionalities of an ERP system.	0.873	0.483
... a time efficient introduction to the basics of an ERP system.	0.872	0.399
The LMS enables me to learn wherever I want.	0.832	0.295
... to repeat content as often as I want.	0.736	0.228
The LMS requires motivating myself to complete the tasks.	0.718	0.255
The LMS represents a very good preparation for the work packages.	0.969	0.469
... a very good preparation for the theoretical tests.	0.713	0.192
The LMS imparts a good understanding for business relations.	0.828	0.367
... basic knowledge for the handling of an ERP system.	1.000	0.551

CFI = 0.7193; TLI = 0.6941; RMSEA = 0.0898; RMSR = 0.6127[3]

Table 3 Construct correlations

Dimension	1	2	3	4	5
1 Information quality					
2 System quality	0.745				
3 Service quality	0.830	0.799			
4 Use	0.486	0.441	0.557		
5 User satisfaction	0.726	0.554	0.649	0.461	
6 Net benefit	0.736	0.527	0.759	0.571	0.756

All correlations are significant at the 0.001 alpha level

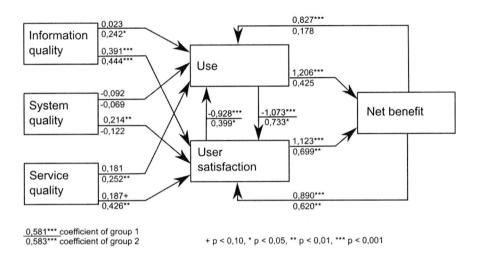

Fig. 3 Regression within the ISSM for both groups

The exogenous latent factors *information quality* (IQ), *system quality* (SYQ) and *service quality* (SEQ) are supposed to have an impact on the actual *use* (USE) of the LMS and the *satisfaction of users* (SAT). In our study we could proof some of these correlations. A strong and highly significant impact of IQ on SAT can be seen in both groups, slightly higher in group 2. From the common opinion in the literature and the common sense this was to be expected [26–29]. Students of group 2 depend in a higher degree on the information provided through the LMS, therefore the impact on SAT is higher for them. But also for group 1 IQ represents the highest determinant for SAT.

For this reason lecturers and operators of a LMS should pay particular attention to the accuracy, relevance, timeliness, usefulness, and completeness of information on the LMS to increase user satisfaction. Learners are more likely to be satisfied when they find high quality information that facilitates the learning process by helping them understand, internalize, and absorb course material [30].

The Impact of IQ on USE however is not that strong and only of acceptable significance for group 2. It has to be stated that the use of the LMS was mandatory for all learners, which explains to a certain degree the difficulty to measure this dimension. As recommended by DeLone and McLean we also tried to measure the intention to use. Those items however showed too low factor loadings to be included in the simultaneous equation model. Another difficulty in measuring use is the significant difference between self-reported use and actual use. User who use a system often and for a long duration tend do underestimated the actual time spent with the system in contract to users who only use is rarely and for short session, which tend to overestimate their spent time [31, 32]. Additionally Urbach and Müller [29] summarize the meta study of Petter et al. [17] by stating that only a moderate support can be found to support the hypothesis that USE can be explained by IQ.

System quality (SYQ) shows very low and negative regression on both dimensions for both groups, except for SYQ on SAT in group 1. Again the meta-analysis by Petter et al. [17] shows only mixed support for the explanation of USE by SYQ in previous studies. While a total of nine studies reported a positive association with system use, seven studies reported nonsignificant results for this model path [29]. The explanation of SAT by SYQ however shows strong support in previous studies. Our study can confirm this for group 1. The reason for the nonsignificant and negative impact in group 2 of our study could not be explained.

SEQ, which amongst others consists of items concerning the support, shows relatively high regression on USE and SAT for group 2. This can be explained by the higher dependence of those learners on the support by tutors and operators of the LMS. Thus operators of a LMS should look for possibilities to enhance the perceived service quality. This could be done through high quality, fast and reliable responses to support inquiries of learners concerning the learning content and the LMS itself.

The impacts of SAT on USE and vice versa show contrary results: highly negative and with strong significance for group 1 and positive but lower and with only moderate significance for group 2. One possibility to explain that case would be the interpretation in the specific context of university students as learners. As the LMS is the only way for learners to prepare for the working packages its use can be seen as mandatory. Students tend to behave according to the minimization principle. They try to reach their target with the least possible input or effort. Thus using the LMS a lot does not result in a higher satisfaction but a lower one. This explains the highly significant negative regression between the dimensions USE and SAT, as well as in the other direction. Students who perceive the information quality as high, experience higher satisfaction and thus don't have to use the LMS very often and for a long duration. Students however which are not satisfied with the LMS, maybe because they find the content not comprehensive, and see a lack in support may be forced to spend more time on the LMS and suffer from frustration, or a negative satisfaction. This however applies only to learners of group 1. The reason for the different results in both groups is not clear for the authors so far.

USE shows highly significant and strong impact on NET as well as vice versa for group 1. Group 2 however doesn't support this hypothesis. Once again those findings reconfirm the meta-analysis by Petter et al. [17] where most studies reported significant associations between USE and NET but six studies reported nonsignificant results.

The highest impacts can be found between SAT and NET, and in the other direction from NET to SAT. Satisfied learners experience a high benefit, and are therefore even more satisfied.

Recapitulatory we can say that our study showed similar results to the average of the meta-analysis conducted by Petter et al. [17] and leads to the following conclusion. The quality of the learning content on the LMS and the support for learners through communication on the LMS are the most important influences for the perceived learning outcome. Especially when attendance class duration is reduced, those become more relevant.

4 Analysis of Importance of Functionalities and Features

We will now have a more detailed look on which components of the LMS gain importance from the learner's point of view with declining attendance class duration.

Figure 4 shows the results on selected items concerning their level of agreement and their importance. We can see that both groups were satisfied with the quality of the content and ascribe this item a very high importance. For students of group 2, the quality of the content was understandably even more relevant. In item IQ2 in the shown graph we can see a significant drop in the level of agreement. Students who depend more on the LMS tend to be more critical with the way

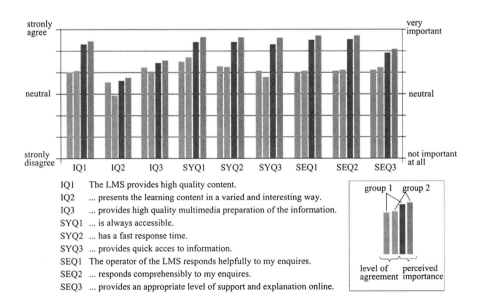

IQ1	The LMS provides high quality content.
IQ2	... presents the learning content in a varied and interesting way.
IQ3	... provides high quality multimedia preparation of the information.
SYQ1	... is always accessible.
SYQ2	... has a fast response time.
SYQ3	... provides quick acces to information.
SEQ1	The operator of the LMS responds helpfully to my enquires.
SEQ2	... responds comprehensibly to my enquires.
SEQ3	... provides an appropriate level of support and explanation online.

Fig. 4 Differences in level of agreement and perceived importance

information gets presented. Those again estimate the importance of that item slightly higher than group 1. The next item supports these findings as students of group 2 are more demanding in concerns of multimedia preparation of the information. The next two items of the dimension system quality, accessibility without interruption and fast response time of the website are more important for learners who are more contingent on the LMS. Item SYQ3 shows that the necessity for quick access to information rises with lower attendance class duration and is also of higher importance. The three selected items concerning service quality all demonstrate the higher perceived importance of relevant and comprehensive support online whether static (glossary) or dynamic (support forum).

In open questions about what learners criticize or would enhance on the LMS there was no noticeable difference between the two groups. Most common statements were to shorten the theoretical input and provide more illustrations and video screenings instead, better support during the e-learning sessions through lecturers and tutors and detailed individual feedback about mistakes in the working packages. Another point that was mentioned by some learners was the demand for audio instructions during the video screenings. However this was also surveyed in the questionnaire, where participants gave it a very low rating in concern of the importance.

Participants of the second part of the study estimated their personal learning success a little bit lower on average (4.86 compared to 5.26) on a seven-point Likert-type scale (1 = strongly disagree, 7 = strongly agree) which could also be seen in the evaluation of the test results concerning theoretical knowledge.

5 Summary and Conclusion

The effectiveness of end user training is considered a critical success factor in the implementation process of an ERP-System. End user training is not only the most time and cost consuming part of the implementation period but also an important aspect for new employees [33]. E-Learning allows cost savings through reduced trainer, travel and opportunity costs. Furthermore it offers a certain degree of adaption possibilities concerning the pace and intensity of learning. The main cost drivers in blended learning scenarios, once the LMS and its content are created, are fees for instructors. Results of this study show that a reduction in face-to-face session duration in blended learning scenarios does not cause a significant loss in the learning outcome, perceived by learners as well as measured in test results. Dropout rates were even lower for learners with shorter instructor led class duration. In order to achieve high learner satisfaction and high learning success in blended learning scenarios, high information quality and helpful and fast support are critical success factors. Especially when reducing instructor led class duration those gain importance to learners. Thus the main effort should be focused on integrating rich multimedia content with educational information that facilitates learning and understanding of course material.

References

1. Mediengruppe, K.: Einsatz von ERP-Lösungen in der Industrie. Konradin Mediengruppe, Leinfelden Echterdingen (2009)
2. Leyh, C., Winkelmann, A., Lu, J.: Exploring the diversity of ERP systems—an empirical insight into system usage in academia. Proceedings of the Americas Conference on Information Systems, Detroit (2011)
3. Venkatesh, V.: One-size-does-not-fit-all: teaching MBA students different ERP implementation strategies. J. Inf. Syst. Educ. **19**, 141–146 (2008)
4. Antonucci, Y., Corbitt, G., Stewart, G., Harris, A.: Enterprise systems education: where are we? where are we going. J. Inf. Syst. Educ. **15**, 227–234 (2004)
5. Boyle, T., Strong, S.: Skill requirements of ERP graduates. J. Inf. Syst. Educ. **17**, 403–412 (2006)
6. Hawking, P., McCarthy, B., Stein, A.: Second wave ERP education. J. Inf. Syst. Educ. **15**, 327–332 (2004)
7. Peslak, A.: A twelve-step, multiple course approach to teaching enterprise resource planning. J. Inf. Syst. Educ. **16**, 147–155 (2005)
8. Noguera, J.H., Watson, E.F.: Effectiveness of using an enterprise system to teach process-centered concepts in business education. J. Enterp. Inf. Manag. **17**, 56–74 (2004)
9. Harun, M.H.: Integrating e-Learning into the workplace. Internet High. Educ. **4**, 301–310 (2002)
10. Galagan, P.: The e-learning revolution. Training & Development **54**, 25–30 (2000)
11. Baker, J.: An investigation of relationships among instructor immediacy and affective and cognitive learning in the online classroom. Internet High. Educ. **7**, 1–13 (2004)
12. Gupta, S., Bostrom, R.P.: End-user training methods: what we know, need to know. Proceedings of the 2006 ACM SIGMIS CPR conference on computer personnel research: Forty four years of computer personnel research: achievements, challenges & the future, ACM, pp. 172–182 (2006)
13. Arbaugh, J.B., Desai, A., Rau, B., Sridhar, B.S.: A review of research on online and blended learning in the management disciplines: 1994–2009. Organ. Manag. J. **7**, 39–55 (2010)
14. Budka, P., Ebner, M., Nagler, W.: Hochschule-Strukturen, Rahmen und Modelle für die Lehre mit Technologien. Lernen und Lehren mit Technologien—Ein interdisziplinäres Lehrbuch, pp. 1–9 (2011)
15. Kerres, M.: Medienentscheidungen in der Unterrichtsplanung. Zu Wirkungsargumenten und Begründungen des didaktischen Einsatzes digitaler Medien. Bildung und Erziehung **53**, 19–39 (2000)
16. DeLone, W.H., McLean, E.R.: The DeLone and McLean model of information systems success: a ten-year update. J. Manag. Inf. Syst. **19**, 9–30 (2003)
17. Petter, S., DeLone, W., McLean, E.: Measuring information systems success: models, dimensions, measures, and interrelationships. Eur. J. Inf. Syst. **17** 236–263 (2008)
18. Iivari, J.: An empirical test of the model of information system success. Database Adv. Inf. Syst. **36**, 8–27 (2005)
19. Sun, P.C., Tsai, R.J., Finger, G., Chen, Y.Y., Yeh, D.: What drives a successful e-Learning? An empirical investigation of the critical factors influencing learner satisfaction. Comput. Educ. **50**, 1183–1202 (2008)
20. Bharati, P., Chaudhury, A.: An empirical investigation of decision-making satisfaction in web-based decision support systems. Decis. Support Syst. **37**, 187–197 (2004)
21. DeLone, W.H., McLean, E.R.: The DeLone and McLean model of information systems success: A ten-year update. J. Manag. Inf. Syst. **19**, 9–30 (2003)
22. Kankanhalli, A., Tan, B., Wei, K.: Contributing knowledge to electronic knowledge repositories: An empirical investigation. Mis Quarterly **29**, 113–143 (2005)
23. Sugianto, L., Tojib, D.: Modeling user satisfaction with an employee portal. Int. J. Bus. Inf. **1**, 239–255 (2006)

24. Dillman, D., Smyth, J., Christian, L.: Internet, mail, and mixed-mode surveys: the tailored design method. John Wiley & Sons, New York (2008)
25. Gebering, D.W., Anderson, J.C.: An updated paradigm for scale development incorporating unidimensionality and its assessment. J. Mark. Res. **25**(2), 186 (1988)
26. Ives, B., Olson, M.H., Baroudi, J.J.: The measurement of user information satisfaction. Commun. ACM **26**, 785–793 (1983)
27. Baroudi, J., Orlikowski, W.: A short-form measure of user information satisfaction: a psychometric evaluation and notes on use. J. Manag. Inf. Syst. **4**, 44–59 (1988)
28. Doll, W.J., Xia, W., Torkzadeh, G.: A confirmatory factor analysis of the end-user computing satisfaction instrument. Mis Quarterly **18**, 453–461 (1994)
29. Urbach, N., Müller, B.: The updated DeLone and McLean model of information systems success. In: Dwivedi, Y.K., Wade, M.R., Schneberger, S.L. (eds.) Information Systems Theory: Explaining and Predicting Our Digital Society, pp. 1–18. Springer, New York (2012)
30. Lin, H.-F.: Measuring online learning systems success: applying the updated DeLone and McLean model. Cyberpsychology & behavior **10**, 817–820 (2007)
31. Payton, F.C., Brennan, P.F.: How a community health information network is really used. Commun. ACM **42**, 85–89 (1999)
32. Collopy, F.: Biases in retrospective self-reports of time use: an empirical study of computer users. Manage. Sci. **42**, 758–767 (1996)
33. Umble, E.J., Haft, R.R., Umble, M.M.: Enterprise resource planning: implementation procedures and critical success factors. Eur. J. Oper. Res. **146**, 241–257 (2003)

Part IV
ERP Implementation and Integration

Does Predefined ERP Implementation Methodology Work for Public Companies in Transitioning Country?

Adnan Kraljić, Denis Delismajlović and Tarik Kraljić

Abstract The main objective of this paper is to answer a question "Does predefined ERP implementation methodology work for state owned companies in transitioning countries?" The focus will be on state owned companies from Bosnia and Herzegovina, as it is typical transitioning company. Paper will treat selected issues which could trouble ERP implementation trough predefined ERP implementation methodology for SAP ERP. This paper presents observations/remarks based on experience of authors in SAP ERP implementation projects in public sector in Bosnia and Herzegovina. Author's goal is to provide useful insight into predefined ERP implementation methodology (in theory) and issues that arise in real life ERP projects. Also, it should provide structural knowledge for all stakeholders involved in the process of ERP implementation in public sector.

1 Challenge Known as ERP Implementation

Enterprise resource planning (ERP) system is a business management system which comprises integrated sets of comprehensive software, which can be used, when successfully implemented, to manage and integrate all the business functions within an organization. These sets usually include a set of mature business applications and tools for financial and cost accounting, sales and distribution,

---

A. Kraljić (✉) · T. Kraljić
International Burch University Sarajevo, Sarajevo, Bosnia and Herzegovina
e-mail: akralic@ibu.edu.ba

T. Kraljić
e-mail: tkraljic@ibu.edu.ba

D. Delismajlović
University of Zenica, Zenica, Bosnia and Herzegovina
e-mail: denisdelismalovic@gmail.com

materials management, human resource, production planning and computer integrated manufacturing, supply chain, and customer information [1].

So, the main feature of ERP is computer-based integration of the whole organization into one system and database. It provides higher efficiency, real time reporting, as data entered in one module of the system are immediately accessible for other organization's functions. Figure 1 presents typical functional ERP architecture.

People often contemplate ERP as software provided out of box. We consider ERP more as a concept. The target of each ERP implementation in organization is to benefit by improving business operations and ease decision making process. Also it is important to state that there is no magic in ERP software. ERP's benefits

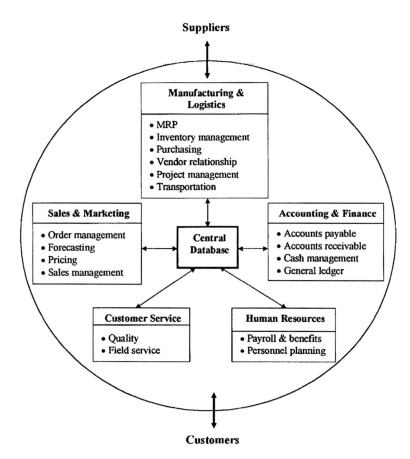

Fig. 1 Typical ERP system architecture

are a direct result of effective preparation and implementation, and appropriate use. This seems obvious, but nine out of 10 companies don't get it right the first time around [2].

2 Story about ERP Implementation

ERP implementation is set of activates, normally leading to the fully operating system. It mixes business, technical and clerks' sides which should work harmonized during the implementation. Every employee in the company is involved in ERP implementation process; either they are technical support in company (IT department) or the end users of information system. Obviously it is not easy to achieve. There are many examples of ERP implementation failures.

The world of IT and business consulting is full of stories of ERP projects gone wrong. Companies such as Whirlpool, Hershey Foods, and Allied Waste Industries have had exposed court cases against ERP software vendors (such as SAP A.G. and Oracle) because of their unsuccessful implementations.

It is interesting that according to a statement cited in an ITWorld.com article, Waste Management claims SAP deceived it by creating "fake software environments" for product demonstrations. The project went bad almost immediately after a sales agreement was signed in October of 2005. Though SAP promised a pilot version of the system would be up and running by Dec. 15, 2006, "it is not even close to being completed today" [3].

Another famous story about SAP implementation failure is Shane Co. The family-owned jewelry retailer that sought bankruptcy told a U.S. judge the company's decline was triggered partly by delays and cost overruns for a $36 million SAP AG inventory-management system.

SAP, the world's biggest maker of business-management software, took almost three years to install and implement the system instead of one year, while costs "ballooned" to $36 million from a projected maximum of $10 million, Shane said in papers filed in U.S. Bankruptcy Court in Denver [4].

In general an implementation is seen as successful if it is completed within budget and time with meeting all the implementation deliverables as measured by ROI, KPIs etc. In any ERP implementation lots of variables are involved like personnel (business side, technical side, support side, users), implementation partner (for example local integration software PeopleSoft, JD Edwards, Salesforce.com etc.), and implementation strategy [5]. With a number of issues that arise together, in a few months to a year or so for implementation, it is important to address critical factors that shape an implementation. Also, as we mentioned previously, it is important not to underestimate the nature of public institution and all bureaucracy you have cope with during the implementation.

3 No One is Immune—Country Specific Issues of Public Sector

There is no industry or activity that is not influenced by current situation in Bosnia and Herzegovina. Complex picture of transitioning post conflict country will be described in next few paragraphs. The stress will be on state owned companies.

In Bosnia and Herzegovina there are some big state owned companies that implemented an ERP or are in the process of implementation. According to SAP User Community in B&H SAP ERP is the main ERP vendor for big public companies. If it could be useful information for someone we will name those companies: EPBiH, BH Telecom, JP EPHZ HB, HT Mostar, Clinical center University of Sarajevo.

One of the issues of public sector in B&H is very complex stakeholder structure due to political system as a result of post conflict situation. (Dayton and Paris political agreement resulted in four different levels of government – 14 governments, 180 ministers; 1 prime minister per 300 000 people, one the most complex and expensive governmental body in the world). According to the 2005 CMI report, this bloated public sector accounts for 54 % of the annual GDP—more than in any other European country [6]. Another issue is widely spread corruption as a one of the common characteristics of post socialist developing country. After the war in B&H and privatization which was proceed doubtfully and obscure hundreds of state owned companies finished in bankruptcy. However, still few state owned companies, mainly utility and telecom companies, are the backbone of country's economy. Unfortunately, public sector in Bosnia and Herzegovina is very complex and due to the last surveys one of the most corrupted in Europe, especially in its employment policy.

As mentioned previously 54 % of GDP is consisted of public sector what implies the importance of this sector and long term consequences if fraud is part of it. Same report states that corruption pattern in B&H is characterized by (a) high level of public concern with corruption, (b) low level of public trust in the governments, (c) state capture and conflict of interest, (d) public administration inefficiencies reflected in widespread bribery in public offices, (e) distorted business environment and (f) a significant burden on poor households, exacerbating poverty and inequality. Public tenders (defined by public procurement law) could provide opportunity for corruption if they are done with a lack of transparency [7]. Also process of choosing the bid winner is complex with not strict definition of vendor selection criteria. According to the World Bank report, in the most cases in B&H, tender policy is that price values for more than 70 % of possible points that vendor can earn. This leads to artificially low price that ensures wining the bid, but do not ensure the quality of service.

4 How ERP Vendors Want to Help Implementations

So, as seen from previous chapter, much of the time ERP software vendors are the targets for blame when expected results do not occur.

ERP vendors state that only following a tested implementation methodology is a prerequisite for successful ERP implementation. All implementation methodologies e.g. Oracle Application Implementation Methodology (AIM), Accelerated SAP (ASAP) etc. suggest at least five phases of ERP implementation: Define; Design; Build; Transition; and Go Live & Support [8]. To avoid those uncomfortable situations ERP vendors developed predefined ERP implementation methodologies. One of the most famous is delivered from biggest ERP vendor SAP. It is ASAP methodology (ASAP – Accelerated SAP). In next few paragraphs we will describe ASAP methodology in more details.

Accelerated SAP (ASAP) is SAP's standard implementation methodology. It is consisted of 6 phases, and those are: Project preparation, Blueprint, Realization, Final preparation, Go-Live Support and Run. It is serial relationship, so predecessor phase has to be completed in order to move on next phase. In Fig. 2. those phases are shown.

This roadmap is a step-by-step guide that incorporates experience from many years of implementing R/3. Along with that, Accelerated SAP contains a multitude of tools, accelerators and useful information to assist all team members in implementing R/3. Quality checks are incorporated at the end of each phase to easily monitor deliverables and critical success factors. ASAP is delivered as a PC-based package, so that—if required—an implementation project can begin prior to having an R/3 System installed [9].

We will give more details regarding each phase.
Project Preparation

Goal of this phase is to plan our project and lay the foundations for successful implementation. It is at this stage that we make the strategic decisions crucial to your project: define your project goals and objectives, clarify the scope of your implementation, define your project schedule, budget plan, and implementation sequence, establish the project organization and relevant committees and assign resources

Fig. 2 ASAP phases

Business Blueprint

During this phase we create a blueprint using the Question & Answer database (Q&Adb), which documents your enterprise's requirements and establishes how your business processes and organizational structure are to be represented in the SAP System. We also refine the original project goals and objectives and revise the overall project schedule in this phase.

Realization

In this phase, we configure the requirements contained in the Business Blueprint. Baseline configuration (major scope) is followed by final configuration (remaining scope), which can consist of up to four cycles. Other key focal areas of this phase are conducting integration tests and drawing up end user documentation.

Final Preparation

After project realization phase, we complete our preparations, including testing, end user training, system management, and cutover activities. We also need to resolve all open. At this stage we need to ensure that all the prerequisites for your system to go live have been fulfilled.

Go Live & Support

In this phase we move from a pre-production environment to the live system. The most important elements include setting up production support, monitoring system transactions [8].

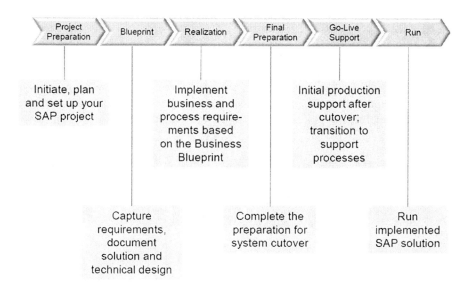

Fig. 3 Phase objectives

Table 1 ERP implementation in transitioning country in state owned companies—Expected objectives for each ASAP phase and constraints that occurs in practice

Phase	Excepted objectives	Constraints in practice regarding the phase objects
Project preparation	Defined your project goals and objectives	Unskilled project managers
	Clarified the scope of your implementation	Corruption in tendering procedure (inadequate tendering procedure)
	Defined your project schedule, budget plan, and implementation sequence	Poorly written tendering documentation Leak of project management knowledge (no clear goals and objectives)
	Established the project organization and relevant committees and assign resources	Poorly prepared project work break structure Employee does not care about resource spending —state money. Budget and project schedule planned with no serious approach
Blueprint	Created blueprints using the Question & Answer database (Q&Adb)	Too much/little time spent on blueprint preparation due to lack of project management knowledge, and requirements set by political not business persons/reasons No localize ASAP documentation for smaller countries (example Bosnian language) Leak of business process mapping skills Leak of professional business environment in state owned companies, which support this extremely important phase Managers and supervisors mostly not centers of competence
	Mapped business processes	
	Overview of all business process	
Realization	Configured the requirements contained in the Business Blueprint	Leak of project management Leak of change management (Change management not consider as important)
	Conducted unit tests Conducted integration tests Prepared end users documentation	Responsibility issue—"there is someone else who will do it" Integration test not taken seriously from end users Very slow internal knowledge and information transfer— several managers has to sign document to be approved .

(continued)

Table 1 (continued)

Phase	Excepted objectives	Constraints in practice regarding the phase objects
Go–Live support	Moved from a pre-production environment to the live system	Help desk not established by the company
		Defined communication channels not respected
	Includes setting up production support, monitoring system transactions	Often, poor management decision made under huge pressure of Go Live phase
		Employees working habits—mistakes are there to be hidden
Run	Optimizing overall system performance	No optimization and improvements
		Lack of understanding that the ERP system is "live" system
		After project is finished all ERP story ends.
		Problems with tendering procedure for support
	Permanent business process optimization	No competent support in country as Bosnia and Herzegovina— low spending on consultant education

Run
Optimizing overall system performance and obtaining permanent business process optimization.

Phase objectives shown in Fig. 3, (Table 1).

5 Most Threatening Constraints in Practice Regarding ASAP Methodology

In next few paragraphs we will discuss the most prominent constraints from the list above.

Inadequate tendering procedure for state owned company—The Public Procurement Law adopted in 2004 generally complies with the main principles of the EU public procurement system. However, in practice procurement process for public companies still provide significant space for fraud. One of the most questionable aspects of public tendering law is determining price as the most important factor in bidding. So winning the bid is based significantly, if not exclusively on price. This leads to artificially dropping the price of some offers so companies are in the risk to become uncompetitive if the price is set according to the real market price for the project scope. This opens the door for system integrators which are not skilled to provide ASAP methodology, in other words, cannot provide skilled SAP consultants who can implement ASAP methodology in SAP ERP implementation.

No localization for ASAP documentation for smaller countries (example Bosnian language)—ASAP methodology provides dozen of documents well written in English language. It is profound help for consultants and substantially accelerates the process of implementation. Unfortunately, this documentation is not translated on local languages of small, transitioning markets as Bosnian SAP market is.

Time consuming decision making flow process (from bottom to top) — Decision makes process in such companies can be very slow. It obviously does not support name of SAP standard methodology—**Accelerated SAP**. One reason could be very complex and deep organization structure. Specific to some public companies is lack of using of modern information infrastructure, like e-mails. Another example is using of internal mail service for paper notices delivery. Also, the nonprofit approach is deeply rooted in employees of public companies in B&H (no real responsibility and valuation by working achievements).

Working habits of management and employees—Probably someone would ask what communism has with ASAP. However, as former communist country, Bosnia and Herzegovina kept some of the practices from that period (especially in state owned companies). These habits could include: no real authority of the management, work is not valuated by achievement but personal relations; there is no incentive by employees to make some efforts to improve their work environment because they are not paid by their working performance and commitment (salary is determinate by salary coefficients for each working position. Coefficient is provided by legislation and internal company HR documents and it could be steady for years). Another problem is unqualified employees with lack of knowledge and practice in business domain they are hired for. The reason for this could be corruption in employment process (some public companies advocate publicly that they prefer daughters and sons of their current employees in hiring process. All this influence that ASAP methodology is not executed in theoretically described manner.

Leak of professional business environment in state owned companies—ASAP methodology requires business educated professionals who can follow ASAP predefined tasks. Very often employees in state owned companies do not have appropriate skills that can support ASAP activities. Even if the project managers deliver tasks to their employee the feedback is missing or is delivered in very poor manner.

Leak of change management (Change management not consider as important)—Change management is a process which aim is to make easier implementation, as well as transition during ERP project. Since ERP project is usually very complex, change management can play significant role to improve employees to understand why the project has been implemented and to make organizational changes and BPR easier. These activities can be summed into 3 basic ones: education of employees, communication among stakeholders and involvement in project process. Lack of change management can affect quality of project implementation, and make results smaller.

6 Conclusion

As it is stated in abstract the main objective of this paper is to answer a question "Does predefined ERP implementation methodology work for state owned companies in transitioning countries?" We tried to answer on this question with experience gained with several projects in state owned companies done in Bosnia and Herzegovina. We will call it hands on experience. As we are working as SAP consultants, we chose SAP Accelerated methodology as referent methodology for our paper. We found it relevant as it is provided by the biggest ERP vendor—SAP A.G. In general ASAP methodology is well developed with hundreds of well-structured documents which support all ERP implementation activities. But in practices for state owed companies it hardly works. As SAP consultants we got impression that ASAP methodology is constructed for private professional business environment which can be easily found in developed countries, but not in state owned companies in transitioning country. At the end we will state the most remarkable constrains we found in applying ASAP methodology in ERP implementations;

- Inadequate tendering procedure for state owned company
- No localization for ASAP documentation for smaller countries (example Bosnian language)
- Time consuming decision making flow process
- Working habits of management and employees
- Leak of professional business environment in state owned companies
- Leak of change management (Change management not consider as important)

We believe this paper could be useful in further ERP implementations and research.

References

1. Sheu, C., Yen, H.R., Krumwiede D.W.: The effect of national differences on multinational ERP implementation: an exploratory study. TQM Bus. Excell. **14**(6), 641–657 (2003)
2. Midrange, E.R.P.: There Is No Magic in ERP Software: It's in Preparation of the Process and, p. 8. People, September (1998)
3. itbusinessedge.com: Whos to blame for failed ERP project that prompted lawsuit, http://www.itbusinessedge.com/cm/blogs/all/whos-to-blame-for-failed-erp-project-that-prompted-sap-lawsuit/?cs=11588 (2021)
4. Bloomberg.com: Shane says SAP costs helped cause jeweler's decline, http://www.bloomberg.com/apps/news?pid=newsarchive&sid=awweg53wmmJw&refer=germany (2012)
5. Bhagwani, A.: Critical Success Factors In Implementing SAP ERP Software, An EMGT Field Project report submitted to the Engineering Management Program and the Faculty of the Graduate School of The University of Kansas (2009)
6. U4.no: Corruption and Anti-Corruption in Bosnia and Herzegovina (B&H); www.u4.no/helpdesk/helpdesk/query.cfm?id=221 (2012)

7. Worldbank, Bosnia and Herzegovina Diagnostic Surveys of Corruption, World Bank; http://www1.worldbank.org/publicsector/anticorrupt/Bosnianticorruption.pdf (2012)
8. Nazir, M.M.: ERP Implementation in Oil Refineries. Daily Business Recorder, Karachi (2005)
9. Miller, S.: Asap Implementation at the Speed of Business: Implementation at the Speed of Business. Computing McGraw-Hill,New York (1998)

A Team-Oriented Investigation of ERP Post-Implementation Integration Projects: How Cross-Functional Collaboration Influences ERP Benefits

Daphne Rich and Jens Dibbern

Abstract The benefits companies achieve by implementing an ERP system vary considerably. Many companies need to adapt their ERP integration solution in the post-implementation stage. But after the completion of such a usually very complex integration project, benefits do not emerge by all means. A misfit between the organization and the IS, especially the aspect of cross-functional team collaboration, could explain these divergences. Using an initial theoretical framework, we conducted a single case study to explore the team-oriented perceptions in a post-implementation ERP integration project. To analyze the benefits and the influences in greater depth we disentangled the integration benefits into their particular parts (process, system and information quality). Our findings show that post-implementation ERP integration changes are not always perceived as beneficiary by the involved teams and that cross-functional collaboration has an important influence.

1 Introduction

In recent years, many companies have decided to invest in the implementation of an integrated Enterprise Resource Planning (ERP) system with the objective of handling business processes with a single IT system company-wide. Such a shared information system (IS) is therefore used by many different departments and functions across a company and is not limited to departmental boundaries anymore. Actual experience shows that the net benefits of such an integrated ERP system do not always have to be positive [1]. One explanation can be found in the

---

D. Rich (✉) · J. Dibbern
University of Berne, Berne, Switzerland
e-mail: daphne.rich@iwi.unibe.ch

J. Dibbern
e-mail: jens.dibbern@iwi.unibe.ch

fit between the organization and the IS [2]; especially in team collaboration [3, 4], as the way of cross-functional operating is considerably changed by the implementation of an ERP system [5]. Business processes and the execution of work functions are more interconnected, standardized and coupled. The teams using the ERP-systems are forced to work more multi-functionally and the execution of one work step has a direct influence on the work of other teams [6–8]. Research conducted at the process of initial ERP implementation projects show that system integration along with cross-functional team collaboration (enabled by integration) is highly important for on-going system success [3, 4, 6].

One aspect, which had previously received little attention, is that after the completion of an ERP implementation, system integration is usually not completed. In the majority of cases it remains to be an illusion to have one ERP system as a single integration solution [9]. Legacy systems and stand-alone solutions persist and need to be interfaced with the ERP system [10, 11]. Additionally, an ERP system has to be adapted continuously to new business processes and environmental changes. Further integration projects are required to standardize and broaden the system landscape. Such integration projects taking place in the post-implementation phase of an ERP system are rarely studied in literature.

Based on extant research findings, the changes of an implemented ERP integration solution, caused by an ERP post-implementation integration project, are supposed to have an impact on the perceived ERP benefits, in particular, if they cause or go along with changes in the way cross-functional teams collaborate [3, 4]. To explain these previously not investigated interrelationships, our study specifically takes the perspective of the teams involved in the execution of a specific business process affected by the integration changes. The objective is to find out (a) how a change in the existing ERP integration solution affects the perceived integration benefits by the involved teams and (b) how the modified cross-functional collaboration influences the perception of the integration benefits.

Given the exploratory nature of this research, a single case study is conducted in a Swiss transportation operator company that planned to extend its existing ERP system with new functionality to improve system integration for its procurement and payment process. Data were gathered two to three months after the introduction of the new integration solution. In this way, an understanding of the perceptions of the integration changes and benefits of the new solution by the three involved teams was achieved. The next chapter introduces the theoretical framework that served as a basis for our exploratory analysis.

2 Theoretical Background

The importance of a fit between the organization of a firm and the information systems has been recognized in IS literature [2] and confirmed in the ERP context [5, 12, 13] repeatedly. It is highly acknowledged that the integration achieved by the implementation of an ERP system generally leads to on-going ERP system usage

[14] and therefore to greater benefits for the whole organization [8, 15, 16]. However, detailed investigations show that the net benefits of increased integration are not always positive [1]. Analyzing these findings, the aspect of cross-functional collaboration emerges. The case studies conducted by Goodhue et al. [4] show that interdependence and differentiation of organizational subunits influence the achieved benefits of a newly implemented enterprise system. Following these findings, Gattiker and Goodhue [3] confirmed their findings by a quantitative study.

Although it is well stated that an ERP system and its integration solution are not stable after the implementation [13], all known research analyzing cross-functional collaboration in connection with ERP integration benefits concentrates on the stage of initial ERP implementation only. While Strong and Volkoff [1] highlight that "[...] a misfit is not a stable object. It changes over time, whether through changes to the ES or some aspect of the organization, or a reframing of the issues", they do not analyze the effect of these changes in-depth.

Adapting the presented findings to the context of post-implementation ERP integration projects, an initial conceptual framework is developed to guide the qualitative exploration of the perceived integration benefits (see Fig. 1). The basic assumption is that every team affected by an integration project perceives specific changes of the ERP integration solution that comprises all ERP system modules and the linkages between the ERP system and other business applications required by a team to fulfill the specific business workflow. Based on the research conducted in the ERP implementation context [15–17] the teams are supposed to notice benefits due to higher integration. Furthermore, changes in integration also influence cross-functional collaboration [6] that is assumed to influence the intensity of the perceived benefits [1, 3, 4]. To open up the opportunity to analyze the benefits and the influences in greater depth we disentangled the integration benefits into their particular parts, such as process, system and information quality as opposed to other studies that mostly treated them on a aggregated level. Our framework is built on the components of the IS Success Model [18, 19]. As we expect benefits at the process level to be important too we add process quality [20, 21] in addition to system and information quality.

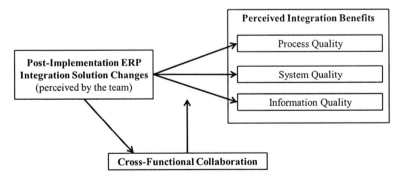

Fig. 1 Theoretical framework

3 Research Design

3.1 Methodology

Guided by the initial theoretical framework, an exploratory approach was chosen by conducting a qualitative single case study. This approach seemed to be appropriate, as the research field is new and our study strives for answering "why" and "how" questions [22, 23]. Data were collected observing an ERP post-implementation integration project. Semi-structured interviews were conducted within three involved teams affected by the integration changes. The semi-structured approach permitted us to additionally raise issues suggested by our theoretical framework [14]. In order to improve validity of our findings [24] we complemented the interviews with observation sessions in the different teams and a process document analysis.

3.2 Data Collection and Analysis

Data Collection. The setting of the case study is a large Swiss company in the traffic logistics industry. The company decided on a corporate-level to harmonize its procurement and payment process across the group by initializing the ERP integration project "Procure to Pay" (P2P). Figure 2 gives an overview of the addressed process supported by the ERP-system SAP. On the company-level, the reasons for initiating the project were basically (a) the poor process quality as well as missing process standardization and optimization due to large divisional differences in process handling, and (b) the ending of the support life cycle of the old accounts payment information system. To overcome these shortcomings, the five main targets guided the project: (1) one company-wide standardized process chain, (2) higher process automation, (3) user friendliness, (4) full SAP integration and, (5) a consistent approval process. Therefore, formerly manually performed tasks or work steps supported by legacy systems were replaced by additional SAP solutions.

Figure 3 illustrates the major process modifications. Before the implementation of the new integration solution, purchase orders were set up by the enquirer via

Fig. 2 "Procure to Pay" (P2P) process overview

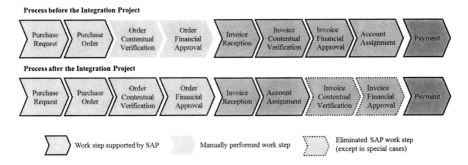

Fig. 3 Process modifications

SAP and then processed by the purchasing department. The enquirer had no opportunity to check the correctness and status of the order in SAP. Furthermore, the financial approval process of purchase orders was executed manually varying from division to division, i.e. in some divisions project leaders approved the orders verbally, in other divisions they signed an order form and some had no approval process at all. Instead, every invoice had to be checked and approved afterwards. In the new workflow, the invoices are automatically booked if the invoice amount is equal to the order price. The main advantages of the new workflow are that wrong orders can be detected earlier, that depreciations can be reduced by preventing miss-deliveries, and that invoices are paid earlier so that the company does not miss cash discount deadlines. Mainly three employee groups can be distinguished that were affected most by the changes: (1) the line teams purchasing material (especially the project teams responsible for large infrastructure projects), (2) the purchasing department, and (3) the accounts payable department.[1]

Our study was conducted in the first project rollout phase in the infrastructure department involving around 9,000 employees. One team of every affected department (project department, purchasing department and accounts payable department) was studied. To become acquainted with the daily workflows, one of the end-users of every team was observed and the working steps were documented. In a second step, four to six end-users of every team were interviewed (see Table 1). The sample is characterized by variety in age, gender, time of employment and role. The interviews were held face-to-face, tape-recorded and transcribed. The recorded workflow served as a basis for the interview discussions. In order to get a thorough understanding of the system, the integration solution and the business processes, project team meetings and system training sessions were attended for half a year and pre-interviews were conducted during the project roadshows.

Data Analysis. All workflow documentations and the interview data were carefully interpreted in order to explore whether and how ERP integration changes influence the perceived integration benefits. Codes were assigned to all remarks

---

[1] The department responsible for the payment transactions is not affected by the changes.

Table 1 Interview sample

Studied departments	End-users interviewed
Project department	2 team leaders
	2 project leaders
Purchasing department	4 purchasers responsible for different product groups
Accounts payable department	1 team leader
	5 accounts payable administrators

Table 2 Coding examples

	Code	Interview statement (EU = end-user)
Perceived integration benefits	*Process quality*	"The time required to accept an invoice [by SAP] is reduced" (accounts payable department employee)
		"With the approval process it takes longer, sometimes, until the order is sent out to the goods provider" (purchasing department employee)
	System quality	"After logging onto the dashboard [in SAP] as newbie, I was really [surprised], it was very comprehensible" (purchasing department employee)
		"I believe that the most important aspects are that it [the new SAP module] is not self-explanatory [...]" (purchasing department employee)
	Information quality	"Frequently, people [from the project department] made a purchase requisition without adding a purchasing price [...] This is not possible with P2P anymore" (purchasing department employee)
		"I believe that you don't find much more information [in SAP].that before."(purchasing department employee)

considered relevant. Initial code assignments were revised, abstracted, and consolidated during the coding process. For this purpose, Table 2 demonstrates the coding by means of the perceived benefits illustrates by an interview quote. Once a relatively concise set of codes had been established, the relationships between the codes were reviewed to ensure that they did not exhibit inconsistencies.

4 Results

4.1 Post-Implementation ERP Integration Solution Changes

The main changes the three departments are confronted with are outlined in Fig. 4. The project teams validate and accept the purchase orders instead of the invoices. The purchasing department is not directly affected by process changes but the purchasing workflow is automatized and supported by a new user interface with an

Fig. 4 Main process changes by department

Process before the Integration Project

Purchase Request → Purchase Order → Order Contentual Verification → Order Financial Approval → Invoice Reception → Invoice Contentual Verification → Invoice Financial Approval → Account Assignment → Payment

	Purchase Request	Purchase Order	Order Contentual Verification	Order Financial Approval	Invoice Reception	Invoice Contentual Verification	Invoice Financial Approval	Account Assignment	Payment
Enquirer / Project Office			(x)			x		x	
Manager / Project Leader				(x)			x		
Purchasing Department		x							
Accounts Payable Dept.					x				

Process after the Integration Project

Purchase Request → Purchase Order → Order Contentual Verification → Order Financial Approval → Invoice Reception → Account Assignment → Invoice Contentual Verification → Invoice Financial Approval → Payment

	Purchase Request	Purchase Order	Order Contentual Verification	Order Financial Approval	Invoice Reception	Account Assignment	Invoice Contentual Verification	Invoice Financial Approval	Payment
Enquirer / Project Office	x		x				(x)		
Manager / Project Leader				x				(x)	
Purchasing Department		x							
Accounts Payable Dept.					x	x			

overview of all orders to be processed. Due to the automated invoice accounting and payment the responsibility for the correct account assignment is switched from the project team to the accounts payable department. As a rule, the account details are already completed by entering the order information, but the last check can only be conducted by the accounts payable team regarding the new integration solution.[2]

The interviews show a more differentiated picture of the changes directly perceived by every team. It is important to gain a basic understanding of these changes to be able to better relate to the perceived benefits (see Table 3).

4.2 Perceived Integration Benefits

The analysis of the interviews first shows, that the integration solution changes affect every team differently. In summary, for the project department and the purchasing department, the effects are beneficial. By having a deeper look at the different categories, not every quality aspect is affected positively (see Table 4). For the project department there is no big advantage seen regarding the system quality, for the purchasing department the information quality perceived is overall quite similar. Studying the interviews of the accounts payable department, in summary, the team

---

[2] **Exceptions**:
- Orders without goods receipt: the project team needs to confirm that the ordered service was delivered.
- Invoices without order reference: the project team still needs to verify and approve the invoice in this case because no assigned order was verified/accepted before.

Table 3 Perceived integration solution changes within the departments

Department	Perceived integration solution changes
Project department	• New SAP "must-field" with the e-mail address of the enquirer in the purchase requisition form • Replacement of invoice verification/approval (at the end of the process) for purchase order verification/approval (at the beginning of the process) • Possibility to change invoice details directly in the system instead of writing a system notice to let the details be changed by the accounts payable department
Purchasing department	• A new SAP "must-field" with the e-mail address of the enquirer in the order form that allows the system to allocate the right approver automatically by a predefined rule (the approver was selected manually by the project team with no clear rule before) • New workflow user interface "Dashboard" with an overview of all purchase orders in the process and especially with the new functionality to directly receive orders rejected by the accounts payable department where the amount invoiced is higher than the amount of the order (was handled by an excel sheet before)
Accounts payable department	• New scanning software focusing only on four "must fields" • New automated invoice validation by only checking the four "must fields" (validation had to be performed manually with a special software before) • New workflow user interface "Dashboard" where everybody sees the whole invoice pool (the invoices could be individually assigned before) • Automated transfer of scanned invoices with an order reference and no goods receipt to the payment department (all these invoices had to be processed manually in SAP because account details were missing due to the fact that the purchase orders were not checked by the project team before) • Responsibility for the correct account allocation as a standard for every invoice received (was handled individually before, mostly delegated to the project team due to the fact that they received every invoice for verifying and approving anyway)

Table 4 Perceived integration benefits

Benefit category	Tendency of perceived integration benefits by the team		
	Project department	Purchasing department	Accounts payable department
Process quality	↑	↑	→
System quality	→	↑	→
Information quality	↑	→	↓

does not notice remarkable benefits at all. The quality of information even decreased. Our findings confirm the research results gained in the ERP implementation context stating that an increased level of integration is not always perceived as beneficial [1, 3, 4]. In the following paper section we analyze whether these divergent perceptions can be explained by aspects of cross-functional collaboration. Thereby, the division of the benefits into the three categories may help in finding a convincing explanation of the influences.

4.3 The Influence of Cross-Functional Collaboration

Collaboration between the Purchasing and the Project Department. Due to the possibility of checking the purchase orders in the beginning of the process, the project teams' dependence on the purchasing department is reduced. This new situation mediates the influence on the perceived information quality positively: faulty data insertion by the purchasing department can be corrected early.

> Before P2P someone wrote the wrong order reference number [...] manually on the order form. He did not write nicely so that a "3" became an "8". [...] Until the go-live of P2P the number [this wrong entry by the purchasing department] has always been stored wrongly.
> (Project team leader)

The integration development is also perceived positively regarding information quality by the purchasing department although they are more dependent on the project team now than before. This increased control is not seen as responsibility constraint but as support enhancing the sense of security instead.

> It is very good, that it [the order] goes back to the line management before it is transferred to the goods provider. So the people have still the possibility to check it substantially and financially. In the end, *they* know that it is ok. I like that.
> (Purchaser responsible for working cloths and security equipment)

> Already *there*, they [the project team members] see if we make a mistake and, thus, we have less incorrect product deliveries. [...] And that is an improvement at the bottom line because all the [goods] exchanges [...] cost money and time.
> (Purchaser responsible for infrastructure construction projects)

On the other hand, this increased dependency of the purchasing department on the actions of the project team is simultaneously influencing the effect on the perceived process speed negatively. The new integration solution would be even more beneficial if the collaboration were to be improved.

> The effect is, that the process time is longer again, because before [the go-life of the new integration solution] we knew that within some minutes the order I generated arrived at the goods provider. Now, in consequence of the new approval [strategy], the process time is once more dependent on people, if they are present, if the substitution is updated [in SAP]. If nobody is doing that it can last about one or two weeks—or even longer—until the order is finally at the goods provider.
> (Purchaser responsible for electricity)

Collaboration between the Accounts Payable and the other Departments. The collaboration at the end of the process is perceived differently. The project team is comfortable with the new situation. They feel more independent by having the opportunity to change entered invoice data directly in the invoice form.

> This is an advantage because before [P2P] we had to return [the invoice] to the accountant and explain in a notice to whom the amount has to be paid. Now I can enter it on my own. This is more efficient. There is less effort needed, typing in a number than writing an instruction. Before, it took always around one week until it came back again. Now I can complete it immediately.
>
> (Project leader)

Analyzing the accounts payable department the missing benefits perception can be also explained by a mediating influence of collaboration. On one hand, they perceive a negative effect on information quality and no benefit regarding process quality due to wrong system entries of the project teams and the purchasing department. Wrong or missing entries in the order form prevent the automatic transferring of the invoice to the payment department. Faulty invoice details entries by the project team sends the invoice back to the accounts payable department. So the perceived potential quality is greatly suffering due to aspects of collaboration and increased dependency. At the end, this also enhances (despite a more integrated system landscape) manually performed work around solutions as phone calls, e-mails etc. to communicate with the other department.

> It happens that people [of the project team] reject [an invoice], although they could do it [the correction] themselves. It is important, we take the time to call someone and explain it. That just takes time. Sometimes it would be easier to simply change the invoice [...].
>
> (Accounts payable team leader)

Interestingly, as in the purchasing department, the accounts payable department too perceives a positive influence of the collaboration on the effect of the integration change on information quality regarding enhanced control. Also for the accountants the sense of security is enhanced.

> Due to the fact that we are accountants now, the [...] approvers have to give a clearer reason why they reject something [...].
>
> (Accounts payable administrator)

All together, the following interesting findings emerge:

- Interdependence influences the effect of the integration changes on the perception of *information quality positively* if it is connected with an additional security effect (e.g. data entries will be checked by another team and thus the entering department feels safer). This is especially relevant for the departments with a supportive role (i.e. the purchasing department and the accounts payable department).
- Interdependence influences the effect of the integration on the perception of *information quality negatively* if the work of a team is more reliant on system data entries of another team. This mediating effect is much stronger if the teams do not *trust* each other.

[The project leaders] don't have any clue what they have to do by checking an invoice.
(Purchaser responsible for infrastructure construction projects)

Yes, we trusted them [purchasing department]. [...] then these incidences happened [regarding severe faulty entries] and we were urged to check the orders [more seriously].
(Project team leader)

- Interdependence influences the effect of the integration changes on the perception of *process quality negatively* due to the fact that autonomy is lost. For example, a next work step can only be executed if the other department completed its work steps: waiting times and a deceleration of the process speed are the result. Previously, the teams were more flexible in executing their workflows.
- The perceived effect of the integration changes on *system quality* is not affected by cross-functional collaboration.

Our findings especially help to explain why the ERP post-implementation integration solution changes are only partly perceived as beneficiary by the purchasing and the accounts payable department. Additionally, they give a reason for the extremely positive results of the project team regarding process and information quality. They do not regard the new tasks as extra work[3] but appreciate the gained autonomy.

5 Discussion

The benefits companies achieve by implementing an ERP system vary considerably. Many companies need to adapt their ERP integration solution in the post-implementation stage. But after the completion of such a usually very complex integration project, benefits do not emerge by all means. Our research paper may help to explain these differences.

In summary, our findings show that post-implementation integration changes are not always perceived as beneficiary by the involved teams and that cross-functional collaboration has an important influence. The potential quality benefits are recognized clearly but they are influenced by collaboration aspects so that the actual effects are neutralized or in the worst case inversed. On the other hand, cross-functional collaboration also strengthens the perceived benefits in some cases. Increased interdependence between the different teams due to a tightened integration solution is not always influencing the benefits perception positively. Differences between the created benefit categories emerge. Interdependence influences the effect of the integration changes on the perception of process quality

---

[3] This was a concern of the project team stated before the go-live of the new integration solution.

negatively and the effect on the perception of information quality either positively or negatively. The perception of system quality is not influenced at all.

5.1 Contributions

Based on the research focusing on the fit between the organization of a firm and the ERP system [2, 5, 12, 13] we expand the findings explaining varying benefit achievements [1, 15, 16] by studying ERP integration projects. The importance of cross-functional aspects regarding integration at a team-level [3, 4, 6], are confirmed in the post-implementation context. Thereby, the partitioning of the perceived benefits enables us to explain effects in more detail at a process, system and information level. Additionally, the organization-oriented findings of Nicolaou [25]—studying the effect of post-implementation changes on a firm's performance—are deepened.

From a practical point of view, the findings on the perceived benefits and the cross-functional collaboration are interesting. The potential integration benefits perceived by every team are essential during the planning of the integration project. By involving the affected teams in an early planning stage, e.g. communication and training can be adapted specifically for every team to achieve the greatest possible benefit. It is important to take also interdependencies into account. The project team has to analyze clearly where work flexibility is limited due to a higher degree of integration. If cross-functional interdependence is enhanced, a firm should invest in the building of trust among the involved teams.

5.2 Limitations and Research Outlook

We recognize that this study is subject to limitations. (1) We use limited data from one integration project in one company. While this helps to control for heterogeneity, it otherwise limits generalizability. (2) We only studied one ERP system, which may limit generalization to other ERP packages. (3) We only investigated the mediating influence of cross-functional collaboration. Other factors characterizing a team may be relevant. For example, the accounts payable team is characterized by a high fear to lose the job due to the automation achieved by the new integration solution. This aspect may have an influence on the negative perception, too. (4) Our data were collected two to three months after the go-live of the new integration solution. The findings may therefore be influenced by "teething troubles".

Additional conceptual and empirical research is needed to revise our findings in another post-implementation integration project in another company. Additionally, it would be valuable to investigate the end-user perspective as we stated during the interviews that not every team member perceives the same benefits due to the integration solution changes.

References

1. Strong, D.M., Volkoff, O.: Understanding organization-enterprise system fit: a path to theorizing the information technology artifact. MIS Q. **34**, 731–756 (2010)
2. Orlikowski, W.J.: Learning from notes: organizational issues in groupware implementation. Technical report. Center for Coordination Science, MIT, Cambridge (1992)
3. Gattiker, T.F., Goodhue, D.L.: What happens after ERP Implementation: understanding the impact of interdependence and differentiation on plant-level outcomes. MIS Q **29**, 559–585 (2005)
4. Goodhue, D.L., Wybo, M.D., Kirsch, L.J.: The impact of data Integration on the costs and benefits of information systems. MIS Q. **16**, 293–311 (1992)
5. Robey, D., Ross, J.W., Boudreau, M.-C.: Learning to implement enterprise systems: an exploratory study of the dialectics of change. J. Manage. Inf. Syst. **19**, 17–46 (2002)
6. El Amrani, R., Rowe, F., Geffroy-Maronnat, B.: The effects of enterprise resource planning implementation strategy on cross-functionality. Inf. Syst. J. **16**, 79–104 (2006)
7. Galbraith, J.: Competing with Flexible Lateral Organizations. Addison-Wesley, Reading (1994)
8. Davenport, T.H.: Mission Critical: Realizing the Promise of Enterprise Systems. Harvard Business School Press, Boston (2000)
9. Sandoe, K., Corbitt, G., Boykin, R.: Enterprise Integration. Wiley, New York (2001)
10. Alshawi, S., Themistocleous, M., Almadani, R.: Integrating diverse ERP systems: a case study. J. Enterp. Inf. Manage. **17**, 454–462 (2004)
11. Themistocleous, M., Irani, Z., O'Keefe, R.M.: ERP and application integration: exploratory survey. Bus. Process Manage. J. **7**, 195–204 (2001)
12. Davenport, T.H.: Putting the enterprise into the enterprise system. Harvard Bus. Rev. **76**, 121–131 (1998)
13. Markus, M.L., Tanis, C.: The Enterprise system experience—from adoption to success. In: Zmud, R.W. (ed.) Framing the Domains of IT Research: Projecting the Future…Through the Past, pp. 173–207 Pinnaflex Educational Resources, Inc., Cincinnati (2000)
14. Furneaux, B., Wade, M.: An exploration of organizational level information systems discontinuance intentions. MIS Q. **35**, 573–598 (2011)
15. Peslak, A.: A study of information technology integration. J. Inf. Syst. Appl. Res. **4**, 19–27 (2011)
16. Seddon, P.B., Calvert, C., Yang, S.: A multi-project model of key factors affecting organizational benefits from enterprise systems. MIS Q. **34**, 305–328 (2010)
17. Markus, M.L.: Paradigm shifts—E-business and business/systems integration. communications of the association for information systems 4. http://aisel.aisnet.org/cais/vol4/iss1/10/ (2000)
18. DeLone, W.H., McLean, E.R.: The DeLone and McLean model of information systems success: a ten-year update. J. Manage. Inf. Syst. **19**, 9–30 (2003)
19. DeLone, W.H., McLean, E.R.: Information systems success: the quest for the dependent variable. Inf. Syst. Res. **3**, 60–95 (1992)
20. Zellner, G.: A structured evaluation of business process improvement approaches. Bus. Process Manage. J. **7**, 203–237 (2011)
21. Berente, N., Vandenbosch, B., Aubert, B.: Information flows and business process integration. Bus. Process Manage. J. **15**, 119–141 (2009)
22. Miles, M.B., Huberman, A.M.: Qualitative Data Analysis: An Expanded Sourcebook. Sage publications, Newbury Park (1994)
23. Yin, R.: Case Study Research. Sage publications, Thousand Oaks (2003)
24. Benbasat, I., Goldstein, D.K., Mead, M.: The case research strategy in studies of information systems. Manage. Inf. Syst. Q. **11**, 369 (1987)
25. Nicolaou, A.I., Bhattacharya, S.: Organizational performance effects of ERP systems usage: the impact of post-implementation changes. Int. J. Acc. Inf. Syst. **7**, 18–35 (2006)

Part V
ERP Landscape

Analysis Pattern for the Transformation of ERP System Landscapes by SaaS

Kurt Porkert and Howard Sutton

Abstract The best possible fulfilment of demands upon IT landscapes requires the systematic analysis of both the business requirements and the way in which the ERP system and its integrated applications should be transformed. A pattern for the analysis can assist in: identifying and evaluating the current system status; estimating the possible improvements with respect to using SaaS and selecting the most advantageous solution. The proposed analysis pattern is based upon documented user applications of SaaS implementation and enabling it's integration in the ERP landscape.

1 Introduction

The current popularity of "Cloud Computing" has also renewed company's interest in "Software as a Service" (SaaS). In many cases such offers are for IT "Landscapes" in which ERP, ECM and other Business applications are closely connected.[1] Analogous to other landscapes, innovation often changes an ERP landscape. In Enterprise Architecture Frameworks [1] this can include the architectural levels of applications, their platforms and the infrastructure.

The decision whether an On-Premise-ERP-Solution should be supplemented replaced by SaaS is an issue for strategic IT planning. According to [2] the appropriate planning activities are: clarifying the need for action and the

---

[1] ERP software und ERP systems are not consistently defined and contain a different number of functional modules and other components [3].

K. Porkert (✉) · H. Sutton
Pforzheim University of Applied Sciences, Business School, Pforzheim, Germany
e-mail: kurt.porkert@hs-pforzheim.de

H. Sutton
e-mail: howard.sutton@hs-pforzheim.de

determination of the objectives for changing the current status; and the determination of the type of changes required with respect to sourcing. For these activities a pattern for analysis is proposed which can help answer a number of questions. Why should an existing ERP landscape be transformed? Is SaaS an appropriate or perhaps the best type of transformation? How can the most appropriate SaaS offer be selected?

2 The Identification and Evaluation of Weaknesses in ERP System Landscapes

The degree of change necessary in an ERP landscape is determined by considering a number of system analyses whose focus can be derived from the architecture of the enterprise architecture framework. Table 1 shows the types of analyses described in [2] which have been grouped into areas, together with the reasons for the weaknesses derived from [4].

The above mentioned analyses are able to identify specific deficiencies from both external and internal causes. Numerous surveys [4], performed by software providers, have demonstrated that in large companies all the weaknesses mentioned can occur simultaneously. In such companies complex heterogeneous IT landscapes evolve through insufficient coordination/co-operation and result in partially obsolete, incomplete und inflexible solutions which caused excessive costs. In larger medium sized companies the main weaknesses were found to be of

Table 1 Relevant analyses and weaknesses in ERP landscapes

Area	Analysis	Weaknesses
Compliance with business demands	Functional analysis, risk and security analysis, compliance-analysis	Missing or inappropriate functionality, insufficient user support, security deficits, none compliance of regulations, deficient data availability
Quality of the structure of the application landscape	Ballast analysis, redundancy analysis, heterogeneity analysis, conformity analysis, integrations gap analyse, data dependence analysis, economic analysis	Functional ballast, functional redundancy, unjustified complexity, heterogeneous applications, inadequate integration, expensive solution
Quality of the technical platform	Flexibility analysis, integration capability analysis, technical status analysis, risk and security analysis, compliance analysis	Poor platform condition, no standard platforms, insufficient scalability, insecure platform, poor integration of platform, heterogeneous platforms
Suitability of operations/deployment	Economic analysis, costs/expenditure comparison	Deficient competence in operations, insufficient technical or organizational infrastructure, expensive cost of operations

a functional or security nature and were caused by the company's growth and/or demands from their business partners. For small sized companies the surveys indicated that the main deficits were to be found in high costs, insufficient user support and unused or obsolete data.

To appreciate the magnitude or importance of the identified weaknesses a criticality analysis should be performed which will indicate the disadvantages on the following three levels:

- Resource efficiency: reduced effectiveness of the IT solution and employees,
- Process efficiency: impaired co-operation between employees; slower, more expensive process, poor process results,
- Market efficiency: competitive disadvantages.

When the established weaknesses reason that immediate actions are necessary, then the primary goal of any transformation is to eliminate those deficits. It is now a question of determining which type of transformation is the most suitable.

3 The Potential to Rectify the Weaknesses Using SaaS

An analysis of the types of transformation [5] demonstrates what needs to be changed and how this will affect the size of the ERP landscape, the software and hardware used as well as the responsibility and location for operations (see Table 2).

SaaS offers a possibility for changing both the responsibility for operations and the location of operations. Such services have been offered as a business model since the end of the 1990s, the functionality of the software is provided over the

Table 2 Types of transformations for ERP landscapes

Classification	Types of transformation
Object for transformation	ERP system, a system additional application, ERP platform, ERP hardware
Impact upon the size of ERP landscape	Increase or decrease in the number of software solutions, replacement of current solutions
Type of software used	Replacement of current solutions by changing the software type; between proprietary standard software, open-source-software, individual software solution
Software or hardware products used	Replacement of current software/hardware product by another or use of another version of the product
Responsibility for operations	Change between central/decentral or between internal/external responsibility, or between different external variations e.g. "service from one provider only" or a "general contractor as service provider"
Location of operations	Change between central/decentral or between internal/external locations, or between different external locations.

internet and thereby differentiating itself by the Multi-Tenant-Architecture from the ASP concept. According to [6] SaaS, this corresponds to a "layer model" for Cloud Services. In addition, "Infrastructure as a Service" (IaaS) or "Platform as a Service" (PaaS) are alternative changes to ERP landscapes [7].

Various deployment models are available for SaaS which are differentiated by operational responsibility, operational location and typical Cloud Services characteristics. Whereas the models "Public Cloud" and "Virtual (Outsourced) Private Cloud" refer to both external operational responsibility and location, the model "Private Cloud" refers to external operational with an internal operational location [8]. A pure "Private Cloud" model refers to both internal operation responsibility and location and, in comparison to the other models, does not represent an outsourcing solution.

The model "Public Cloud" is available to many users and offers standard services as Multi-Tenant Solutions which are available over the internet. This enables favourable conditions for: a quick, user controlled scaling of resources; high availability together with payment based upon the use of the solution which often results in a low price. This model requires a stable and quick internet connection but is often unable to fulfil the security requirements of the user. It is an appropriate alternative when standard services are used and only low level security is necessary for the data.

There are principally three variants of "Private Cloud". The first variant is when the customer performs everything themselves, the second is when the provider performs the service at the customer either at the customers location or in house. It is evident that variants one to three are accompanied by an increasing security risk.

To what degree SaaS is suitable for reducing the deficits in an ERP landscape depends upon the company's sourcing strategy [2]. When SaaS is consistent with this strategy the appropriateness of SaaS can be determined using an analysis of the existing conditions. Favourable conditions for using SaaS are: highly dynamic set of requirements, the absence of expertise for the operational activities for the IT solution, the necessity for quick implementation of new software [7–10].

The Kiviat diagram in Fig. 1 can help to recognise whether SaaS could be used for a specific set of demands. When all the points lie on the outside boundary then SaaS is ideal for the case in question.

When it is evident through using the above fulfilment profile that SaaS could be used, then the next step should be to consider whether the actual transformation goals can be fulfilled by SaaS.

An evaluation of 65 user's reports [11, 12] identifies the typical objectives for implementing SaaS in ERP system landscapes. The size of companies in the reports were: smallest (10.8 %), small (12.3 %), medium sized (55.4 %) and large (21.5 %). The companies were in the following sectors: industry (28 %), wholesale/retail (9 %), services (57 %) and others (6 %). The results indicate that company's pursued a number of objectives, primary and subordinate, to eliminate the weaknesses in their systems (see Table 3).

Analysis Pattern for the Transformation of ERP System

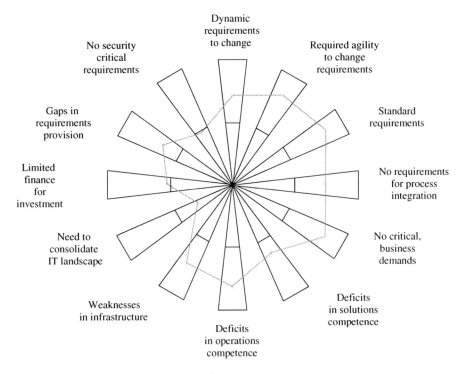

Fig. 1 Fulfilment profile of SaaS model with respect to defined conditions (increasing from the centre to the outside), based upon an exemplary transformation

Table 3 Grouping the SaaS objectives, based upon the fore mentioned user reports

SaaS objectives	Weaknesses eliminated
Reducing the costs of provision (sourcing)	Missing operational competence, insufficient technical and/or organizational infrastructure, excessive operational costs
Increasing flexibility	Insufficient technical status, inability to scale the operations, slow system changes
Consolidation	Insufficient conformity to standards, functional ballast/redundancy, inappropriate system complexity, heterogeneity of hardware/software, insufficient integration
Elimination of gaps	Missing/inappropriate functionality, poor data availability, security problem, insufficient conformity to regulations

To select the most appropriate services for the SaaS model both the respective objectives together with other requirements are necessary.

Fig. 2 Relative frequency of SaaS objectives named in the 65 transformation cases

4 Decision Criteria for Using SaaS

In 54 % of the documented cases it was decided to use a complete SaaS ERP solution. Of the remaining cases: 12 % decided upon SaaS for ERP system components; 12 % for CRM systems or system components, 14 % for ECM system components and 8 % for other supplementary application systems. The decisions to use SaaS assume that the respective goals (Fig. 2) could be fulfilled.

The reasons and conditions described for using SaaS correspond, in many cases, those scenarios presented [8] for using Cloud Services. Reducing costs by converting investment costs into running costs was the most commonly mentioned goal, especially by the small companies. The avoidance of incremental fixed costs was also frequently mentioned by users who wished to increase their flexibility; this can be achieved because SaaS components can be paid for when they have actually been used and specific components can be implemented and/or changed at short notice.

Medium sized companies, in particular, implemented SaaS for complete business applications to reduced costs. This was achieved through consolidating complex, heterogeneous, insufficiently integrated ERP system landscapes and those which did not correspond with the strategic requirements. Consolidation in very large companies corresponded to using SaaS as a supplement for ECM extensions to the ERP system.

Analysis Pattern for the Transformation of ERP System

Table 4 Supplementary criteria to implementation goals for using SaaS

Criteria for	Examples
Additional functional service requirements	Degree of availability of the mandatory/optional functions, ability to customise functions, functional ballast, ability to extend the functionality, compliance
Additional none functional service requirements	Prices, methods of determining costs, references, security of information, performance, reliability, ability to adapt to users requirements, ability to integrate additional applications, customer friendliness, capability to be re-integrated, amount of detail in the service level agreements
Requirements on the service management	Quality of the security management (especially identity management and emergency management), change management, incident handling, capacity management, SLA Management, service desk, contract management (preparation, control, dissolution)
Requirements for the service provider	Technical competence, financial stability, image, dependence upon other providers, certification, willingness to be audited, willingness to provide information regarding locations, operations, current law/regulations and service management.

The goals of flexibility and consolidation were mentioned in numerous user reports and were associated with the intention of standardising business processes or eliminating previous deficits. The second most frequently mentioned reason to extend or replace "On-Premise ERP systems" was the reduction of deficits in the current software functionality, this referred to both data availability and information security. SaaS was also able to provided additional functionality which enabled either new business areas to be accommodated in a flexible way at low cost; or SaaS was able to provide functions which only an external provider could supply at the required quality level.

For example, Web Services for external checks for creditworthiness; congestion reports for transportation; or data for auctions and stock markets. SaaS as a Business Continuity Service is also mentioned as useful in reducing system unavailability ("down time").

When the objectives of the system appear to be achievable, it is still necessary to analyse in detail whether any additional demands [8, 9, 13, 14] upon the service, it's management and the service provider can be fulfilled (see Table 4).

An analysis of the relevant functional service requirements is naturally dependent upon the specific user's situation. For the none functional service requirements the emphasis is upon the costs and operating expenses. To compare the costs the TCO method is useful, enabling a complete and transparent analysis of the relevant cost items. It can sometimes also be useful to compare the amount of work required (in time units) or the solutions competence requirements. Special notice should be made of the effects of the; strategic, operative, financial, security and social requirements upon the service and its management [7–9, 14]. For specific models, the differences in requirements upon the service management need to be considered.

5 Conclusion

The decision whether SaaS should be implemented for ERP system landscapes should result from an analysis which considers both the potential benefits/ advantages and disadvantages. Primarily the benefits result from the negation/ resolution of current system deficits. The analysis pattern presented eases the identification and evaluation of typical weaknesses in existing ERP system landscapes. Known analysis patterns for IT landscapes and decision making concepts for cloud computing together with published data from SaaS user reports form the basis for the paper. A number of implementation scenarios have been derived from these sources, showing which weaknesses in ERP landscapes can be resolved using SaaS. The frequency with which these scenarios are used varies for large and small sized companies. The potential of SaaS to eliminate the weaknesses depends upon the degree to which the ERP landscape fulfils the listed conditions. The selection of the appropriate SaaS variant is based upon the analysis of the groups of criteria presented, which include functional and none functional service requirements as well as requirements upon the service management and provider. The use of the analysis framework can be supported by using either EAM tools or specific check lists [15] to both document and evaluate of the decision process.

References

1. Rowekamp, P.: EAM Frameworks. In: Keuntje, J. H., Barkow, R. (eds.) Enterprise Architektur Management in der Praxis, pp. 215–228. Symposion Publishing, Düsseldorf (2010)
2. Hanschke, I.: Strategisches Management der IT-Landschaft—Ein praktischer Leitfaden für das Enterprise Architecture Mangement. Hanser, München, Download-Anhang zum Buch A: Analyse-Muster. http://files.hanser.de/hanser/docs/20100621_21621165557-63_Hanschke Download-Anh%C3%A4nge_final.zip (2010)
3. Bradford, M.: Modern ERP Select, Implement and Use Today's Advanced Business Systems, 2nd edn. Lulu Press, Raleigh (2010)
4. Porkert, K.: Analyse der IT-Landschaft—kein Thema für Kleinunternehmen? In: Haubrock, A., Rieg, R., Stiefl, J. (eds.) Zweite Aalener KMU-Konferenz—Beiträge zum Stand der KMU-Forschung, pp.323–343. Shaker, Aachen (2011)
5. Knümann, G.: Application Transformation—Lösungspfade für eine optimierte Anwendungslandschaft. White Paper, BearingPoint GmbH, Frankfurt. http://www.cio.de/fileserver/idgwpcionew/files/310.pdf (2010)
6. Mell, P., Grance, T.: The NIST definition of cloud computing—recommendations of the National Institute of Standards and Technology. Special Publication 800-145, NIST, Gaithersburg. http://csrc.nist.gov/publications/nistpubs/800-145/SP800-145.pdf (2011)

7. Lenart, A.: ERP in the cloud—benefits and challenges. In: Wrycza, S. (eds.) Research in Systems Analysis and Design: Models and Methods. 4th SIGSAND/PLAIS EuroSymposium 2011, pp. 39–50. Springer, Berlin (2011)
8. BITKOM (eds.): Cloud Computing—Evolution in der Technik, Revolution im Business. Leitfaden, Berlin, http://www.bitkom.org/files/documents/BITKOM-Leitfaden-Cloud Computing_Web.pdf (2009)
9. Benlian, A., Hess, T.: Chancen und Risiken des Einsatzes von SaaS—Die Sicht der Anwender. In: Benlian, A., Hess, T., Buxmann, P. (eds.) Software-as-a-Service, pp. 174–187. Gabler, Wiesbaden (2010)
10. Lechesa, M., Seymour, L., Schuler, J.: ERP Software as Service (SaaS): factors affecting adoption in South Africa. In: Møller, C., Chaudhry, S. (eds.) Re-conceptualizing Enterprise Information Systems, LNBIP, vol. 105, pp. 152–167. Springer, Heidelberg (2012)
11. Porkert, K.:Einsatzszenarien der Cloud-Services nach Angaben in publizierten Anwenderberichten. Unpublished documentation, Pforzheim University, Pforzheim (2012)
12. Porkert, K.: Entscheidungskonzept für die Transformation einer IT-Landschaft durch Cloud-Service-Einsatzszenarien. In: Barton, T., Erdlenbruch, B., Herrmann, F., Müller, C., Schuler, J. (eds.) Management und IT, pp. 133–150. News & Media, Berlin (2012)
13. Henneberger, M., Strebel, J., Garzotto, F.: Ein Entscheidungsmodell für den Einsatz von Cloud Computing im Unternehmen. In: HMD—Praxis der Wirtschaftsinformatik 44, 275, pp. 76–84 (2010)
14. Terplan, K., Voigt, C.: Cloud Computing, mitp, Heidelberg (2011)
15. Schott, A.: Darstellung und Bewertung betrieblicher Anwendungslandschaften mit integriertem Cloud-Computing unter Verwendung der Software planningIT. Unpublished thesis, Pforzheim University, Pforzheim (2011)

Part VI
ERP: Cost-Benefit Analysis

Automated Testing of ERP GUI: A Cost-Benefit Analysis

Johannes Keckeis, Jan-Peter Eberle, Kurt Promberger and Pascal Erhart

Abstract This paper summarizes the execution and evaluation of an automated graphical user interface test. A state of the art Enterprise Resource System serves as test subject and a vendor-specific capture and replay tool is applied in order to execute the test. The test specification requires the tester to create a big variety of very individual test subprograms which can be combined to fulfill greater purpose. Evaluation is bound to a five stage spiral model, containing quantitative methods, such as a ROI calculation, and qualitative methods, like the ISO 9126-1. Each stage is individually assessed and weighted for the object of creating one combined cost benefit valuation.

1 Introduction

As enterprise resource planning (ERP)-systems are more and more common in these days, it's testing has gained an equivalent amount of importance. Nicolas Carr identified the reliability of complex IT-Systems as a key factor for a company's success, especially the more the company relies on the use of complex IT-Systems such as ERP-systems [1]. The main purpose of software testing is to discover errors or any kind of flaw in the tested program or application, but it can

---

J. Keckeis (✉) · J.-P. Eberle · K. Promberger · P. Erhart
University of Innsbruck, Innsbruck, Austria
e-mail: johannes.keckeis@uibk.ac.at

J.-P. Eberle
e-mail: jan-peter.eberle@uibk.ac.at

K. Promberger
e-mail: kurt.promberger@uibk.ac.at

P. Erhart
e-mail: pascal.erhart@uibk.ac.at

be applied to a big variety of objectives. Stress tests, usability tests, security tests or graphical user interface tests are some common examples of black box testing. Black box testing requires no profound knowledge about the tested software code [2]. The great complexity of an ERP-system, or comparable information-systems, does not allow for a complete system test covering every single feature of the system, since the costs of testing would clearly exceed the benefit of a completely tested system. Test automation is a technique to extend the test coverage and reduce the required resources. But even automated testing is limited to a certain degree of coverage because test automation requires more preparation than manual testing, automation is not always efficient. The main subject of this paper is the cost benefit analysis of an automated graphical user interface test of an ERP-system. Since costs and benefits have both, qualita-tive and quantitative effects, different approaches in measuring are applied. A specifically prepared five stage model for evaluating different types of costs and benefits supports the process of creating an impartial assessment framework. The five coherent stages cover quantitatively measurable features such as the comparison of automated and manual testing in hours of workload, as well as qualitative features like usability or understandability of the test tool assessed by indicators identified in the ISO 9126-1 [3]. All stages together contribute for a most impartial cost benefit analysis.

2 Methodology

In order to evaluate different aspects of a cost benefit analysis, a variety of methods are deployed. The distinct methods are represented in a specifically designed five stage evaluation model for the specific purpose of evaluating the costs and benefits of automated GUI testing: (Fig. 1).

The methodology is best explained, referring to each of the stages in this model. Stage I avails itself a quantitative approach. Measurable facts, such as the time required for the test preparation and the execution compose the basis for further evaluation. The definition of the test specifications, which are pre-supposing for preparation and execution of the test, are not part of this stage, because this task happens independently in both automated and manual test process. Therefore simple measuring of the duration (in hours, days or weeks of workload) is sufficient for assessing stage I. Automated testing should display a remarkable difference between the duration and execution of the test program. As execution of automated tests does not require any kind of supervision, the main aspect for evaluation of this stage needs to be the preparation duration. The second stage is needed for comparison with manual methods of GUI testing. In order to identify the duration for preparation and execution of a similar test, manual testing needs to be done additionally. If the test case is too extensive for manual testing, a sample test case should be specified, so that additional costs are minimized. Exclusively of relevance for the assessment in this stage is the difference in workload between manual and automated testing of the same test case. Stage I and II serve the

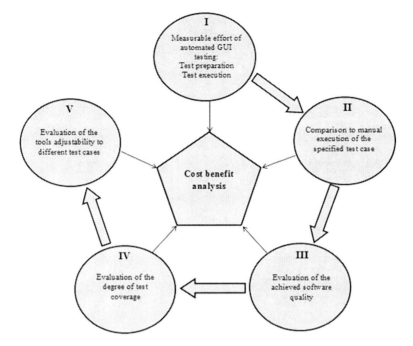

Fig. 1 Stages of cost-benefit analysis

quantitative evaluation of automated software testing and could be applied to any type of software testing. Measuring and comparing expenses of automated testing influence only the evaluation of costs. Savings in costs due to test automation do not inevitably mean a benefit. In stage III a qualitative approach for evaluation is taken into account. Based on the ISO 9126-1 [3], a framework for evaluating software quality, key indicators for software testing respectively its specifications are identified by Zeiss B. 2007 [4].

This framework embodies the separate categories for evaluating the test case. In comparison with the ISO 9126-1, Zeiss' framework delivers evaluation aspects which suit the different aspects of software testing appropriately. Reusability is a category, which was not covered in the ISO 9126-1, but has been added due to its great importance in software testing. Evaluation of the test case in stage III combines all adequate categories and subcategories of this model and contributes for the qualitative influence on the cost benefit analysis [3, 4] (Fig. 2).

Although Zeiss' framework incorporates the degree of test coverage, this specific criterion is revisited in stage IV due to its quantitative character. Test coverage needs to be defined in the test specifications and can be expressed as a percentage number. 100 % test coverage can only be achieved by considering every single application and functionality of the tested software. There is a strong interrelation between the degree of test coverage and the expenditure in preparation and execution of the test, which is assessed in stage I. In order to evaluate the

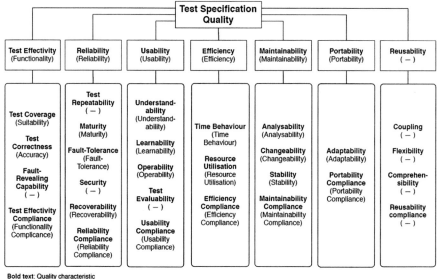

Fig. 2 Framework of evaluation software test specification

degree of test coverage, the influence on stage I has to be taken into account. Although the benefit of completely tested software cannot be neglected, the costs do not justify such a holistic approach [5].

The final stage considers the aspect of utilizing the test tool in different test cases. After the testing is done, the preparation of the test program should not become worthless for additional test. Therefore this stage evaluates the test tools capability of being utilized individually for differing test cases. As a qualitative property, the adjustability is measured to provide for possible benefits of the test tool. Test design and test programs need to be defined in a way, that a repeated usage in a variety of test scenarios can be realized. If the test tool does not allow for this feature, the evaluation of the tool must not be positive, not least because testing is automated in order to raise efficiency and productivity [6].

3 Use Case: Automated Testing of Comarch ERP Enterprise 5

3.1 Specification of the Test Procedure

The test procedure covers several steps of the traditional value-chain in logistics and includes the core modules of an Enterprise-Resource-System. As the basis for evaluation, the creation of the master data (product, supplier and customer), the procurement process and the sales process were used. This test procedure has been chosen due to its practical relevance as well as facile reproducibility and clear quantification [7]. Furthermore processes described above allow the manufacturer already in the early development stages to perform the analysis in order to keep adaptation and error correction costs as low as possible [5, 8].

3.2 Test Case

For the test case Comarch ERP Enterprise 5 and a suitable tool for GUI-testing were applied. The test automation tool provides record and playback features that allow to interactively record user actions and replay them back any number of times. Therefore the results can be compared to the expected actions and help to identify potential for improvements and troubleshooting. For better handling the business process were split in several subprograms (e.g. the procurement process is mapped by using 83 subprograms). This enables the test-person to build combinations of different subprograms, reuse previously used components and moreover a better traceability and transparency. To Validate the manual actions generally the mean of 10 test-runs was taken in account.

4 Results

As an answer towards the question whether a test automation tool provides a cost reduction or not, it can be stated that at the positive effects (higher coverage, less working hours, etc. [8]) had occurred. According the results of the test case, the costs for the development of test automation tool—compared to manual methods—are more than acceptable. Details will be explained in the following paragraph.

4.1 Stage 1: Test Preparation and Execution

The preparation of the test scenario took a total of 85 min to complete. This includes 80 min for creation of subprograms and 5 min to finalize the test-suite (contains the subprograms). The range of the subprograms covers the previously described basis for evaluation.

A single sequence of the test suite required 32.60 min (mean of 10 test runs). For comparison, the manual execution by a person takes 21.23 min. Depending on the assumption that a automated execution doesn't need any supervision, we can calculate the reduction of loan costs using the following formula.

$$reduction = (n * t_{manual\ execution}) - t_{preparation} \qquad (1)$$

e.g. (test case)

$$reduction_{test\ case} = (10 * 21.23\text{min}) - 85\text{min} = 127.3\text{min} \qquad (2)$$

By transformation of the formula the number of repetitions where a reduction of loan costs is existent can be calculated. Due to the following calculation a reduction of the loan cost can be reached after the fourth repetition of the test automation tool.

$$number\ of\ repetitions = \frac{t_{development}}{t_{manual\ execution}} \qquad (3)$$

e.g. (test case)

$$number\ of\ repetitions = \frac{85\text{min}}{21.23\text{min}} = 4.0 \qquad (4)$$

In conclusion the time consumption needed for test preparation and execution is on a lower level while using the test automation tool. Based on the scale effect of repetitions and subsequently re-using of the existing subprograms (modular structure of the test suite) it is possible to realize a significant cost reduction with much less effort.

4.2 Stage 2: Comparison to Manual Execution

Performing the process steps manually requires less time that is needed for the automatic execution with the test suite. In sum, however, much more loan costs incurred, cause e.g. no time for monitoring is taken into account by using the test automation tool. Thus, despite a longer execution time, has an positive effect on saving cost, especially with complex test scenarios. To consider is that the playback speed is slower than user's actions. Therefore, the test suite blocks the ERP program for longer than the manual execution would require. Increasing the playback speed of the test program and an execution outside normal working hours might be potential improvements.

4.3 Stage 3: Evaluation of Achieved Software Quality

According to the ISO 9126-1 [3], software quality can also be defined by measuring the amount of errors detected during the test. For the test case study an ERP system within an advanced life cycle stage was used. Therefore after 10 runs, no unexpected behavior or errors of the system were detected. In summary the the impact of this step on the assessment of the case study is neutral because no applicable information was retrieved.

4.4 Stage 4: Degree of Test Coverage

Generally we intended to use the key business processes (procurement, production, and fulfillment [9]) for the test scenario. Due to the high complexity and individual structure of the production and financial processes we skipped this business process. Thus in the test scenario an adequate level of test coverage has been achieved. The goods cycle of e.g. a trading company could be covered by test automation tool. Here, the degree of coverage, in addition to other indicators, is representative of the test scenario's value and contributes positively to the evaluation of the test suite.

4.5 Stage 5: Tool Adjustability

Similar to the degree of test coverage, the benefits of automated testing are additionally indicated by its adjustability. It could be shown that a modular structure of test programs reduces the development time and later the adaptability significantly. The reason for this is the reusability of previously developed individual components. Thus a high degree of adjustability was achieved. The test tool applied in the test scenario satisfied this criterion very well and ensures the usage in any thinkable scenario.

5 Future Work and Limitations

As future work we plan to investigate how to rate the weighting of the parameters. A factor analysis and a qualitative analysis (expert interviews) should help us, to be able to rate and weight the five parameters: (Table 1).

This table shows an example in weighing the different stages of our model. Regarding the fact, that expenses for preparation and execution significantly gain importance by comparing them to the arising costs of manual ways, stage I let alone is weighed with 10 % and stage II with 30 %. Achieved software quality weighs 20 % due to its non neglectable influence on the benefits of automated

Table 1 Proportional rating table

Stage of model	Description	Weighted proportion (%)
I	Preparation and execution	10
II	Comparison to manual testing	30
III	Achieved software quality	20
IV	Degree of test coverage	15
V	Adjustability to different test cases	25

software testing. Assessing the degree of test coverage with 15 % is justified by its varying influence on costs as well on benefits. Of great importance for upcoming work with test tools is it's adjustability which also means reusability. Easy to adjust tools facilitate the future application and are a key factor for the evaluation of the cost benefit analysis. Establishing a standardized benchmarking and assessment system harmonizing with the test scenario above is one of the next major goals, which will also help to improve the value of our approach.

As limitation for our test case it should be noted that we focused on a specific ERP system and used selected business processes. As future work and to eliminate the limitations above, we seek to extend the width of our sample processes as well as to shift towards other ERP systems if there will be a test automation tool available. Establishing a standardized benchmarking and assessment system which harmonized with test scenario above is one of the next major goals, which will also help to improve the value of our approach.

6 Conclusion

Automated testing of ERP-systems is due to the complexity of these systems a compound task to do. This study focused a black box testing approach in the form of a GUI-test. Reducing the complexity for the tester allows for more efficient testing, since the software code of the ERP-system does not need to be fully comprehended. Black box testing concentrates solely on the input and output of the tested program and includes the user in order to imitate his or her typical behavior for testing the programs interaction with its characteristic environment [10]. Evaluating the test automation for ERP-Systems has the purpose of exposing the costs and benefits of this testing procedure. The five stage model in this study regards quantitative features, such as the measuring of working hours for preparation and execution, as well as qualitative features, like the usability of the test tool, and can be applied as a guideline for evaluation. In order to demonstrate the usage of the model, a test scenario has been specified, which includes very common user interactions with the ERP-system. The tested ERP-system can be described as state of the art and provided a stable and suitable environment for the test case. Especially the comparison with manual methods of software testing showed that test automation saves workload and raises test efficiency. By means of modular testing, the degree of test coverage can easily be adjusted and is therefore a big qualitative advantage of automated testing. Assessing the tools adjustability to different test cases is the last stage of the model and serves the purpose of evaluating the test tool itself. Due to the results of this study, as well as technological improvements assembled in state of the art test tools, automating software tests can clearly be recommended.

References

1. Carr, N.G.: It doesn't matter. Harv. Bus. Rev. **81**(5), 41–49 (2003)
2. Myers, G.J.: Methodisches Testen von Programmen. Oldenbourg, München (2001)
3. International Standard Organization (ISO/IEC): Informational technology—product quality—part 1: quality model. (iso/iec 9126-1) (2001)
4. Zeiss, B., Vega, D., Schieferdecker, I., Neukirchen, H., Grabowski, J.: Applying the ISO 9126 quality model to test specifications—exemplified for TTCN-3 test specifications. In: Proceedings of the Software Engineering, pp. 231–244 (2007)
5. Dustin, E., Rashka, J., Paul, J.: Software Automatisch Testen: Verfahren, Handhabung Und Leistung. Xpert. press : Security/Entwickler, Springer (2001)
6. Sebastian Wieczorek and Alin Stefanescu: Improving testing of enterprise systems by model-based testing on graphical user interfaces. In Proceedings of the 2010 17th IEEE International Conference and Workshops on the Engineering of Computer-Based Systems, ECBS '10, IEEE Computer Society, pp. 352–357, Washington, DC (2010)
7. Huang, C.-Y., Chang, J.-R., Chang, Y.-H.: Design and analysis of gui test-case prioritization using weight-based methods. J. Syst. Softw. **83**(4), 646–659 (2010)
8. Menzel, M.: Software-Testautomatisierung: Leitfaden für die effziente Einführung. AV Akademikerverlag (2006)
9. Magal, S.R., Word, J.: Essentials of Business Processes and Information Systems. Wiley Publishing, Hoboken (2009)
10. Frühauf, K., Ludewig, J., Sandmayr, H.: Software-Prüfung - eine Anleitung zum Test und zur Inspektion (5. Aufl.). vdf, (2004)

Utilizing Enterprise Resource Planning in Decision-Making Processes

Bahram Bahrami and Ernest Jordan

Abstract This paper reports on findings from a research project investigating Enterprise Resource Planning (ERP) and its utilization on decision-making processes in Australian organizations. The focus of the study is to reveal if and how the vast amount of data, which is generated by ERP systems, could improve decision-making processes on strategic and tactical levels. The findings are based on data consists of information collected in two phases by semi-structured interviews and survey. Findings from two phases of data collection is used to build a System Dynamics model as an exploratory vehicle to verify findings and formulate practical scenarios to help managers utilizing enterprise systems for their more strategic benefits such as decision-making.

1 Introduction

1.1 ERP Definition and Evolution

In recent decades, the term ERP has been used by both practitioners and academics in divergent applications and as a result it has acquired number of different meanings and also allowed for confusion regarding the meaning of the term. In fact, the term ERP itself could have contributed to the confusion, as 'Resource Planning' is not the main purpose of acquiring ERP systems.

ERP is a set of integrated, configurable information systems applications software that can be bought 'off-the-shelf' and tailored by an organization in order

---

B. Bahrami (✉) · E. Jordan
Macquarie University, Sydney, Australia
e-mail: m.j.bahrami@gmail.com

E. Jordan
e-mail: gpt@mq.edu.au

to integrate and share its information and related business processes within and across functional areas [1]. Such off-the-shelf packages (as opposed to applications built in-house) help organizations manage important aspects of their business, such as accounting, finance, manufacturing, distribution, human resources and sales [2, 3]. ERP eventually enables organizations to achieve inter-organizational supply chains [4, 5] by evolving into Extended ERP systems that can exploit technological advances in the areas of internet and electronic commerce, and support inter-organizational processes on an extended network of supplier and distributors [6].

The fundamental capabilities of ERP systems come from transaction processing and structured record keeping of those transactions, and not 'planning' as the name Enterprise Resource Planning suggests. Although planning and decision support applications can be optional add-ons, they are not the core capabilities of the system [7]. However such features and capabilities are the most valuable benefits that ERP adopters expect from their investment on ERP to gain competitive advantages. This research is an investigation to see if and how these benefits are materialized in practice among Australian organizations in the first tier of ERP market.

2 Research Methodology

This research is a preliminary step to examine the extent to which adapters of ERP systems benefit from potential decision support characteristics of such systems. The aim is to investigate the problem from different perspectives such as user expectations, exhibition of decision support features in ERP systems and actual realization of such benefits in practice within Australian organizations.

Decision support characteristics of ERP systems and its utilization in practice has not been the focus of notable number of research both in industry and academia spheres. The lack of knowledge and theory on the underlying research question is the main reason to design this research as a two-stage study based on qualitative and quantitative methods. In the first stage of this research qualitative methods are utilised to investigate the current status of Australian organisations and industry practitioners in regards to utilizing ERP systems towards decision making process. In this stage, semi-structured exploratory interviews with purposefully selected participants were conducted in order to cater for the lack of underlying knowledge and theories and comprehensive studies on the main subject of the research in the Australian context.

In the second stage, gained insight from the qualitative stage is utilized to provide necessary foundation to make effective use of qualitative methods to investigate the subject in more depth and details.

Finally, based on findings from the qualitative and quantitative data analysis a theoretical System Dynamics (SD) model was built. The use of SD approach provides key insights into the interactive behavior of system elements over times that are normally not obvious through non- systematic approaches. The theoretical model in addition to establishing a holistic view of studied incorporating factors and parameters, provides a vehicle to conduct sensitivity analysis, policy experimentation and simulation in order to offer insight and to formulate practical guidance into better utilization of ERP data towards decision-making.

This paper briefly presents findings from the first and second stages of the research, however it primarily focuses on explaining the underlying login behind the SD model and on findings from the modeling exercise.

3 Modeling

3.1 System Thinking and Modeling Methodology

The systems thinking and modeling methodology used in this study was based on the SD methodology initially developed by Jay Forrester and others at the Massachusetts Institute of Technology in the late 1950s. Such an approach aims to understand the behavior of complex systems over time and deals with internal feedback loops and time delays that affect the behavior of the entire system [8].

It should be noted that this model is exploratory, in that it examines a theoretical model developed from observations and findings from exploratory interviews and survey results. The model, therefore, should not be considered comprehensive and final.

4 System Structure and Parametric Model

This section describes the conceptual model constructs and their relationships. Causal loops for each construct are analyzed and Causal Loop Diagrams (CLDs) are then used to construct Stock and Flow diagrams, which are the building blocks of the parametric model. In CLDs the emphasis is more on internal relationship between variables and less on exogenous variables. However, any relevant exogenous variables are displayed in the diagrams.

4.1 Implementation Issues

Implementation issues—including time and cost overrun and integration—are at the heart of this model. These issues, problems and obstacles have been the subject of numerous surveys, case studies and reports in both academia and industry [9–14]. These studies focused mainly on critical success factors impacting the successful implementation of ERP, and they often failed to investigate existing interactions between parameters across the whole system. In the conceptual model developed for this research, implementation issues were analyzed as high-level parameters interacting with the rest of the system over time. Figure 1 shows the causal loop model for implementation issues based on the findings in previous phases of this research.

Two reinforcing feedback loops in this model represent growing and declining actions. The first reinforcing loop shows that management and executives' involvement and support results in fewer implementation issues, which could improve management support and commitment to the project. Management and executives' involvement and support could decrease implementation issues and successful implementation, and fewer operational issues is a contributing factor to improving management support and their active involvement. This loop has been identified as a major critical success factor for systems implementation success in general and to ERP implementation specifically [15, 16].

The second reinforcing loop shows that implementation issues such as cost and resources and integration could have a direct impact on the cost of ownership, which in turn contributes to more issues arising in implementation. This loop is supported by both the findings of this research and the literature.

4.2 Cost of Ownership

Cost of ownership of a system consists of implementation, running and upgrade/maintenance costs. This cost is significantly influenced by the success of the project's implementation. Any technical or non-technical implementation issues

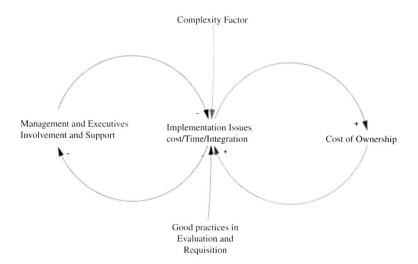

Fig. 1 Causal loop: implementation issues

usually lead to greater cost, and greater cost and a tight budget can increase the difficulty of implementation. This creates a reinforcing loop, which is depicted in Fig. 2. The findings from survey data analysis indicated significant correlation between these parameters.

Cost of ownership is influenced by a balancing loop, which includes maintenance and upgrade. Maintenance and upgrade activities cause increased cost, which increases the problems with implementation. However, organizations facing difficulties with implementation, such as technical, process and integration issues, tend to decrease their upgrade and maintenance activities, thereby causing a balancing loop.

4.3 Maintenance

Maintenance, changes and upgrades activities cause the cost of ownership to increase, which in turn increases the project's implementation cost. At the same time, increased difficulties in implementation mean that maintenance, changes and upgrades become less frequent due to lack of resources. This is a balancing loop which works against the reinforcing loop between implementation issues and cost of ownership. These two causal loops are depicted in Fig. 3.

Maintenance, changes and upgrades are also strongly influenced by exogenous variables such as ongoing technological advancement and changes, and ERP vendors' and adopter's mergers and consolidations. These variables have been explained in more detail in previous chapters.

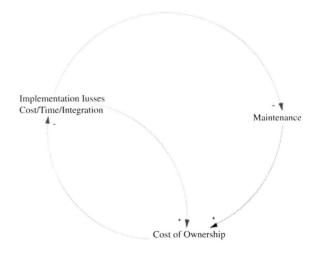

Fig. 2 Causal loop: cost of ownership

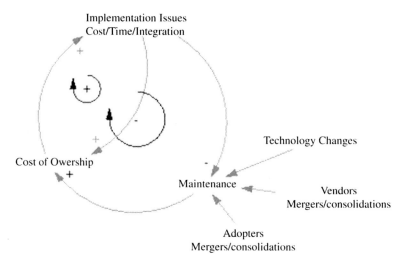

Fig. 3 Causal loop: maintenance and upgrade

4.4 Maturity

The process of adaptation between organizations and ERP system is referred to as maturity. This process is often long and sometimes never ending. Findings of this research showed that the process of maturity in ERP implementation is always under the negative impact of increasing cost of ownership, constant maintenance, and upgrade and implementation issues. At the same time, maturity could lead to executives and managers acquiring a more positive perception of ERP systems, which eventually leads to their involvement and support in the ERP implementation and adaptation process. The increase in managerial involvement could decrease implementation problems. These causal links are depicted in Fig. 4. In the causal diagram there is one reinforcing loop and one balancing loop, working against each other.

4.5 Perception

Executives' and managers' perception of an ERP system is influenced by how the system is being implemented and used, particularly in terms of the system's more strategic benefits. The factors impacting managers' and executives' perceptions, based on both my findings and the literature, are captured in the causal loops presented in Fig. 5.

Perception is impacted by four loops. The first reinforcing loop shows that increasing positive perception encourages managers to gain more training and ultimately knowledge, which in turn leads to leveraging the system beyond its transactional capabilities and more towards strategic benefits.

Fig. 4 Causal loop: maturity

Another reinforcing loop involves positive perception increasing management involvement and support in the adaptation process. This has a direct impact on reducing implementation issues, which in turn reduces the cost and leads to gaining maturity, which helps increase the positive perception. Two other reinforcing loops within the big loop indicate the direct impacts of cost and implementation issues on perception.

4.6 Management Knowledge and Training

One of the important factors influencing the adaptation process of enterprise systems, and utilizing them to their full potential, is the level of management knowledge and training about these systems. Our findings and the literature suggest this factor is influenced by two reinforcing loops, as shown in Fig. 6. On one side it helps to utilize the system beyond its transactional capabilities, thus providing strategic benefits that lead to change management perception in a positive way. This positive perception then leads to increased management knowledge and training by providing the required resources.

On the other side, the cost of ownership influences the budget allocated to training, and so the cost of ownership has a negative causal relationship with this variable.

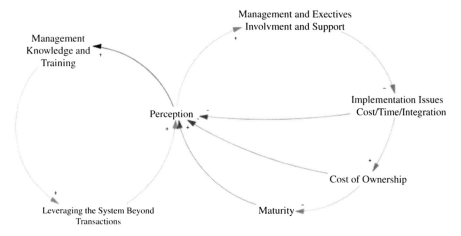

Fig. 5 Causal loop: perception

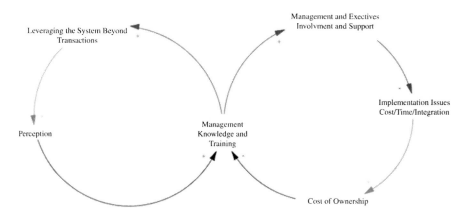

Fig. 6 Causal loop: management knowledge and training

4.7 Management and Executives' Involvement and Support

The literature investigating ERP from different aspects highlights that a key success factor is management and executives' involvement and support at the time of implementation and during the life of the system. Our findings also showed that greater management involvement and support reduce implementation difficulties and eventually create the reinforcing loop on the left-hand side of Fig. 7. Another reinforcing loop on the right-hand side of Fig. 7 shows the impact of this variable on good practices in evaluation and requisition. The positive impact leads to fewer implementation issues, which eventually increases management involvement and support.

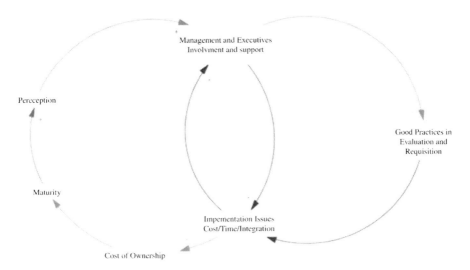

Fig. 7 Causal loop: management and executives' involvement and support

5 Dynamic Modeling

SD model was built based on building blocks explained in causal loop diagrams earlier. The main objective in building the model was to examine how the interaction between different system elements and their causal relationships creates a dynamic system. The model was also used to perform sensitivity analysis in order to design strategy and policies to facilitate the greater use of ERP systems for their strategic benefits, beyond the usual transactional and operational benefits.

The ability to experiment with various policies and situations provided both theoretical and practical benefits, and enhanced our insight into the system's behavior in terms of its structure, exogenous variables values and causal effects.

5.1 Model Structure

The basic structure of all reservoir variables was assumed to follow the rules and equations represented in Figs. 8 and 9 and the equations presented in the subsequent paragraph.

The value of Reservoir Variable at any given time (t) is equal to its value in a fraction of time earlier (t−dt) plus the change rate in dt. This was defined in the model with the following formulas:

Reservoir Variable (t) = Reservoir Variable (t − dt) + (Change Rate) * dt

Where Change Rate = Reservoir Variable * (Positive Change + Negative Change)

Reservoir Variable Initial Value = 100

Fig. 8 Basic reservoir structure

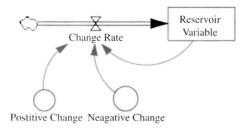

Imp Complexity Factor is an exogenous variable used for testing the sensitivity of the system towards the complexity of the system. For the first simulation we used a constant value for this variable.

Other variables in this model translated reservoir variables values into factors that were used to calculate other variables in the model. Each of these was a function of the reservoir variable that they translated. We used that same logic to construct all the translation variables in this model. We assumed that all reservoir variables changed between the values 70 and 130, with 100 the equilibrium and initial value. Translating this range to factors that impacted on other variables in the model was based on a curve that was almost neutral around 95–105, and then slowly increased or decreased depending on the value of reservoir variable (Fig. 10). In the model all factors were the same translation of reservoir variables.

5.2 Reference Mode

The first step of experimenting with the constructed model was to define the problem this model represents. This problem definition in SD terminology is called the reference mode. The reference mode may contain actual variables from collected data and abstract variables representing qualitative information. In the reference mode we assumed that exogenous variables "technology changes", "vendors' merger and consolidation" and "adopter merger and consolidation" followed an upward trend, represented in Fig. 11. This trend was not based on any historical quantitative data and purely represented past experience and expected trends. In the reference mode we could not make similar assumptions for other exogenous variables because all could have different values based on system adopters and environmental circumstances. Therefore we left the other six exogenous variables as 0, and leave their impacts to be discussed in the sensitivity analysis section.

Another two exogenous variables with initial inputs for the reference mode were "implementation cost factor" and "running cost factor". Implementation cost factor represented the initial cost of adopting the system, which reached a maximum in the first few years and gradually reduced to 0. This is represented in Fig. 12. This trend was not based on any historical quantitative data and purely represented past experience and expected trends.

Utilizing Enterprise Resource Planning

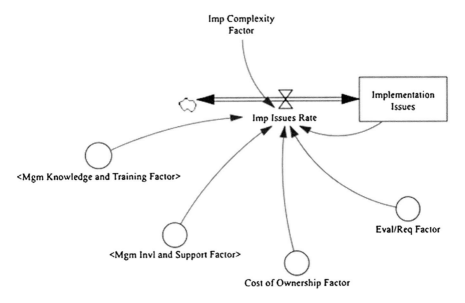

Fig. 9 Implementation issues structure

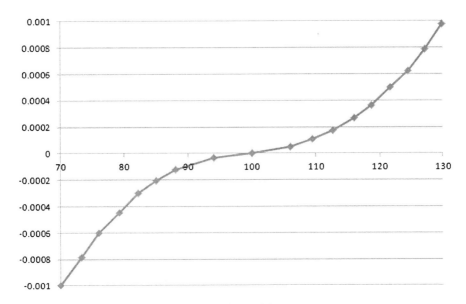

Fig. 10 Standard translation function across the model

Running cost factor represented the ongoing cost of adapting the system. This cost could go up the first few years and then stabilised for the rest of system's life (Fig. 13). Once again this trend was not based on any historical quantitative data, but represented past experience and expected trends.

Fig. 11 Exogenous variables (technology changes, merger and consolidation) over time

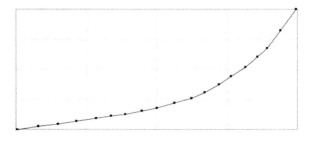

Fig. 12 Exogenous variables (implementation cost) over time

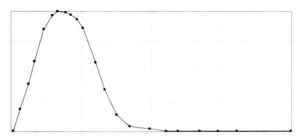

Fig. 13 Exogenous variables (running cost) over time

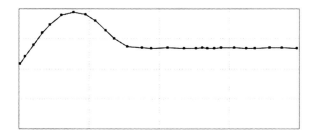

5.2.1 Simulating Reference Mode

We ran the model for 100 months in the reference mode, with exogenous variables values as described in this section. Most variables behaved as per expectations, verifying that the model structure had no major defect and could be used to analyze the impact of other variables as they were added individually into the simulations. Figure 14 shows some the system outputs for the reference mode.

Cost of evaluation, acquisition and implementation initially increased rapidly in the first few years and then dropped to a level of ongoing cost. This started to increase from period 50 again as more system change, maintenance and upgrade was required due to the age of the system.

Increasing cost of maintenance and upgrade level variable was a result of an increase in three exogenous variables: "technology changes", "vendors' merger and consolidation" and "adopter merger and consolidation". The impact of increasing cost of maintenance, upgrade and change, along with the cost of ownership initially caused implementation issues to increase exponentially, which

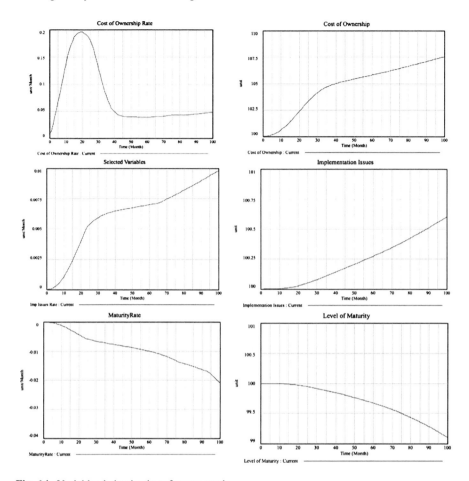

Fig. 14 Variables behavior in reference mode

in turn had a negative impacts on maturity. This in turn caused a decline management perception, management support, management knowledge and training, and eventually led to less chance of leveraging the system beyond its transactional capabilities (Fig. 14).

5.3 Scenarios

The reference mode presented in the previous section provided a realistic result based on the findings in the early part of the research. Using the SD model we tried to run different scenarios in which we changed this situation based on different values/trends given to variables. We considered the reference mode as a non-ideal situation, although it more or less represented what we had found in the qualitative and quantitative data analysis.

We conducted two simulated scenarios, which we called "ideal" and "promising". The ideal scenario presented a situation where all variables were moving in the right direction, system implementation was done with reasonable cost and effort, and it had matured by the time its strategic benefits, such as helping management to make better decisions, were realized. In the promising scenario we tried to improve the reference mode so that it more closely represented the current situation, with realistic and reasonable strategies. This scenario should be the one to be used for practical improvements in real-life implementation.

5.4 Sensitivity Analysis

We used sensitivity analysis tool in our SD modeling tool. By examining all variables, it was evident that implementation complexity factors and exhibition of decision support functionality and features were having major impa ct in changing the system output towards positive territory.

This result indicated once again the importance of successful implementation on all other variables in the process of adaptation between organization and enterprise systems. It was also clear that the tool and its functions and features played a significant role in achieving higher degrees of utilization of ERP systems towards decision making. At the same time, maintenance and upgrade policy and changes made to the model didn't seem to significantly impact on trends.

6 Contribution

This research was designed to investigate the topic from three different perspectives: expectations, exhibition and realization. Based on our findings stakeholders and users of enterprise systems perceive substantial importance in the potential of ERP to improve the decision-making process, at both strategic and operational levels, by providing necessary information and the tools and capabilities necessary to enhance the decision-making process (expectations). However, in practice, this positive perception doesn't materialize to an acceptable degree among first-tier ERP adopters in Australian organizations (realization). Also, from participants' perspectives, ERP systems provide few capabilities and features for decision support (exhibition). Further investigations into these three main categories revealed some of the factors that prevent the realization of these benefits. These factors and their potential impacts and interactions were discussed previous sections and are briefly summarized here.

Users and stakeholders expressed their high expectation of enterprise systems and the potential impact on the decision-making process and decision quality.

However, this expectation has not generally led to the inclusion of ERP decision-support features and capabilities among the main objectives for investment in ERP. In another words, decision-support features of ERP do not play an important role in the evaluation and requisition process.

In addition, participants do not perceive that ERP systems provide capabilities that help improve their decision-making process or that provide information to help managers and users make more informed decisions. In the context of this research, adopters' high expectations do not match the exhibition of capabilities and features in ERP systems. This is despite the fact that an increasing number of enterprise systems have been introducing business intelligence modules and decision-support capabilities in recent years. Future research could investigate the barriers and obstacles preventing organizations from using these tools in practice.

Although a lack of exhibition of decision-support features and capabilities was among the reasons found for not realizing such benefits in practice, further investigation into the problem suggested that the numerous obstacles and difficulties of the ERP adaptation process are among the main factors preventing utilization of ERP towards more strategic benefits. One of the greatest obstacles is probably achieving a reasonable level of integration across enterprise processes and data. In many cases this has led to decoupled or semi-integrated ERP implementation, a major compromise on one of the main objectives of investing in ERP. Decoupled modules, along with a department-centric mentality, contribute to the downgrade of valuable ERP data; rather than being utilized in organization-level strategic decision making, these data are being used for departmental day-to-day operations.

One of the exogenous factors having impacts on the research topic is the increasing numbers of ERP vendors and customers being merged, bought or consolidated. As a result, continuous changes in ERP systems, the need for integration between different ERP systems and the consolidation of data from different sources consume a good portion of allocated budgets to ERP programs, preventing organizations reaching the maturity stage in their adaptation process.

Other major factors affect management training and systems' user-friendliness. Although most participants recognized the impact of ERP systems for making better decisions, the majority of managers and decision makers had no official training in using EPR, interpreting data or recognizing the potential benefits to be gained by using BI modules. In addition, although many ERP vendors have invested in making their systems user friendly and have equipped them with intuitive report writers and BI modules, most legacy systems and older versions of enterprise systems used by first-tier ERP adapters lack any such features. Even for those systems with effective user-interface and BI modules already in place, these features are not easily accessible due to users' lack of training or awareness.

Building the SD model served to provide better understanding of the phenomenon in its entirety, using a systematic approach. In addition, the sensitivity analysis highlighted the strength of the model's sensitivity towards implementation. This means efforts in reducing complexities in both implementation and the ongoing adaption process will successfully reduce the cost of ownership in the long term, eventually leading to an increased rate of maturity and greater utilization of the system for decision making. Such a situation happens only with favorable conditions in exogenous variables, such as the exhibition of decision-making capabilities and features. A system that exhibits features and capabilities for decision making with manageable implementation issues could lead to the exponential growth of utilizing such systems towards their strategic benefits.

References

1. Davenport, T.: Mission Critical: Realising the Promise of Enterprise Systems. Harvard Business School Press, Cambridge (2010)
2. Kumar, K., Hillegersberg, J.: ERP experiences and evolution. Commun. ACM **43**, 23–26 (2000)
3. Kumar, V., Maheshwari, B., Kumar, U.: Enterprise resource planning systems adoption process: a survey of Canadian organisations. Int. J. Prod. Res. **40**, 509–523 (2002)
4. Boonstra, A.: Interpreting and ERP implementation project from a stakeholder perspective. Int. J. Project Manage. **24** 279–295 (2005)
5. Akkermans, H.A., Bogerd, P., Yücesan, E. and van Wassenhove, L. N.: The impact of ERP on supply chain management: exploratory findings from a European Delphi study. Eur. J. Oper. Res. **146** 284–301 (2003)
6. Gupta, M., Kohli, A.: Enterprise resource planning systems and its implications for operations function. Technovation. www.sciencedirect.com (2004)
7. Jacobs, F.R., Bendoly, E.: Enterprise resource planning: development and directions for operations management research. Eur. J. Oper. Res. **146**, 233–240 (2003)
8. Radzicki, M.J., Taylor, R.A.: Origin of system dynamics. Jay W. Forrester and the History of System Dynamics. http://www.systemdynamics.org Retrieved 23 Oct 2008
9. Bingi, P., Sharma, M., Godla, J.: Critical issues affecting an ERP implementation. Inf. Syst. Manage. **16**, 7–14 (1999) (Summer)
10. Brynjolfsson, E., Hitt, L.: Paradox lost? Firm-level evidence on the returns to information systems. Manage. Sci. **42**(4), 541–558 (1996)
11. Brynjolfsson, E., Hitt, L.: Beyond the productivity paradox. Commun. ACM **41**(8), 49–55 (1998)
12. Buckout, S., Frey, E., Nemec, J.: Making ERP succeed: Turning fear into promise. J. Strategy Bus. **15**, 60–72 (1999)
13. Davenport, T.H.: Putting the enterprise into the enterprise system. Harvard Bus. Rev **76**, 121–131 (1998) (July/August)
14. Davenport, T.: Mission critical: Realizing the promise of enterprise systems. Harvard Business School Press, Cambridge (2000)
15. Houdeshel, G., Watson, H.J.: The Management Information and Decision Support (MIDS) system at Lockheed Georgia. MIS Quarterly **11**(1), 128–140 (1987)
16. Watson, H.J., Annino, D.A., Wixom, B.H., Avery, K.L., Rutherford, M.: Current practices in data warehousing. Inf. Syst. Manag. **18**(1), 47–55 (2001)

Part VII
Critical Success Factors

Flexibility and Improved Resource Utilization Through Cloud Based ERP Systems: Critical Success Factors of SaaS Solutions in SME

Ariane Gerhardter and Wolfgang Ortner

Abstract The following paper investigates the changes of the critical success factors of ERP implementations caused by the technology "cloud computing" and by the product innovation in the area of system configuration as well as of the provided services. The methodology used is a differential analysis of the classical ERP system SAP R/3 and the on demand solution SAP Business ByDesign. The purpose of this paper is to examine whether the entrance barriers for small and medium-sized enterprises to the ERP market indeed decrease because of the business model "cloud" and the innovative configuration. As a result of these changes in technology critical success factors of ERP implementation in SME are deduced. Furthermore, specific criteria of a value benefit analysis are selected in order to support decision makers of small and medium-sized enterprises whether to implement a SaaS system.

1 Introduction

A trend caused by the progress and the propagation of internet technology as well as by the increasingly available internet bandwidth can lead to a revolution of the IT market [1]. Information systems are offered under the designations cloud computing, on demand solutions or Software as a Service (SaaS) [2]. Thereby, the customer obtains the standard software solution as a service via the internet [1]. The provider is responsible for operating and maintaining the system whereas the user obtains the needed service and pays a monthly usage fee [3]. This Trend

---

A. Gerhardter (✉) · W. Ortner
FH Joanneum University of Applied Sciences, Graz, Austria
e-mail: ariane.gcrhardtcr@gmx.at

W. Ortner
e-mail: wolfgang.ortner@fh-joanneum.at

"[...] has the potential to transform a large part of the IT industry, making software even more attractive as a service and shaping the way IT hardware is designed and purchased" [4].

The authors *Benlian, Hess* and *Buxmann* outline the following advantages for such business models [5]:

- A cost advantage caused by the lower total costs of ownership.
- A shorter implementation period enabled through the direct obtaining via the internet.
- Free personnel resources that can concentrate on core business.
- Higher flexibility because of the improved support of processes; consequently a faster response to changes on the market is possible.

Target group for on demand systems is mainly small and medium-sized enterprises (SMEs) since these have lower IT know-how and usually lower resources available compared to large businesses. On demand solutions are especially made for those SMEs that don't want to set up an own IT infrastructure [6]. The existing entrance barriers for SMEs on the ERP market should decrease due to the new web-based business model as well as to the simplified and improved configuration of the standard software [7].

1.1 Are SMEs Able to Overcome the Entrance Barriers?

Within this paper it is examined if the existing entrance barriers [8] to the ERP market indeed decrease for SMEs. In order to determine the critical success factors for a SaaS implementation two ERP systems from the same provider are compared. The classical ERP system is represented by SAP R/3 and the on demand solution by SAP Business ByDesign (ByD).

The following research questions are pursued:

- How do critical success factors of ERP implementation change through the web-based business model "cloud"?
- What impact has the innovation of the ERP product (internet technology and configuration model) on the critical success factors?

1.2 Methodology

Based on the initial situation and the outlined research questions, a literature analysis was carried out in order to identify the critical success factors as well as other influencing factors. Within the research specific criteria of a value benefit analysis were established. This value benefit analysis should guide through a structured decision making process for the system that should be implemented [9].

2 Essential Differences Between the Classical ERP System and the SaaS Solution

The major differences between the classical ERP system and the investigated SaaS solution are the customizability of the ERP solution and the concomitant effect on the implementation expenses and in further consequence on the total costs of ownership (TCO).

2.1 Customizability of the ERP Solution

The customizability of the new solution differs from the classical ERP customizability because of its *business orientation*. That means the user doesn't require any technical know-how in order to configure the system. The technical system configurations are made automatically by the system in the background. Regarding this business oriented customizability the following advantages are stated [10]:

- Simplification of the configuration process due to the central configuration for the entire system and the possibility to configure the system in each product lifecycle stage.
- High transparency through disclosure of the entire range of functions in the solution catalogue.
- Users establish their own solution, with a maximum of control of the implementation by the use of commercial language and without necessity of technical specialized knowledge.
- High degree of decision support by integrated services and current knowledge transfer.

The simplified configuration process leads to a decrease of the implementation time. It also enables a short and friction-free knowledge transfer about in-house expiries between customer and manufacturer.

Nevertheless, the high degree of the standardization of the functions should be considered controversially. On the one hand it is a special advantage of SaaS, because the business processes can be extended according to the demand and the solution can be flexibly adapted to the company's growth [11]. Moreover, a reduction of the expenses for updates or release changes can be realized. This count therefore no longer to a critical success factor during the operation as it does with a classical ERP system [8]. On the other hand, the adaptation possibilities of the solution to the company are limited, because the solution disposes only of predefined functions [1].

2.2 Costs

The TCO of a SaaS model can decrease, in comparison to that one of a classical ERP system, according to *Mathew* and *Nair* over a period of 3 years around up to 60 % [12]. In order to verify this statement it requires of a more exact calculation which must be carried out individually for a company in each case for classical ERP and SaaS solution [2].

The cost trend of a classical ERP solution differs basically from that of a SaaS solution (cf. Fig. 1).

By outsourcing the ERP system as well as by the business oriented implementation the investment and implementation costs of a SaaS solution clearly lie under that of the classical ERP solution [13]. Nevertheless, the monthly expenses for the service rent linearly rise with increasing number in users.

The current expenses of the classical ERP solution are proportional for the number of the users, however, the additional maintenance costs show decreasing marginal cost. The conclusion can be drawn that a SaaS solution is worthwhile only up to a certain number in users.

Table 1 represents those properties of SaaS solution that have a considerable impact on the costs of the software.

3 Critical Success Factors for the SaaS Implementation

Those factors which influence the success of an implementation project decisively are understood as critical success factors. The non-observance of these factors can lead to the failure of the implementation project. The success is measured in the dimensions quality, expenses and duration of the implementation [14]. At this point the most high powered critical success factors are shown. In order to determine the critical success factors for the SaaS implementation those of a classical ERP implementation are investigated by a literature analysis (cf. Table 2)

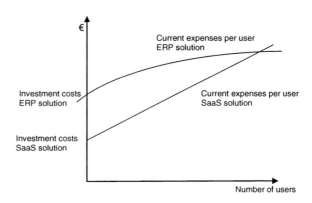

Fig. 1 Cost trend of classical ERP solution compared to on demand model

Table 1 Properties, reasons and impact on costs

Properties of SaaS solution	Reasons	Impact on costs
Fast availability	Enabled through the access via internet	Potential to reduce the implementation costs
Lower training expenditure	By intuitive user interface and product innovation in the area of integrated learning environment	Reduction of the training expenses
Simplified configuration	By predefined functions and processes within the Business Adaption Catalogue	Reduction of the implementation expenses and the duration, reduction of consultant's expenses
Predefined functions and processes	Potentials out of using best practice processes	Reduction of development and implementation costs
Outsourcing of the IT infrastructure	New technology "cloud"	Reduction of the IT personnel expenses, the hardware and software costs, and the current operation costs
Flexible extensibility of the solution	Modular structure of the solution's extent	Reduction of the monthly royalty based on the solution's extent
No additional personnel resources required	Outsourcing of operation and maintenance (updates and release changes) to the provider	Lower operation costs

and then reconceived according to the new influencing factors and the technological settings.[1] A detailed description of the critical success factors for the SaaS implementation is explained at *Gerhardter* [9].

Involvement and training of the users

The participation and early involvement of the end users in the implementation project are with a SaaS system implementation of the same meaning as with a classical ERP system. The purpose of involving and training the users is to avoid media disruptions and to ensure the usage of existing tools [8, 15–19] The non-observance of this critical success factor can lead to high training costs during the operation as well to an increase of the TCO. If the users get to know the system early enough, the greatest possible user benefit from the functionalities of the system can be drawn [11].

In a SaaS solution the training expenses can be considerably reduced by the intuitive usability. A stronger involvement is supported by the learning environment integrated in the system [20]. However, for SMEs this still means that they must invest time in the creation of an acceptance among the employees and also include time resources for training purposes.

---

[1] The designations of the criteria are defined consistently because each author has its individual designation.

Table 2 Literature analysis: critical success factors of a classical ERP implementation

Criteria	Author					
	v. Arb [8]	Blume [15]	Brand [16]	Umble/Haft/ Umble [17]	Esteves/ Pastor [18]	Siegenthaler/ Schmid [19]
Involvement and training of the users	✔	✔	✔	✔	✔	✔
Project management	✔	✔	✔	✔	✔	✔
Commitment of top management	✔	✔		✔	✔	✔
Clearly formulated project objectives	✔	✔	✔	✔	✔	
Method of the implementation approach	✔	✔	✔	✔	✔	
Technical requirements	✔		✔	✔	✔	✔
Risk of consultancy	✔	✔			✔	✔
Reorganization of business processes	✔	✔		✔	✔	
Time and resource management	✔	✔			✔	✔
Contract drafting	✔				✔	

Commitment of top management

For many projects the low interest in the project or the wrong project appraisal of the top management represents a critical success factor. Consequently, a lacking guidance of the project and a too low support of the project team within the project realization of the top managers can arise [8, 15, 17–19]. With a SaaS implementation in SMEs the importance of this success factor can change due to the enterprise's size. Thus the top management will more likely be actively involved in the project realization. However, should the top management not be involved in the implementation project, this critical success factor is of the same importance as by a classical ERP introduction.

Method of the implementation approach

The decision on the method of the implementation approach, between step by step and big bang, influences decisively the success of the introduction of a classical ERP system as well as of an on demand ERP system. With a gradual implementation the implementation expenses as well as the risks which are connected to all departments with the acquisition of a new solution decrease. [8, 15–19] However, an implementation of the entire solution can bring the following advantages for SMEs [21]:

- Requirements of all scopes of business are fulfilled by the implementation of the completely integrated solution.
- The demand to integrate other systems during the implementation is reduced.
- The system interruptions which appear by the phase wise introduction are decreased.

The decision for one of both methods is dependent on company-specific conditions.

Technical requirements

The technical requirements have changed significantly through the web-based business model. Thereby, the design of the system architecture fades from the spotlight, however, data migration, data quality and interfaces to other systems are still considered as critical success factors. Data migration is easier than before because of the innovative services in the system. However, this is still a critical part of each implementation project.

SMEs only recently worry about the security because of the outsourcing of internal data to third parties and the dependence on the provider in which they thereby proceed [1]. However, according to *Grobman* data are stored more secure in a data centers than on premise at some companies. Further risks are internet fail outs, long responding times, high server utilization and bottlenecks in the capacity of the internet connection. These risks can negatively impact the indirect expenses for downtime [2].

Risk of consultancy

The risk of being dependent on the consultant decreases through the innovative service infrastructure for SaaS systems. The model based development enables high transparency of the processes and further simplifies the adaptability. The authors *Zencke* and *Eichin* state that it is possible to set up the solution without any support of consultants [7]. The degree of the consultants' support is determined by SMEs through the choice of one implementation service model and is dependent on their competences to accomplish an implementation project [14].

Dependency on the provider and drafting of the contract

By the web-based business model a new risk evolves: the dependence on the provider. This dependence correlates with the outsourcing of data as well with the operation of the ERP system. As a consequence the following problems can occur [2]:

- Adaptations of the system are not carried out.
- Important legal or organizational updates are not performed on time or not at all.
- The provider becomes insolvent or does not exist any longer, data could get lost.

The last problem is also with a classical ERP system of certain relevance, however, by far not from the range as with a SaaS model. Against a too strong powerlessness or dependence on the provider SME can protect themselves by effective drafting of the contract. The contract should include responsibilities and approaches unambiguously for the tasks but also for borderline cases. Further the technical and organizational risks for a flawless operation of the system are covered by the provider with the contract [22].

Reorganization of business processes

An implementation requires to examine the existing business processes on efficiency and effectiveness and to carry out organizational restructuring measures. This is about the degree of adaptability of business processes. That means which business processes are adapted to the system and where is the system adapted to the processes. [8, 15, 17–19] Because SaaS solution is equipped with predefined business processes, necessary change measures of the organization to the system should be carried out. With the system choice should be decided, what extent the company is willing to adapt the processes to the integrated "Best Practice" processes and whether this adaptation implicates measures of process reorganization [2].

The confrontation of the critical success factors of classical ERP and SaaS implementation outlines how far critical success factors have changed due to the web-based business model and the product innovation. Table 3 summarizes the identified critical success factors of a SaaS implementation.

4 Specific Criteria for a Value Benefit Analysis to Determine the Implementation Effort

Based on the differences of classical and on demand ERP implementation specific criteria of a value benefit analysis are derived. This value benefit analysis should enable SME to assess the effort for each implementation and should support the decision-making process. For this only qualitative criteria that evolved from the underlying perceptions, are considered. A universal value benefit analysis cannot be established because the evaluation of criteria is dependent on company specific influences (e.g. financial situation, size, industry, requirements and objectives).

Table 4 represents an exemplary evaluation of the criteria acquired by an expert workshop. The assessment expresses an answer to the question: how important is this criterion in order to draw the best benefit out of the system and to reduce the implementation effort?

For the value benefit analysis the following steps have to be considered [23]:

1. The partial value benefits u_i of the single solutions (classical and on demand) are established and evaluated along an interval from 0 to 100. The lowest value is represented by 0 and the highest by 100. The subjective reason of this evaluation is outlined in the column *reasons*.
2. The weighting g_i for each criterion has to be done. The sum of that has to be 1.
3. The value benefit of each row is calculated by multiplying the partial value benefits with the responding weighting. The sum of this partial value benefits

Table 3 Critical success factors of a SaaS implementation

• Dependency on provider	• Method of the approach	• Project management
• Technical requirements	• Drafting of contract	• Risk of consultancy
• Reorganization of business processes	• Involvement and training of the users	• Clear formulated project objectives
• Time and resource planning	• Commitment of top management	

Flexibility and Improved Resource Utilization 179

Table 4 Exemplary evaluation of the value benefit analysis

Criterion	g_i	SAP R/3 u_i	Partial Benefit $g_i * u_i$	Reason for SAP R/3	SAP ByD u_i	Partial benefit $g_i * u_i$	Reason for SAP ByD
Implementation	0.14	36	5.04		68	9.52	
Strain on personnel resources (impact on personnel costs)	0.2	30	6	High personnel requirement and costs (internal and external), own IT department	70	14	No IT department, lower personnel requirements due to simplified implementation
Risk of dependency on consultants (impact on consultant costs)	0.15	30	4.5	Complex system, high technical know-how required; hence high dependency on consultants	80	12	Easy configuration, task list as implementation guideline, no technical know-how; hence lower risk of dependency
Reorganization measures of business processes—will of change	0.1	70	7	Reference processes can be adapted to company, reorganization measures moderate, due to moderate degree of standardization	40	4	Choice of processes out of predefined functions, high degree of standardization, high reorganizational measures
Training of users technical know-how (impact on training costs)	0.15	30	4.5	High technical know-how required, due to the system's complexity, elaborated customizing, high training effort	80	12	Little training effort through integrated learning area, Help Center, SAP ByD Community, improved usability
System availability—duration of implementation	0.1	20	2	Development, installation, hardware allocation, elaborated customizing	70	7	No installation, available on demand, no extra hardware required
Operation and maintenance	0.15	70	10.5		60	9	
Dependency on the provider	0.2	90	18	Little risk because system on premise and open source code	30	6	High risk due to outsource of business data, less possibilities for own software development
Effort for updates and release changes (impact on TCO)	0.1	50	5	High effort on resources for updates and releases because system on premise	90	9	Due to standardized functions, no effort on resources because of system outsourcing
Overall value benefit	1		15.54			18.52	

builds the entire value benefit for classical ERP system and SaaS solution. The system with the higher value benefit is considered to be the better decision.

The choice of the criteria is based on the following assumptions:

Strain on personnel resources: High personnel requirements increase the implementation effort and leads to a rise of direct and indirect expenses. A higher effort due to the establishment of an IT department occurs.

Risk of the dependency on consultants: An autonomous completion of the implementation project by the company is basically possible for each system. However, the SaaS solution is easier to implement across the simplified configuration and the increased usability.

Reorganizational measures of business processes—will of change: Elaborated organizational alteration measures are directly proportional to the implementing duration, which further increases the implementation effort.

Training of users—technical know-how: The higher the requirements for technical know-how the higher the effort for training.

System availability—implementation duration: The faster the system is available the faster can the company draw a benefit out of it.

Dependency on the provider: A high dependence on the provider can negatively impact the implementation through e.g. long response times on the productive system. This dependency also contains the risk that can occur across the outsourcing of business data e.g. data security.

Effort for updates and release changes: The higher the degree of standardization, the lower the effort for updates and release changes, which further leads to a decrease of the indirect costs.

Consequently, for this exemplary case, the SaaS solution is the better choice regarding implementation as well as the phase of operation and maintenance. However, to support a concrete investment decision for a company, individual weights for the identified criteria have to be determined to ensure a sustainable decision.

5 Conclusion

The new business model and the innovation of the ERP product have influenced the meaning of the critical success factors for a SaaS implementation. From experiences of previous implementation projects, and the deduced new service models as well as by the application of the web-based system architecture new chances arise for providers to establish in the market of SME. The examination about ERP trends in 2011, carried out by the company *i2s Consulting*, outlined that the public consciousness in Austria and Switzerland was sharpened increasingly for SaaS solutions by the market entry of SAP ByD. *I2 s consulting* predicts that by the increasing number of references and the further progress of application of functionalities in the SaaS mode, the spotlight on SaaS solutions will clearly

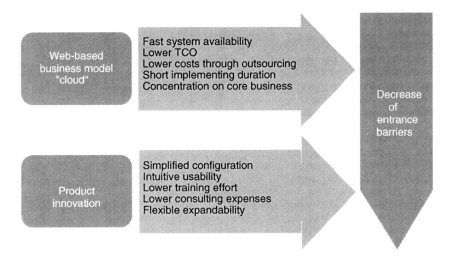

Fig. 2 Decrease of entrance barriers for SME

increase in the ERP sphere within the next 3 years. However, there is still a higher level of acceptance in companies from the service industry than in manufacturing companies. This trend can be presumably put down to the high degree of standardized processes in service industries, because in producing companies the core processes are very company-specific [24].

Also this examination proposes a decrease of the entrance barriers for SME in the ERP market enabled through the business model "cloud" and the innovation in the product area (see Fig. 2).

References

1. Buxmann, P., Hess, T.: Software as a service. In Wirtschaftsinformatik **50**(6), 500–503 (2008)
2. Grobman, J: ERP Systeme On Demand: Chancen, Risiken Anforderungen, Trends. Diplomica®, Hamburg (2008)
3. Saugatuck (2008). Mietsoftware: So profitieren kleinere und mittelständische Unternehmen. SAP AG
4. Armbrust, M., Fox, A., Griffith, R., Joseph, A., Katz, R., Konwinski, A., Lee, G., Patterson, D., Rabkin, A., Stoica, I., Zaharia, M.: A view of cloud computing. Commun. ACM **53**(4), 50 (2010)
5. Benlian, A., Hess, T., Buxmann, P.: Software as a Service: Anbieterstrategien, Kundenbedürfnisse und Wertschöpfungsstrukturen. Gabler, Wiesbaden (2010)
6. Weiss, C.: SAP für KMUs, Business byDesign in Österreich. In Monitor 4 (2011)
7. Zencke, P., Eichin, R.: SAP Business byDesign—Die neue Mittelstandlösung der SAP. In Wirtschaftsinformatik **50**(1), 47–51 (2008)
8. Von Arb, R.: Vorgehensweisen und Erfahrungen bei der Einführung von Enterprise Management Systemen dargestellt am Beispiel von SAP R/3. Bern (1997)

9. Gerhardter, A.: Implementierung von ERP Systemen für kleine und mittelständische Unternehmen im Wandel der Zeit. Bachelorarbeit an der FH Joanneum, Kapfenberg (2011)
10. Hufgard, A., Krüger, S.(2011). SAP Business byDesign: Geschäftsprozesse, Technologie und Implementierung anschaulich erklärt. Galileo Press
11. Walzenbach, M.: Standardisiert aber individuell, http://www.steeb.de/sapbusinessbydesign/wasistbusinessbydesign/kundenindividuell.html
12. Mathew, M., Nair, S.: Pricing SaaS models: perceptions of business service providers and clients. In J. Serv. Res. **10**(1), 51–68 (2010)
13. Türling, F.: Software as a Service: Outsourcing von ERP Prozessen, http://www.erpmanager.de/magazin/artikel_1705_saas_erp_outsourcing
14. SAP AG: Erfolgreich Starten mit SAP® Business byDesignTM: Individuelle Unterstützung für jedes Unternehmen, https://www.sme.sap.com/irj/sme/go/portal/prtroot/docs/library/uuid/c0c505b3f20b2c102fa3d35fa6681991?QuickLink=solution/services/serviceportfoliogolive
15. Blume, A.: Projektkompass SAP®: Arbeitsorientierte Planungshilfen für die erfolgreiche Einführung von SAP®-Software. Vieweg & Sohn, Braunschweig/Wiesbaden (1997)
16. Brand, H.: SAP R/3 Einführung mit ASAP: Technische Implementierung von SAP R/3 planen und realisieren. Addison Wesley Longman, Bonn (1999)
17. Umble, E., Haft, R., Umble, M.: Enterprise resource planning: implementation procedures and critical success factors. Eur. J. Oper. Res. **146**, 241–257 (2003)
18. Esteves, J., Pastor, J.: A Critical Success Factor's Relevance Model for SAP Implementation Project, in: Lau, Linda: Managing Business with SAP: Planning, Implementation and Evaluation, Idea Group, London, pp. 240–261 (2005)
19. Siegenthaler, M., Schmid, C.: ERP für KMU: Praxisleitfaden: Richtig evaluieren und einführen, BPX Edition Dalla Vecchia (2005)
20. SAP BYD Mitarbeiterschulung: Mitarbeiter einfacher und schneller schulen, https://www.sme.sap.com/irj/sme/solutions?rid=/webcontent/uuid/30f70cfe-8426-2c10-c9a5-812b550f29b2
21. Hesseler, M., Görtz, M.: Basiswissen ERP Systeme: Auswahl, Einführung & Einsatz betriebswirtschaftlicher Standardsoftware. W3L, Witten (2007)
22. Wiemann, F.: Wetteraussichten heiter bis wolkig—Cloud Computing Verträge und ihre rechtlichen Fallstricke, http://www.saas-forum.net/blog/gastbeitrag-wetteraussichten-heiter-bis-wolkig-cloud-computing-vertraege-und-ihre-rechtlichen-fallstricke/04082010
23. Vahs, D., Schäfer Kunz, J.: Einführung in die Betriebswirtschaftslehre. Schäffer Poeschel, Stuttgart (2007)
24. i2s Consulting: Business Software Trends: Die Sicht des i2s research, http://erpsurvey.de/blog/2011/02/07/business-software-trends-2011-die-sicht-des-i2s-research/ (2011)

Analysis of the Critical Success Factors for ERP Systems Implementation in U.S. Federal Offices

Asmamaw A. Mengistie, Dennis P. Heaton and Maxwell Rainforth

Abstract Enterprise Resource Planning (ERP) system implementation is a complex information technology project that integrates organization-wide operations. Prior surveys have reported perceptions about factors which are critical to ERP implementation success. But no prior research has empirically tested the relationship between ERP implementation factors (IFs) as independent variables and project success indicators as dependent variables. In the present study the research questions were: (1) is there a statistically significant relationship between an identified set of implementation factors for ERP projects and the empirically reported success indicators? (2) Do specific individual factors predict the level of success? Paper and online surveys were collected from 92 senior level ERP project participants—CIOs, project managers, executives and consultant/developers with experience on Federal ERP implementation projects. The study provided descriptive survey results for ERP implementation success and perceived effectiveness of implementation factors in the environment of U.S. Federal government ERP projects.

1 Introduction

An Enterprise Resource Planning (ERP) system. An ERP system is a complex enterprise information system (EIS) based on the business processes and application integration to automate the flow of material, information, financial resources

---

A. A. Mengistie (✉)
The MIL Corp, Maryland, USA
e-mail: asmamawa@gmail.com

D. P. Heaton · M. Rainforth
Maharishi University of Management, Fairfield, United States of America
e-mail: dhcaton21@gmail.com

M. Rainforth
e-mail: rainforth@mum.edu

and other operational activities within an organization using a common database without physical restriction [26]. Such software applications serve as single source of multiple benefits to the organization, for example data integrity, system control—efficiency; reduce costs; better and faster inventory management; real time operations; integrated information of all parties (other agencies, vendors, clients, employees, agents, distributors etc.); integrated operation locally and internationally; process improvement; paperless office environment and much more [23, 24, 39].

Federal offices implemented or are in the process of implementation one or more of the ERP systems across their agencies in order to streamline financial and administrative systems, allow individual agencies to share information in a standardized way, eliminate multiple systems and reduce duplication and reduce costs. Through the implementation of federal ERP systems, agencies share many business requirements, can manage a budget, recruit people, distribute payroll, generate purchase orders and so on using an ERP solutions which can provide a standard, uniform way of performing office functions, can reduce duplication, produce meaningful information and cut administrative costs [5]. Several government offices have implemented different ERP software application systems with a huge capital investment [39, 47]. According to Sommer [44] the number of U.S. Federal ERP implementations has risen rapidly in recent years such as the U.S. Army, U.S. Navy, NASA, Defense Logistics Agency (DLA), and several other Federal agencies. Public organizations started replacing existing systems and implementing ERP for their operational efficiency [9]. As Wagner and Antonucci [46] indicated, for example, the U.S. Navy expended $3 Billion for its ERP implementation [13]. Blick et al. [7] pointed out that the U.S. federal ERP market climbed from US$2.8 billion in 1998 to US$3.7 billion in 2003.

Even though successfully implemented ERP claims all the benefits mentioned above, there are also times where it may bring disastrous result for those that fail to manage the implementation process [21]. Studies showed that more than 40 % of large software implementations fail, 90 % of ERP implementations are either late or over budget and 67 % of enterprise application initiatives could be considered as unacceptable or unsuccessful [8, 38]. According to Wagner and Antonucci [47] compared to private organizations, federal government ERP implementations experience higher rate of failure. One of the reasons for this failure is that in most cases, the public-sector has adopted much of the generalized private-sector ERP implementation approach and tailored it to the public environment [47].

Understanding the ERP critical success factors (CSFs) in implementing Enterprise Resource Planning (ERP) systems has been a challenging process for both public and private organizations. Prior surveys about CSF's have asked respondents to evaluate the presence of or importance of particular factors that they think are critical to success. But with the exception a few case studies; the prior research has not combined measuring implementation factors (IFs) and measuring project success. This lack of empirical analysis of the relation of success factors to success outcomes is the primary problem which the current study addresses. Another gap seen from the review of the literature is that although, most of the ERP implementation factors (IFs) in the private sector are applicable to success in the public sector; still there are major differences between the two sectors [45]. According to Wagner and Antonucci's [48] case study on the State of Pennsylvania, the integration process of governmental agencies and their systems is quite different from the private sector and requires different approach. In this regard, it is crucial to identify and level the implementation factors of ERP in the public sector in advance for a successful outcome [38].

2 Purpose of the Study

The purpose of this study is to empirically test the relationship between perceived effectiveness of managing IFs (independent variables) in ERP projects and project success results (dependent variables). The present study conducts exploratory statistical tests of the relationships of independent variables to dependent variables—which have not been done before in prior studies.

Additionally, the study addresses the gap that few studies have empirically explored implementation factors of ERP projects in the U.S. Federal government sector. So, a secondary purpose of this study is to analyze the implementation factors that contributed to the success of ERP implementations in U.S. Federal offices, with the aim of communicating implementation guidelines government offices and other stakeholders.

This study is aimed to address the following research questions:

1. Is there a statistically significant relationship between an identified set of implementation factors and the empirically reported success?
2. Do specific individual factors predict the level of success?

3 Literature Review

3.1 Definition of Enterprise Resource Planning

An ERP system is a commercial software package (such as Oracle, SAP, JDE, PeopleSoft, BAAN) that enables the integration of business processes throughout an organization [28, 30]). An ERP system is a complex enterprise information system based on the business processes integration to automate the flow of material, information, and financial resources among all functions within an organization using a common database Kumar [24]. Wallace and Kremzar [48] stated that ERP is an enterprise-wide set of management tools that balances demand and supply, containing the ability to link customers and suppliers into a complete supply chain, employ proven business processes for decision-making. ERP also provides high degrees of cross-functional integration among sales, marketing, manufacturing, operations, logistics, purchasing, finance, new product development, and human resources. ERP is a standardized software application system which users can buy off-the-shelf rather than developing a complex software solutions from the beginning. ERP system is a comprehensive package of software solutions that seek to integrate the complete range of business's processes and functions in order to present a holistic view of the business from single information and IT architecture [17]. ERP packages can be implemented "as is" or customized according to an organization's business requirements.

3.2 Defining Success of ERP Project Implementation

Indicators of success of ERP implementation comprise the dependent variables in the present research. Most project management literature has indicated that the success of a project is indicated by the completion of a project within budget, time and at the expected quality or performance. For example, Duncan [14] indicated that a project can be taken as successful if it meets cost, schedule, and scope objectives. Similarly, Shenhar and Wideman [41] mentioned that in its old axiom a project can be called successful if it is on time, on budget and conformance to its requirements. With one additional criterion Pinto and Slevin [35] indicated that a project can be considered successful if it is on schedule, budget, achieved goals set in advance and accepted and used by the clients for whom the project is intended. According to Deloitte's survey [12] more than 75 % of respondents felt that if the project was delivered on time, on budget, and met business goals and objectives, it was successful.

As discussed above the success of ERP implementation can be measured using different parameter. Wei [50] explicitly pointed out that the following are the most common successful implementation criteria referred in most of the literature.

1. Completion of a project as per the scheduled time frame
2. Completion of the project without exceeding its budget
3. Functionality of the ERP system including modules completion, functionality fitness and security
4. User friendliness of the system such as ease of learning and operation
5. System flexibility for upgrading, integration and customization

On the other hand Heydenrych and Cloete [20] emphasized business impacts rather than project completion criteria; they stated that the indicators for the successful integration of e-commerce and financial information systems in an ERP system are:

- Connected Corporation
- Reengineered Business Processes
- Optimized Processes
- Automated Processes

- Added Value to the Organization
- Added Value to the Customers
- Cut Overhead Costs
- Efficiently Utilized Middleware
- Integrated Services, etc.

Somers and Nelson [43] noted that there are no uniform lists of measurements for the successful ERP project implementation. The success of ERP systems is an obscure and highly subjective concept [35, 52].

3.3 Which Implementation Factors are Critical for Successful ERP Implementation?

In the present study, the independent variables are those implementation factors that other researchers hold to be vital for implementation success. These implementation factors are examined in relation to measures of successful project outcomes, such as being on time and within budget.

Table 1 lists previous studies whose objective was to identify which implementation factors are critical for project success. As can be seen the table, these previous studies have been based on case studies or surveys soliciting opinions of ERP practitioners and experts regarding which implementations factors are most important. No studies have empirically examined whether key ERP implementation factors actually predict project success. Few studies have empirically explored implementation factors in the U.S. federal offices.

An ERP implementation project is not simply running a software application out of a box as it requires a highly complex implementation process [35]. It has its own unique methodology of implementation and follow up. It requires time and other valuable resources before, during and post implementation phases. The complexity of ERP implementation is also depending on the type and size of the organization. The technique and approach of ERP implementation for small organization with few functional departments is different from a big and multinational company with various departments and operational units. The methodology applied for a private organization may be different from government/public organizations.

The prior literature has identified factors that believed to contribute to the success or failure of an ERP implementation in different type and size of organizations. Some of these have been said to be critical and others are optional for the success of the ERP project. CSFs can be understood as the few key contributing factors in the smooth phase by phase implementation of the project [6, 43, 51]. According to Esteves and Pastor [16], in order to achieve success in software project implementations, it is important to define and analyze the most critical factors. Researchers have identified list of critical success factors for ERP implementation and categorized as below [15, 42].

Table 1 Summary of research studies on ERP implementation

Researcher(s), Year	Method of research	Findings
Estevez and Pastor [15]	Qualitative research using grounded theory	Developed a unified model of the CSFs in ERP implementaions and mapped these factors in a matrix with four perpectives as organizational, technological, stratrgic and tatical
Bhatti [6]	Field survey of 53 respondents	Used 65 item instruments that measures seven dimensions of ERP implementation. ERP implementation model developed
Light and Papazafeiropoulou [27]	Case study on 8 companies	Concluded that in adition to the standard project management CSFs other factors specific to ERP implementation include legacy systems, ERP strategy, business process change, and software configuration
Somers and Nelson [43]	Survey of 86 respondents from Fortune 500 companies and other firms that implemented ERP	Identified the CSFs which are the most crucial in ERP implementations and determined which factors are significant at different phases of the project
Chang et al. [9]	Survey of 61 managers and users that implemented SAP Financials	ERP knowledge management is the most problematic factor, followed closely by system development concerns and operational deficiencies
Pabedinskaitė [35]	Qualitative (Survey on ERP Experts in Lithuania)	Identified 16 main factors determining the success of implemention of ERP
Motwani et al. [32]	Comparative case study on 4 firms	Concluded that careful change management, network relationships, and cultural readiness have a positive impact on ERP implementations
Plant and Wilcocks [36]	Case study (longitudinal) on two firms ERP implementations	Emphasis upon the determination of clear goals and objectives at the project outset; and the utilization of interactional vendors of added-value in terms of new business practice knowledge and enhanced project team capability

(continued)

Table 1 (continued)

Researcher(s), Year	Method of research	Findings
Nah and Delao [33]	Case study on two firms ERP implementation	Seven categories of critical success factors were identified and compared the importance of these critical success factors across the phases of ERP implementation and upgrade using four-phase model
Shanks et al. [40]	Case study on two firms—from China and Australia	This study has explored the critical success factors for different phases of ERP systems and finds out that some factors may be important independent of national culture, and some other factors may be culturally dependent
Al-Fawaz et al. [2]	Literature review	The study identifies the most cited success factors in the literature and illustrated their significant importance in ERP implementation

1. Strategic or factors at the planning phase factors
2. Tactical or implementation phase factors and
3. Operational factors

Project managers follow different approaches or models in ERP implementations. Esteves and Pastor's [16] grounded theory method study resulted in an initial unified model of the critical success factors in ERP implementations. In their research, they mapped the CSFs into a four matrix consisting of organizational, technological, strategic and tactical. The *organizational* dimension of this model focuses on the organizational, cultural and business process related factors. The *technological* part defines the required inputs of ERP implementation such as hardware, software and infrastructure. In the *strategic* part defines requirements related to management support, team composition, project scope management and partners' related factors. Finally, in the *tactical* part factors related to business activities with short term objectives. Similarly, Holland et al. [22] suggested an ERP implementation Model organized into strategic-tactical framework. The *strategic* part specifies the need for a project mission, top management support and project schedule outlining individual actions steps for project implementation. In the *tactical* factors on the other hand includes client communication, personnel, business process change, client acceptance monitoring and feedback.

Motwani et al. [32] also did a research using literature review and case study methods and proposed an ERP implementation framework using phase approach.

These phases include pre-implementation or setting-up phase, implementation, and post-implementation or evaluation.

3.4 Federal ERP Overview

Though, there is a general assumption that ERP implementation can bring improvement in the entire organization, successful implementation is a challenging process and different from organization to organization [32]. Factors which contribute to the success of ERP implementation for a private business might not help for federal offices [39]. The model or methodology that vendors or contracting companies used for private business organizations might not be applicable for federal offices.

Citizens, public administrators and agencies expect better service from federal offices [39]. In response to this expectation as well as to increase their employees' satisfaction, reduce costs and improve their performance most U.S. federal offices implemented one or the other ERP applications [7, 39]. As a result, some are successfully implemented and others either failed or still struggling. For example the Federal Bureau of investigation (FBI) and Internal Revenue Service (IRS) implementation projects failed while U.S. General Accounts Office incurred more than $200 million additional budget for its project implementation [10].

Federal ERP projects are different in their environmental, organizational, and individual levels. According to Heintze and Bretschneider [19], at the environmental level, public agencies have a tendency to be more strongly influenced by the political than by the economic environment. This influence imposes a short-term vision, strong measures of accountability, and tasks performed under the watchful eye of the public. At the organizational level, public agencies show more rigid hierarchies and structures, and more paperwork and more red tape. Similarly, at the individual level the motive, incentives and job satisfaction is different compared to individuals in the private sector. Due to this differences, implementing ERP system in the public organizations requires convincing stakeholders about the values of ERP and ready to answer questions such as: Why now? How much will it cost? What will we gain if we do it? What are the risks if we don't do it? and so on [34]. Though, there are differences mentioned above, the basic functionalities of private sector are still applicable in the public sector [46].

On the other hand, due to increase in the public ERP market, the largest ERP vendors started responding by providing more complete organizational systems with public organization's specific requirements and functionalities [11].

Raymond et al. [39.] summarized the motives of ERP implementation in the government environment into four categories.

1. Technological motivations—infrastructure improvement,
2. Operational motivations—business process improvement,

3. Performance motivations—outcome improvement, and
4. Strategic motivations—change in the design and delivery of service.

3.5 Problems of ERP Implementations in the Federal Environment

ERP system implementation is different from the traditional type of information system implementation as the scale, complexity, organizational impact, and the costs are different. For many organizations, the implementation of ERP systems can be a monumental disaster unless the process is handled carefully in advance of its occurrence [18].

The organizational structures of several federal agencies are more complex, consisting of many departments and divisions, each having their own manager, business rules, and processes [46]. This complex nature of federal offices is not only because of internal but also they are reviewed and audited by other federal agencies [28].

In addition to the structural complexity, federal offices are headed by political appointees who are changed frequently so as the project they were managing. These changes in leadership and project objectives will create challenges for maintaining a large-scale ERP implementation focus and top management commitment [49]. Mark [29] also commented that politically appointed CIOs may lack the technical acumen to put forward a coherent strategic vision as a result the responsibility for establishing the strategic direction of IT may be transferred to middle management or private sector project consultants apparently non-influential as CIOs.

4 Survey Research Study

4.1 Survey Instrument

To investigate CSFs for ERP implementation in federal government projects in the U.S., a questionnaire survey was conducted. The study provided descriptive survey results for ERP implementation success and perceived effectiveness of implementation factors in the environment of U.S. Federal government ERP projects. Questions in the paper and online survey asked by project outcomes (dependent variables) and implementation factors (independent variables). From the literature, a list of 16 IFs was selected for this survey. These 16 were grouped into three composite factors: strategic, tactical and operational, as follows:

1. Strategic Factors
   - Project management.

- Top Management Support.
- Project champion.
- Clear goals and objectives.
- Business plan and Vision.

2. Tactical

- Team Composition.
- User involvement and motivation.
- Decision Making Processes.
- Business Process Reengineering (BPR).
- Inter-agency communication and cooperation.
- Change Management.
- Vendor Support.

3. Operational Factors

- User Training and Education.
- Dedicated Resources.
- Technological infrastructure.

4.2 Survey Participants

Targeted samples of 440 experts were selected from U.S. federal agencies that implemented federal ERP systems. Participants consisted of CIOs, project managers and project leads. In Addition to federal employees, consultants who have been working in both private and federal ERP implementations were approached. This sample was selected randomly from list of federal IT project participants regardless of age group, sex and departmental level.

Paper and online survey usable responses were received from 92 senior level ERP project participants—CIOs, project managers, executives and consultant/developers with experience on Federal ERP implementation projects.

4.3 Finding of the Study

The descriptive statistics such as the mean, frequency, percentage, standard deviation and variance were computed to describe the characteristic of the data collected. The data was also further interpreted using correlation and regression analysis techniques. The Pearson product-moment correlation analysis between each independent variables indicated that most of them are significantly correlated.

While calculating regression analysis the 16 IFs as a whole were considered as independent variables to predict the dependent variables. In addition to the 16 IFs the three composite implementation factors (strategic, tactical, and operational factors), which were calculated by averaging the appropriate IFs for the strategic, tactical, and operational phases were taken as independent factors. With regards to the dependent variables, the three success indicators of ERP implementation—time, budget and project objectives were used. Linear regression technique was used for percentage of budget and percentage of project objective achieved dependent variables. However, due to the dichotomous nature of response of the questionnaire logistic regression technique was used for time and over budget dependent variable. In summary:

1. The Omnibus test of model coefficients p value is 0.03 which indicated that the 16 IFs as a whole can be used to predict failure to complete an ERP implementation project within the initial time frame or schedule significantly. The test results whether the 16 IFs as a whole can be used to predict the extent to which an ERP implementation project would exceed its budget indicated as significant. The omnibus test of the regression model was significant ($F(16, 40) = 3.69, p < 0.0005$).
2. A linear regression on the composite factors as independent variables were significant as predictors ($p < 0.0005$). Individually strategic and tactical factors were significantly associated with lower percentages over budget ($p = 0.001$ and $p < 0.0005$, respectively).
3. Linear regression analysis was also used to determine whether the independent variables as a whole can be used to predict the extent to which an ERP project met its objectives successfully (dependent variable) and the result was not significant for both the 16 IFs and three of the composite factors. In other words, both independent variables were not good predictors to determine whether the project objective was achieved in an ERP implementation.
4. The regression coefficients indicated that among the 16 individual IFs the only factor that was a significant predictor was "Project team composition" with p value of 0.037.

5 Discussion of the Findings in Relation to Previous Research

An ERP implementation project is not simply running a software application out of a box but it requires a highly complex implementation process [35]. It requires time, expertise and other valuable resources throughout its implementation process. The complexity of ERP implementation is different from one organization to the other as well as from sector to sector. The technique and approach of ERP implementation used for small organization with few functional departments is different from a big and multinational company with various departments and operational units. The methodology applied for a private organization may be different from government/public organizations [45]. By the same token, the IFs for private sector ERP implementation may or may not apply for the public sector [46].

Therefore, analysis of the IFs for ERP implementation as well as the relationship between these factors shall be studied separately. In relation to this, much work has been done on the implementation factors for ERP implementation in the private sector. However, no prior research had empirically tested the relationship between implementation factors (IFs) as independent variables and project success indicators as dependent variables.

For example, Somers and Nelson [43] did a survey on 86 respondents from Fortune 500 companies and other firms that implemented ERP and identified 22 CSFs which are most crucial in ERP implementations and determined which factors are significant at different phases of the project. Nah and Delgado [33] conducted a case study on two firms ERP implementation and identified CSFs and compared their importance across the different phases of ERP implementation and upgrade. They concluded that the importance of these factors across different phases of ERP implementation and upgrade is very similar. Though, these research studies identified and analyzed the CSFs for ERP implementation, none of them determined statistically significant relationship between the CSFs and validated each of the individual factors to predict the level of success. However, this research has clearly identified the CSFs for federal ERP implementations.

Slevin and Pinto's [42] study included a model for success in project implementation which is defined as $S = F(x_1, x_2,\ldots x_n)\ n\ S\ f,\ldots\ldots, 1\ 2 =$ where S is project success and x_i the critical success factor i. In this model is too general as the size and complexity of projects are different. However, in this study, the success of federal ERP implementation can be represented by the following equation. IFsFERPI = f (x1, x2, x3... xn), where x1, x2, x3... x n are the different IFs for federal ERP implementations. Where, IFsERPI is the Implementation factors for Federal ERP Implementation and f stands for function of. What are the implementation factors (xi) affecting the success of an ERP implementation in U.S. federal offices? From this equation it is possible to understand that the success of federal ERP implementation is a function of different factors. The presence of these factors individually or as whole determines the success of the ERP project.

In addition to this, it was tried to evaluate the relationship between these independent factors. Statistical analysis was also conducted to validate if the individual success factors (independent variables) can predict the success of ERP project in relation to the three success criteria—time, budget and project objective.

This study has identified the top five factors for federal ERP implementations. These include top management support, communication both internal and external (interagency), effective training of end users, effective decision making process and dedicated resources. These implementation factors are particularly useful to practitioners to provide clear guidance and allocate resources wisely in the process of ERP project implementation [40]. Mohan [31] and Al-Mashari et al. [1] explanation strengthens this finding in that the implementation factors for ERP implementation include factors such as developing training strategies, developing a project management plan, obtaining senior management support and involvement throughout the project, and the development of a clear definition of your business processes and requirements.

5.1 Conclusion of the Study

Much has been written about the implementation factors for ERP implementation projects; but no study tested statistically whether there is significant relationship between the set of implementation factors and the empirically reported success indicators. Moreover, each of the individual factors was not validated to check if it can predict the level of ERP implementation success. This study tried to handle these points. From the output and the regression analysis of this study the following can be concluded:

1. Respondents rated the most important factors for ERP implementations in the federal environment. The five important factors were top management support, communication both internal and external (interagency), effective training of end users, effective decision making process and dedicated resources. These ratings can be compared findings of Bhatti [6], Pabedinskaitė [34], Somers and Nelson [43] which indicated that top management support, effective training of end users and dedicated resources are among the top IFs but not interagency communication and effective decision making process. From this it can be realized that some factors are more important in the federal environment ERP implementations, compared to the private sector.
2. The 16 IFs as a whole can be used to predict the failure of a project to complete within the initial time frame and completion of the project within budget. In addition to this the regression test indicated that the three composite independent variables can also predict completion of the project within budget significantly. Both the 16 IFs and composite factors together were not good predictors to determine whether the project objectives were achieved.
3. The result of this finding indicated that 83 % of federal ERP implementations were delayed, 78 % of them were over budget and none of the projects met their targeted objectives more than 90 %. An ERP implementation project can be considered successful if it is on time, on budget and meets its objective [14, 41]. From this it is possible to conclude that several federal organizations didn't achieve success in their ERP implementation projects.
4. So far, no research recommendation has been found that can be used as a guide to avoid the potential for failure completely. However, through conscious consideration of the IFs at each of the ERP implementation phases organizations can minimize the risk for failures.

References

1. Al-Masbari, M., Al-Mudlmigh, A., Zairi, M.: Enterprise Resource Planning: A Taxonomy of Critical Factors. Eur. J. Oper. Res. **146**(2), 352–365 (2003)
2. Al-Fawaz, K., Al-Salti, Z., Eldabi, T.: Critical Success Factors in ERP Implementation: A Review. European and Mediterranean Conference on Information Systems (2008), Al Bustan Rotana Hotel, Dubai. Retrieved February 2012 from http://bura.brunel.ac.uk/bitstream/2438/3336/1/Camera%20Ready%20Copy.pdf
3. AMR Research: The ERP Market Sizing Report, 2006–2011. http://www.gtm.sap.com/uk/solutions/business-suite/erp/pdf/AMR_ERP_Market_Sizing_2006-2011.pdf (2007). Accessed 25 May 2011
4. Archer, K.J., Lemeshw, S.: Goodness-of-fit test for a logistic regression model fitted using survey sample data. Stata J. **6**(1), 97–105. http://www.stata-journal.com/sjpdf.html?articlenum=st0099 (2006). Retrieved May 2012
5. Bearing Point.: Implementing ERP systems in the public sector: nine sure ways to fail or succeed. http://www.purdue.edu/onepurdue/about/documents/implementing_erp_public_000.pdf (2004). Accessed September 2011
6. Bhatti, T.R.: Critical success factors for the implementation of enterprise resource planning (erp): empirical validation. In: Proceedings of the Second International Conference on Innovation in Information Technology (IIT"05), pp. 1–10, Dubai, UAE. https://blog.associatie.kuleuven.be/kwintenjoly/files/2010/05/ERP_implementation_succes_factors.pdf (2005). Accessed November 2011
7. Blick, G., Gulledge, T., Sommer, R.: Defining business process requirements for large-scale public sector ERP implementations: a case study. In: Proceedings of the European Conference on Information Systems, Wirtschafts Universität, Wien. http://people.stfx.ca/x2011/x2011ucb/SAP/ERP%20configuration/configuration%20case/New%20Folder/20000156.pdf (2000). Accessed November 2011
8. Chang, S., Gable, G.: A comparative analysis of major ERP life cycle implementation, management and support issues in Queensland government, Queensland University of Technology, Information Systems Management Research Center, pp. 1152–1166 (2000)
9. Chang, S., Gable, G., Smythe, E., Timbrell, G.: A Delphi examination of public sector ERP implementation issues. In: Proceedings of the 21st International Conference on Information Systems, pp. 494–500. http://portal.acm.org/citation.cfm?id=359640.359793 (2000). Accessed 21 March 2011
10. Chung, Y.: An analysis of success and failure factors for ERP systems in engineering and construction firms. University of Maryland, Faculty of the Graduate School, pp. 3–6 (2007)
11. Deloitte Research: The keys to smart enterprise transformation for the public sector, Deloitte Consulting and Deloitte & Touche. http://www.deloitte.com/dtt/cda/don/content/keys%20to%20Smart%20ET.pdf (2002). Accessed 5 April 2011
12. Deloitte Research: ERP change management survey http://www.deloitte.com/assets/DcomUnitedStates/Local%20Assets/Documents/us_cnsltg_hc_shrmerp_040106.pdf (2005). Accessed 26 May 2011
13. Dinan, M.: Report: federal government IT spending to approach $100 billion per year by 2012. http://small-business-voip.tmcnet.com/topics/smb-voip/articles/47747-report-federal-government-it-spending-approach-100-billion.htm (2008). Accessed 21 May 2011
14. Duncan William, R: Defining and measuring project success, project management partners. http://www.pmpartners.com/resources/defmeas_success.html (2004). Accessed April 2012
15. Esteves, J., Pastor, J.: Towards the unification of critical factors for ERP implementations. In: 10th Annual Business Information Technology (BIT) 2000 Conference, Manchester (2000)
16. Esteves, J., Pastor, J.: A framework to analyze most critical work packages in ERP implementation projects. In: International Conference on Enterprise Information Systems, Spain (2002)

17. Gable, G.: Large package software: a neglected technology? J. Glob. Inf. Manag. 6(3), 3–4 (1998)
18. Grabski, S.V., Leech, S.A.: Risks and controls in the implementation of ERP systems. Int. J. Dig. Acc. Res. 1(1), 47–68 (2001)
19. Heintze, T., Bretschneider, S.: Information technology and restructuring in public organizations: does adoption of information technology affect organizational structures, communications, and decision making? J. Public Adm. Res. Theory 10(4), 801–830 (2000)
20. Heydenrych, G., Cloete, E.: ERP transition to e-commerce: training for a new methodology. In: Proceedings of the 2007 Computer Science and IT Education Conference, pp. 323–334 (2007)
21. Holland, C.P., Light, B.: A critical success factors model for ERP implementation. IEEE Software, (May/June), pp. 30–35 (1999)
22. Holland, C.P., Light, B., Gibson, N.: A critical success factors model for enterprise resource planning systems implementation. In: Proceedings of the 7th European Conference on Information Systems, Copenhagen, Denmark (1999)
23. Jarrar, Y.F., Al-Mudimigh, A., Zairi, M.: ERP implementations critical success factors – The role and impact of business process management. Proceedings of the 2000 IEEE International Conference on Management of Innovation and Technology ICMIT 2000 Management in the 21st Century, pp. 122–125 (2000)
24. Jiang, Y.: Critical success factors in ERP implementation in Finland. Swedish School of Economics and Business Administration, Finland, pp. 5–6 (2005)
25. Kumar, K., Hillegersberg, J.: ERP experiences and evolution. Commun. ACM 43(4), 23–26 (2000)
26. Kumar, V., Maheshwari, B., Kumar, U.: Enterprise resource planning systems adoption process: a survey of Canadian organizations. Int. J. Prod. Res. 40, 509–523 (2002)
27. Light, B., Papazafeiropoulou, A.: Reasons behind ERP package adoption: a diffusion of innovations perspective. In: Leino, T., Saarinen, T., Klein, S. (eds.) Proceedings of the Twelfth European Conference on Information Systems, pp. 1062–1074. Turku School of Economics and Business Administration, Turku, Finland (2004)
28. Management Information Systems in Public and Private Business: An Empirical Test. Management Information Systems, (1990), pp.536–545
29. Mark, K.W.: Information systems technologies: A public-private sector comparison. J. Comput. Inform. Syst. 46(3), 50–56 (2006)
30. Markus, M.L., Tanis, C.: The enterprise systems experience–from adoption to success. In: Zmud, R.W. (ed.) Framing the domains of IT research Glimpsing the future through the past, vol. 173, pp. 173–207. Pinnaflex Educational Resources, Cincinnati (2000)
31. Mohan, S.: Successful systems implementation. White Paper Deloitte and Touche, Public Sector. http:/www.deloitte.com/dtt/cda/doc/content/sys_imp_ps2.pdf (2003)
32. Motwani, J., Subramanian, R., Gopalakrishna, P.: Critical factors for successful ERP implementation: exploratory findings from four case studies. Comput. Ind. 56(6), 529–544. http://www.nuigalway.ie/bis/mlang/readings/ERP (2005). Accessed 18 Apr 2011. Systems/Motwani (2005) Critical factors for successful ERP implementation.pdf
33. Nah, F., Delgado, S.: Critical success factors for enterprise resource planning implementation and upgrade. J. Comput. Inf. Syst. (46), pp. 99–113 (2006)
34. Neely, T.: Leading through an ERP implementation. J. Gov. Financial Manag. 54(4), 38–41 (2005)
35. Pabedinskaitė, A.: Factors of successful implementation of ERP systems. Econ. Manag. 2010(15), 691–697 (2010)
36. Pinto, J.K., Slevin, D.P.: Balancing strategy and tactics in project implementation. Sloan Management Review, (Fall), pp. 33–44 (1987)
37. Pinto, J.K., Slevin, D.P.: Project success: definitions and measurement techniques. Proj. Manag. J. 19(1), 70–71 (1998)

38. Plant, R., Wilcocks, L.: Critical success factors in international ERP implementations: a case research approach. J. Comput. Inf. Syst. **47**(3). http://moya.bus.miami.edu/~rplant/papers/JCIS%202007.pdf (2007). Accessed 15 January 2011
39. Raymond, L., Uwizeyemungu, S., Bergeron, F.: ERP adoption for E-Government : an analysis of motivation. eGovernment Workshop'05 (eGOV05), September 13 2005, Brunel University, West London, UK. http://www.iseing.org/egov/eGOV05/Source%20Files/Papers/CameraReady-4-P.pdf (2005). Accessed 27 May 2011
40. Shanks, G., Parr, A., Hu, B., Corbitt, B.J., Thanasankit, T., Seddon, P.: Differences in critical success factors in ERP systems implementation in Australia and China: a cultural analysis. In: Hansen, H.R., Bichler, M., Mahrer, H., (eds.) Proceedings of the Eighth European Conference on Information Systems, Vienna (2000)
41. Shenhar, A.J., Wideman, R.M.: Improving PM: linking success criteria to project type. AEW Services, Vancouver, BC ©2001. http://www.maxwideman.com/papers/improvingpm/improvingpm.pdf (2001). Retrieved January 2012
42. Slevin, D.P., Pinto, J.K.: Balancing strategy and tactics in project implementation. Sloan Manag. Rev. (Fall), pp. 33–44 (1987)
43. Somers, T.M., Nelson, C.: The impact of critical success factors across the stages of enterprise resource planning implementations. In: Proceedings of the 34th Hawaii International Conference on System Sciences—2001 (2001)
44. Sommer, R.: Public sector ERP implementation: successfully engaging middle-management. Commun. IBIMA **2011** p. 2 (2011)
45. Thomas, G., Jajodia, S.: Commercial-off-the-shelf enterprise resource planning software implementations in the public sector. J. Govern. Financial Manag. http://www.lsiconsulting.com/pdf/COTS_ERP_in_PublSect_0504.pdf (2004). Retrieved 3 March 2011
46. Wagner, W., Antonucci, L.: An analysis of the imagine PA public sector ERP project. In: Proceedings of the 37th Hawaii International Conference on System Sciences—2004
47. Wagner, W., Antonucci, L.: The imagine PA project: the first large-scale, public sector ERP implementation. Inf. Syst. Manag. **26**, 275–284 (2009)
48. Wallace, T.F., Kremzar, M.H.: ERP: making it happen; the implementers guide to success with enterprise. Wiley, New York (2001)
49. Watson, E., Vaught, S., Gutierrez, D., Rinks, D.: ERP implementation in state government. Annals of IT case studies. Idea Group Inc, Hershey (2003)
50. Wei, C.C., Chien, C.F., Wang, M.J.: An AHP-based approach to ERP system selection. Int. J. Prod. Econ. **96**(1), 47–62 (2005)
51. Yingie, J.: Critical success factors in ERP implementation in Finland. Swedish School of Economics and Business Administration, Finland, pp. 5–6 (2005)
52. Zhang, L., Zhang, Z., Banerjee, P.: Critical Success Factors of Enterprise Resource Planning Systems Implementation Success in China, 36th Hawaii International Conference on System Sciences, IEEE (2002)

Part VIII
Business Process

Towards a Framework and Platform for Mobile, Distributed Workflow Enactment Services on a Possible Future of ERP Infrastructure

Dagmar Auer, Dirk Draheim, Verena Geist, Theodorich Kopetzky, Josef Küng and Christine Natschläger

Abstract In this paper we represent a workflow management system architecture that realizes a sweet spot between the robustness of a centralized master workflow management enactment service and the flexibility of distributed disconnected workflow management services. The architecture emerged in a concrete scenario with the requirement that traveling business agents can proceed working with their supporting enterprise application even if they are disconnected from the Internet and therefore disconnected from their enterprise IT infrastructure. So far, the solution deals with the data and workflow state facets of the problem and appropriate data and workflow state synchronization are key characteristics of the solution. On the visionary side, the realized architecture can be turned into a general framework for robust distributed workflow-based systems. Such architecture will generalize the central workflow enactment service to become a hub for distributing not only data and workflow state but also the mobile code that makes

---

D. Auer (✉) · J. Küng
University of Linz, Linz, Austria
e-mail: dagmar.auer@faw.uni-linz.ac.at

J. Küng
e-mail: jkueng@faw.uni-linz.ac.at

D. Draheim
University of Innsbruck, Innsbruck, Austria
e-mail: draheim@acm.org

V. Geist · T. Kopetzky · C. Natschläger
Software Competence Center Hagenberg, Hagenberg, Austria
e-mail: theodorich.kopetzky@scch.at

C. Natschläger
e-mail: christine.natschlaeger@scch.at

up the enterprise application. Then, the crucial element of such an architecture will be a sandbox virtual machine for the distributed slaves that interplay in data, workflow, and code synchronization.

1 Introduction

In this paper we represent a workflow management system architecture that realizes a sweet spot between the robustness of a centralized master workflow management enactment service and the flexibility of distributed disconnected workflow management services. The architecture emerged in a concrete scenario with one of the main requirements being that traveling business agents can proceed working with their supporting enterprise application even if they are disconnected from the Internet and therefore disconnected from their enterprise IT infrastructure. Additional requirements like space constraints on the client side or the necessity to attach certain domain specific hardware to the client and integrate data from said hardware into the workflow precluded the usage of standard solutions available at the time of implementation.

The currently realized implementation, the so-called PreVolution system, is able to deal with the data and workflow state facets of the problem. Appropriate data and workflow state synchronization mechanisms are key characteristics of the solution. This solution can be turned into a general framework for robust distributed workflow-based systems. The aimed for architecture generalizes the central workflow enactment service to become a hub for distributing not only data and workflow state but also the mobile code that makes up the enterprise application. Then, the crucial element of such an architecture will be a sandbox virtual machine for the distributed slaves that interplay in data, workflow, and code synchronization.

The main issue of the paper it to compare the proposed offline-enabling framework with other existing architectural solutions, i.e., the established mainstream ERP infrastructures based on sandbox mechanisms or web-based application and today's cloud computing. An objective of the paper is to bring into question the potential and future role of such ERP infrastructure.

We start in Sect. 2 with a description of the objectives and realization of our asymmetric, data, and workflow state synchronizing ERP solution, i.e., the PreVolution approach. In Sect. 3 we present and discuss our vision to generalize the PreVolution approach to become a full-fledged ERP infrastructure and, eventually, BPM (business process management) platform. We discuss further directions in Sect. 4. We mention important related work throughout the paper. We discuss related work in Sect. 5 and finish the paper with a conclusion in Sect. 6.

2 An Offline-Robust ERP System

In this section we present a concrete offline-robust ERP solution. The challenge was to realize an ERP system in way that is robust against disconnecting the client, i.e., a laptop, from the central IT infrastructure of the enterprise. It was the requirement that the user is able to work with the workflow-based application even in offline phases. Therefore, the solution is a mobile computing solution project [1]—mobility is not about using a wireless network, it is about disconnecting and reconnecting from a network. Actually in the solution concept the client laptops are equipped with wireless internet. The laptops connect as often as possible to the company network to be synchronized as often as possible. However, it is assumed that a steadily sufficient wireless internet connection cannot always be established and therefore the application must be able to deal with this.

The concrete project [2, 3] was conducted with the Austrian Social Insurance company for Occupational Risks—AUVA (Allgemeine Unfallversicherungsanstalt). With more than 5000 employees and more than 4 million customers [4] AUVA is a major Austrian insurance company. One important field of activity of the AUVA is the prevention of occupational risks in enterprises. On a regularly basis or upon request, consultants visit the companies in order to investigate work environments and conditions for safety on site and, eventually, to make recommendations or even to impose obligations.

The purpose of the realized system is the internal planning of the AUVA risks prevention activities and support for the consultants in conducting their company visits. A consultant plans traveling routes consisting of several companies to be visited, proposes this route to a stakeholder and adjusts them with this stakeholder. At the beginning of a business trip the consultant loads relevant data concerning the companies on the traveling route and their employees from the central IT system onto the laptop. On-site the consultant follows rules in order to investigate the workplaces and plants, collects relevant data and generates reports for the visited companies. Back home, the data is evaluated, (additional) reports are made and the final results are loaded back to the central IT system. The software built in this project supports the workflows needed to get all this done.

Figure 1 shows the resulting architecture. The client laptops have all workflow control and business logic that also resides on the server. They have also a local database, i.e., Oracle Database Lite [5]. The interfaces to the work list of the workflow enactment service and the workflow-controlled business logic were provided as web services to the client software [6]. The trick is the design of these interfaces. The client is capable to do some workflow steps that are independent from global workflow relevant data on his own and to defer the communication of the workflow progress. This way a degree of freedom is gained that allows for offline progress of workflows. The clients use their workflow control, business logic, and database only in periods they are offline, i.e., not connected to the company network. If a client is connected to the network, it uses the workflow control and business logic at the server and is in this way accessing the server

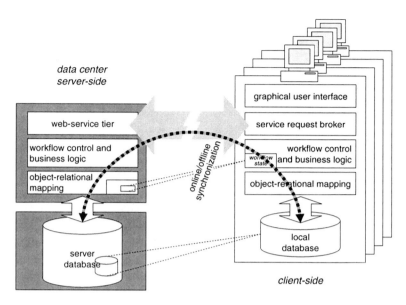

Fig. 1 A service-oriented system architecture for distributed workflow

database. The user has to initiate an update of the laptop's local database before he disconnects the client from the network. Synchronization takes place. The trick is that the synchronization mechanism looks at the task in the user's work list of the workflow control and only uploads data to the laptop's database that is actually needed for the currently impending business trip.

2.1 Realization Issues

When a client reconnects to the company network the data which has been accessed and manipulated in the meantime must be synchronized again. Conflicts are resolved with cooperation of the user. The human computer interaction of the user cooperation has been improved with the notion of context-based conflict resolution—an application of data provenance considerations [7, 8]. The system makes the user aware of the object net that is the context of a manipulated data set and the dialogue in which the manipulation occurred. The description of the synchronization makes clear that it required more than a database replication mechanism to realize it. The context-based conflict resolution developed for the offline-robust ERP system has been described in [2].

In a first version of the system the workflow enactment service was realized on the basis of an early version of the BizTalk server. In the current version the workflow enactment server is realized as a particularly lightweight and flexible matrix-based implementation. The overall business process network is interpreted as a state machine and the whole workflow enactment knowledge is captured in a matrix of state transitions on business process activities, i.e., workflow states. This easy solution does not target scalability with respect to the amount of workflow states; however, it is particularly scalable and maintainable with respect to the amount of realized innovative enactment service features like the treatment of security issues, role-based access management and synchronization. An in-depth description of this architecture of the workflow enactment service and its advantages with respect to technical scalability can be found in an SCCH technical report [9].

3 On a Possible Future of ERP Infrastructure

The following discussion is about none other than the question of how to make established ERP infrastructure fit for the demands of an ever more networked, agile and mobile business world. Furthermore, cloud computing has been turned into reality. Many experts expect that cloud computing to dramatically increase flexibility and quantity of outsourcing initiatives. Major companies currently invest enormous amounts of money into huge on-demand data centers. Even if cloud computing does not take off as a sourcing paradigm, its conditions and technologies—high-end network bandwidth, high-end transfer protocols, server and desktop virtualization—are available and ready to change the face of compute services and IT infrastructure. The transformation of data centers into private clouds is in the nearest future. It is important to discuss whether the desire for a next-generation ERP infrastructure is overtaken by the cloud computing trend.

3.1 Deep Standardization

We believe in the importance and power of what we call deep standards or deep standardization [10, 11] for the success of technologies in general and IT technologies in particular. In the field of information technologies official or quasistandards are often shallow. Shallow standards may define a concrete technology in the context of one of the many tiers that make up software architectures, e.g., HTML5, CSS3, Java, XML etc. Even if a standardization effort addresses a whole complex tier of technology we would rather call it a shallow standard. An example of that is plain CORBA, i.e., the initially defined CORBA without those parts that specify a component model, which horizontally addresses a plethora of phenomena for the field of distributed object computing. The same is true for service-oriented architecture (SOA) [12].

However, what really boosts the widespread use of mature technology and further technological innovation are standards that crosscut separated concerns, i.e., standards that define for a certain domain of technology or application domain the several components of an architecture and the interplay of these components.

We call such standards deep standards or deep standardization. There are important positive examples for deep standards in the field of information technology, e.g., the OSI and TCP/IP families of standards which are definition of the whole network stack. Other examples of deep standards are the domain-specific component models of enterprise applications, i.e., is the open EJB (Enterprise Java Bean) standard and the CORBA component model.

In the field of information technology we have seen other strictly-defined holistic architectures that are no official standards and are even not perceived as standards, although they actually had a major standardizing impact in their field. Actually, it is the field of ERP system development and governance, where we see examples of this. In the mid-level computer range we had the successful and widespread AS/400[1] technology stack. Its holistic design of a fully integrated operating and database system OS400[2]/DB2, the virtual machine tier TIMI (technology independent machine interface) and the 4GL programming language RPG (Report Generator) are teamed together for the purpose of rapid application development and particularly robust execution [13]. In its heyday, the AS400 architecture worked like a successful standard in its domain, i.e., the domain of domain-specific and unique selling points creating software development for medium and also fast growing enterprises. Remember how a whole domain-specific software development industry, i.e., the so-called ISVs (independent software vendors), emerged on the basis of and around AS400.

Similarly, the SAP system from the start was a holistic architecture for developing, testing, distributing and re-distributing, running and monitoring enterprise application code. From the start, its architecture was oriented towards realizing ERP as SaaS (Software as a Service) [1] and, therefore, lessons learned from the SAP architecture are extremely important for the current discussion of cloud computing and cloud-based ERP [14, 15].

SAP is so successful because of its IT and software infrastructure concept. The maturity is in strictly defined tool-supported interplay between its components for developing, transporting, running and monitoring software. This is so for customers who exploit SAP as SaaS and for customer that privately host SAP. If SAP is used as SaaS, the role of the SAP infrastructure as a SaaS infrastructure is obvious. Even if SAP is run privately, customers benefit from the additional services provided by the overall SAP infrastructure concept and support in the global context like capabilities for bug and problem monitoring and reporting.

As the above AS400 and SAP examples proof it is possible at one point in time to grasp all requirements and appropriate technological solutions for them and to integrate them into a single technological well-balanced vision and architecture. This is what deep standardization is about and the examples show that it is no mere fiction. Of course, the environment of each domain and therefore its requirements change. From time to time it might be necessary that an established architecture is

---

[1] Today's System i.
[2] Today's i5OS.

fundamentally rethought and refactored or even completely obsolete. Today, we are faced with ever-shorter innovation cycles. Nevertheless we believe that deep standardization is not outdated and still possible. In the rapidly changing technological environment of today we surely need sophisticated approaches to make deep standardization a still working concept. The discussion of this and proposals on how to achieve this, e.g., by a systematic streamlining moderation of changes, is beyond the scope of this paper and conducted elsewhere [10]. For the time being it is sufficient to understand that we use the notion of deep standardization as the overall objective that drives our discussion of possible future ERP infrastructure.

3.2 Sweetspot Architecture for Robust Workflow-Based Systems

In order to understand the key ingredients of the proposed architecture we will discuss several possible platforms and architectures for ERP infrastructure, i.e., mainstream ERP infrastructure as established by classic SAP installations, the PreVolution framework, web application architecture, mainstream cloud computing and academically discussed P2P distributed workflow approaches, and will compare them with the proposed future ERP infrastructure. Considered aspects encompass mobility, scalability and additional aspects like maturity. A summary of the discussion is also given as a table of the several architectures properties at the end of Sect. 3 in Fig. 4.

The Mainstream ERP Infrastructure. Diagram (i) in Fig. 2 illustrates the mainstream ERP infrastructure as established by the SAP R/3 architecture. The architecture is a client/server or master/slave architecture. A stub is installed at each client to provide locally basic services of the platform. An important role of the stub code is to serve as an interpreter of GUI code. In the SAP infrastructure this part of stub code is called SAPGUI, of course, today also browser-based GUI is supported for SAP. But the stub is also the host for additional distributed services of the platform, e.g., monitoring and reporting capabilities.

The PreVolution Approach. In the PreVolution approach—see diagram (ii) in Fig. 2—the GUI code necessary for the client is installed and always executed at the client. This is contrast to approach (i) where the necessary GUI code is always send via the network and interpreted at the client side. Furthermore, in approach (ii) the business logic code is redundantly installed at the server and the client. Also, workflow state and data is copied and redundantly maintained at the client. Whenever the client is offline, the business logic is executed at the client with the private copy of data and workflow state. The necessary workflow enactment service is considered part of the business logic in this illustration. Upon reconnection, a mature synchronization for data and workflow state takes place as described in Sect. 2 and [2]. In contrast to this, in approach (i) the business logic is always

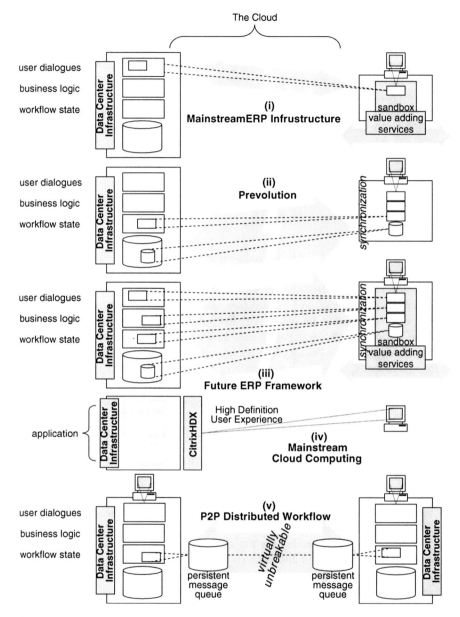

Fig. 2 Platforms and architectures for ERP infrastructure

called via the network and executed at the server. Data and workflow state are maintained exclusively at the server—regardless of possible caching.

Mobility, Scalability, and Maturity. The approach presented in diagram (iii) is the attempt to combine the advantages of approaches (i) and (ii). The advantages of

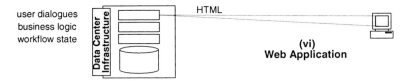

Fig. 3 Web application architecture

approach (ii) over approach (i) is that it enables offline work. The advantage of approach approach (i) over approach (ii) is that it needs no roll-out of new software versions. Approach (ii) must be enhanced by a software distribution concept and mechanism to make it a scalable working solution. This software distribution advantage approach (i) has in common with web-based application architectures as sketched in diagram (vi) in Fig. 3 and also mainstream cloud computing architecture—see diagram (iv) in Fig. 2. Furthermore, approach (i) is assumed to offer additional value adding services that are distributed over the stubs of the connected clients. These services are an advantage over approach (ii) and the web application and cloud solution. If these distributed services were about monitoring the GUI interpreting role of the stub only, this argument in favor of approach (i) were obsolete. However, we believe that a mature ERP infrastructure needs defined distributed services in the future, e.g., for client hardware and security monitoring [16].

Approach (iii) is a solution for ERP that is mobile, scalable, and mature. It can be classified as truly mobile because it addresses offline phases of work. It is scalable, because it systematically addresses the problem of software distribution. The maturity of such a future platform should show in two aspects: First, in the existence of distributed value-adding services, and second, in the definition of all of its components and services, basically in terms of appropriate APIs (application programming interfaces), as an open standard—in the sense of deep standardization as described in Sect. 3.1. In particular, maturity would show in the definition of a workflow enactment service interface against for the coordination of user dialogues and therefore realization of workflows. In general, such an ERP infrastructure should show all features that we expect from today's business process management platforms as described in [17, 18].

The characterizing feature of approach (iii) is the fact that it enables offline-phases. It generalizes the concept of an offline-robust ERP system as described in Sect. 2 to the level of an ERP platform or infrastructure. Therefore, we call approach (iii) an offline-enabling ERP infrastructure and mean with this the whole bundle of generalized data/code/state distribution/synchronization plus the value adding services as described above in the sequel.

Cloud Computing. Cloud computing is not a vision, it is mainstream technology. Whether it takes off is rather a question of economic issues, i.e., business models, sourcing, pricing, and not a technological question anymore. Given today's network bandwidth and stability and state-of-the-art middleware [19] like Citrix HDX (High Definition User Experience) [20] combined with latest desktop and server virtualization technology, it is possible to run virtually all applications that are relevant for today's enterprise computing in the cloud, as depicted by diagram (iv) in Fig. 2. Even security issues that are often heard as unresolved for cloud computing are not a technological concern. Technologically, security is improved by cloud computing through better governance of IT and software assets. Legally, with respect to data privacy, question might be open, but we do not want to delve into this topic here—we feel that at least sometimes security arguments are used to obfuscate a sourcing debate [21, 22].

IT supporting for defined processes and structured data have always been run server-based to benefit from the robustness of data center infrastructure. Major chunks of decision support applications and the field of office automation needed locally installed solutions in the past. At least, the data part of office automation was always supported with high-quality storage services in professional settings and enterprise content management (ECM) solutions emerged to improve control over the mass of non-structured data that emerged in the informal processes backed by office automation [23]. Now, with cloud-based desktop virtualization, it is absolutely no problem anymore to run office automation completely server-based. Given this, data center quality is available for the full range of enterprise applications now.

Despite its technological maturity, current cloud computing—as compared to approach (iii)—does not offer turnkey support for offline phases yet. The possibility, e.g., to edit documents on- and offline (as announced by Google [24]) is certainly one building block for that kind of support.

We now come up with the central claim of our discussion on possible future ERP infrastructure: *The need for an offline-enabling ERP infrastructure boils down to the question of network ubiquity.*

Ubiquity [25] of network services is amenable to render the vision of an offline-enabling ERP platform obsolete. Ubiquity of network services has several facets:

- *Technological facet.* First, this is a question of mere spatial distribution. Second, it is a question of quality of service, i.e., network availability. We have seen dramatic growth with respect to both of these aspects in the past decade.
- *Economic facet.* This facet is simply about costs of network services.
- *Organizational facet.* This is about the question, whether there are scenarios, e.g., of legal nature, that enforce offline phases.

Therefore, only future can tell whether such a platform is needed or not.

P2P Distributed Workflow. To complete the discussion and this way reinvestigate the given arguments we also compare the approaches (i) through (iv) with a fictional P2P (peer-to-peer) distributed workflow platform as depicted in diagram (v).

All solutions (i) trough (iv) are client/server solutions, with cloud computing enabling ultra-thin clients. All solutions offer data center quality of service for those components that run at the server-side. Note that data centers invest a lot in redundancy, take-over and backup technologies to provide data safety and high availability of compute services. There is no need for solution (iii) if enterprise applications are used on basis of network owned by the enterprise only. Then, the

	Mobility	Scalability	Additional Assets
Mainstream ERP	—	explicitly addressed	client-side value adding services
Prevolution Architecture	explicitly addressed	—	—
Future ERP Infrastructure	explicitly addressed	explicitly addressed	client-side value adding services
Web Application Architecture	—	per se	current mainstream
Mainstream Cloud Computing	—	per se	future mainstream
P2P Distributed Workflow	—	• particularly expensive • restricted to peers	virtually unbreakable network

Fig. 4 Summary of properties of discussed ERP platforms and architectures

data center can, at least in principle, ensure availability of the network service. If a third-party network is involved, solution (iii) applies. P2P distributed workflow is a nice idea, but to achieve the same quality of the overall solution as approaches (i) through (iv) it is necessary to provide the same data center infrastructure at each site that hosts components of the distributed system as depicted in diagram (v). Most likely, such an architecture might apply to B2B (business-2-business) scenarios with process coordination spawning internals of several organization beyond mere coordination or EDI (electronic data interchange) [26] between organization. Though such scenarios have by far not been usual to date, the comparison with scenarios (i) through (iv) is instructive.

Also, P2P distributed workflow technology does not solve *per se* the problem of possible network downtimes of involved third-party networks. Therefore solution (v) exploits persistent message queues well-known from the OLTP (online transactional processing) [27, 28] field and established VAN (value-added networks) technology from the EDI [26] field (Fig. 4).

4 Further Work

The design of a new ERP infrastructure can be harmonized with our vision of cloud-based software engineering CASE 2.0 [10]. CASE 2.0 is about consolidating all software engineering artifacts and tools containing code and programming environments as a web of views onto a single underlying model (SUM) that resides on the cloud. CASE 2.0 enriches Orthogonal Software Modeling (OSM) [29], which has its roots in the KobrA [30] method by process-related considerations and transports it into the cloud. With respect to CASE 2.0 the stubs of the envisioned ERP platforms can be considered standardized detached views and therefore fit the concept.

5 Related Work

The context-based conflict resolution approach developed for the offline-robust ERP system has been described in [2]. For a discussion of related work of the data synchronization aspect, e.g., [31, 32], please also have a look at [2]. In contrast to all the example related work discussed in this section [33–36] the offline-enabling ERP framework proposed in this paper is not a P2P distributed workflow management framework. The point is that our framework is a distributed framework, but distribution by no means immediately enforces a distribution of equal components. Our framework is a client/server architecture in the strict sense of an asymmetric master/slave architecture. The goal of using the term P2P framework for the other many approaches that are usually discussed in the community is exactly to emphasize this difference.

The approach described in [33] motivates distributed workflow enactment for inter-enterprise usage by improved failure resilience and increased performance. Whereas increased performance does not seem to be a valid motivation due to the fact that workflow enactment plays a marginal role in the application load mix only, the failure resilience argument is clearly out-of-date. High availability is a concern that can be separated. It is achieved by the executing platform rather by the application itself through a high-availability cluster solution or by the takeover capabilities of today's state-of-the-art redundant virtualization platforms like VMware [37].

The approach described in [34] is agent-based. Again, the approach is motivated by efficiency and robustness. The approach relies on a metaphor of autonomous agents. The approaches in [35] and [36] deal with the aspect of robustness by establishing self-healing mechanisms for a distributed workflow enactment service.

Only recently, we have proposed a unification of service-oriented computing and distributed object computing in [38]. This unification is not a deep standardization in the sense of Sect. 3.1, it analyses and bridges the gap between the service-oriented and the object-oriented metaphors. Its elaboration has been motivated by the mass of object-oriented programming for devices that connect to service-oriented portals. The tools and techniques developed along the lines of this unification can be exploited in the implementation of the envisioned offline-enabling ERP platform as well as in the implementation of a P2P distributed enactment service but must not be mixed with either of them.

6 Conclusion

In this paper we have described the objectives and the solution of the offline-robust ERP system PreVolution. The solution was centered around a redundant multi-tier enterprise application architecture and based on a context-oriented synchronization approach.

Given the success of the PreVolution project[3] this paper discussed the feasibility of generalizing the basic architectural notions to a value-added ERP infrastructure. The aim was to understand the possible role of this ERP infrastructure and to argue in favor of its usefulness. We discussed the concept also against the background of other possible solution architectures, i.e., mainstream ERP infrastructure, web-based applications, mainstream cloud computing and a fictional P2P distributed workflow management framework.

We came up with the central claim that the need for an offline-enabling ERP infrastructure boils down to the question of network ubiquity.

Acknowledgments Thanks go to the PreVolution team at SCCH (Software Competence Center Hagenberg GmbH) and the team at AUVA. The PreVolution project was approx. a 35 person year effort. Crucial parts of the PreVolution project, i.e., approx. a third, have been funded by the FFG (Forschungsförderungsgesellschaft Österreich—Research Funds Agency Austria).The publication has been partly written within the project "VerticalModel Integration (VMI)" which is supported within the program "Regionale Wettbewerbsfähigkeit OÖ 2007–2013" by the European Fund for Regional Development as well as the State of Upper Austria. This work was further supported in part by the Austrian Science Fund (FWF) under grant no. TRP 223-N23.

References

1. Lee, Y., Kim, Y., Choi, H.: Conflict resolution of data synchronization in mobile environment. In Lagan, A., Gavrilova, M., Kumar, V., Mun, Y., Tan, C., Gervasi, O. (eds.) Proceedings of ICCSA 2004—the 4*th* International Conference on Computational Science and Its Applications. Volume 3044 of Lecture Notes in Computer Science. Springer, Berlin, pp. 196–205 (2004)
2. Draheim, D., Natschläger, C.: A context-oriented synchronization approach. In: Electronic Proceedings of the 2nd International Workshop in Personalized Access, Profile Management, and Context Awareness: Databases (PersDB 2008) in Conjunction with the 34th VLDB Conference, pp. 20–27 (2008)
3. Pichler, M., Rumetshofer, H., Wahler, W.: Agile requirements engineering for a social insurance for occupational risks organization: a case study. In: Proceedings of the 14th IEEE International Requirements Engineering Conference, RE'06. IEEE Computer Society, Washington, pp. 246–251, September (2006)
4. AUVA: Austrian social insurance for occupational risks. We care for your safety (2000)
5. Oracle: Adding mobile capability to an enterprise application with oracle database. White paper, Oracle (2007)

---

[3] The PreVolution project was granted 2*nd* place of the GC (Gesundheitscluster Österreich— Healthcare Cluster Austria) Genius Award—research and development category—in 2009.

6. Kopetzky, T., Draheim, D.: Workflow management and service oriented architecture. In: Proceedings of the Nineteenth International Conference on Software Engineering & Knowledge Engineering (SEKE'2007). Knowledge Systems Institute Graduate School, Boston, pp. 749–750, July 9–11 (2007)
7. Buneman, P., Khanna, S., Wang-Chiew, T.: Why and where: a characterization of data provenance. In Van den Bussche, J., Vianu, V. (eds.) Proceedings of ICDT 2001—the 8*th* International Conference on Database Theory. Volume 1973 of Lecture Notes in Computer Science. Springer, Heidelberg, pp. 316–330 (2001)
8. Foster, J.N., Karvounarakis, G.: Provenance and data synchronization. IEEE Data Eng. Bull. **30**(4), 1321 (2007)
9. Draheim, D., Illibauer, C., Kopetzky, T.: Specification of business processes and realization as web services. Technical Report SCCH-TR-0810, Software Competence Center Hagenberg (2010)
10. Atkinson, C., Draheim, D.: Cloud aided-software engineering—evolving viable software systems through a web of views. In: Mahmood, Z., Saeed, S. (eds.) Software Engineering Frameworks for Cloud Computing Paradigm. Springer, New York (2013)
11. Draheim, D.: CASE 2.0—on key success factors for cloud-aided software engineering. In: Proceedings of MDHPCL the 1*st* International Workshop on Model-Driven Engineering for High Performance and Cloud Computing. ACM Press, New York (2012)
12. Draheim, D., Lee, I., Park, C., Song, I.: The service-oriented metaphor deciphered. J. Comput. Sci. Eng. **4**(4), 253–275 (2010)
13. Soltis, F.G.: Fortress Rochester: The Inside Story of the IBM Iseries. System iNetwork, Loveland (2001)
14. Mell, P., Grance, T.: The NIST definition of cloud computing. Natl. Inst. Stand. Technol. **53**(6), 50 (2009)
15. Buyya, R., Yeo, C.S., Venugopal, S., Broberg, J., Brandic, I.: Cloud computing and emerging IT platforms: vision, hype, and reality for delivering computing as the 5th utility. Future Gener. Comput. Syst. **25**(6), 599–616 (2009)
16. Harrison, K., Bordbar, B., Ali, S., Dalton, C., Norman, A.: A framework for detecting malware in cloud by identifying symptoms. In: Proceedings of EDOC' 2012—the 16*th* IEEE International Enterprise Distributed Object Computing Conference. IEEE Press, New York (2012)
17. Atkinson, C., Draheim, D., Geist, V.: Typed business process specification. In: Proceedings of EDOC' 2010—the 14th IEEE International Enterprise Computing Conference. IEEE Press, New York pp. 69–78, October (2010)
18. Draheim, D.: Business Process Technology: A Unified View on Business Processes, Workflows and Enterprise Applications, 1st edn. Springer, Berlin (2010)
19. Bernstein, P.A.: Middleware: a model for distributed system services. Commun. ACM **39**(2), 8698 (1996)
20. Citrix: Balancing desktop virtualization with Citrix HDX media stream and Intel core and Intel core vPro processors. Citrix White Paper, Citrix (2010)
21. Carr, N.G.: IT doesn't matter. Educause Rev. **38**, 2438 (2003)
22. Carr, N.G.: Does It Matter? Information Technology and the Corrosion of Competitive Advantage. Harvard Business Press, Boston (2004)
23. Draheim, D.: Smart business process management. In: Fischer, L. (ed.) 2011 BPM and Workflow Handbook. Future Strategies, Digital edition. Workflow Management Coalition, February (2012)
24. Google: Announcing your two most requested features: offline document editing and drive for iOS (June 2012). http://googledocs.blogspot.co.at/2012/06/announcing-your-two-most-requested.html
25. Weiser, M.: The computer for the 21st Century. IEEE Pervasive Comput. **1**(1), 1925 (2002)
26. Emmelhainz, M.A.: EDI: Total Management Guide, 2nd edn. Wiley, New York (1992)
27. Bernstein, P.A., Newcomer, E.: Principles of Transaction Processing—For the Systems Professional. Morgan Kaufmann, San Francisco (1997)

28. Gray, J., Reuter, A.: Transaction Processing: Concepts and Techniques, 1st edn. Morgan Kaufmann Publishers Inc., San Francisco (1992)
29. Atkinson, C., Stoll, D., Tunjic, C.: Orthographic service modeling. In: Proceedings of 3M4SE' 2011—the 2nd International Workshop on Models and Model-driven Methods for Service Engineering, IEEE International, pp. 67–70, August (2011)
30. Atkinson, C., Bayer, J., Bunse, C., Kamsties, E., Laitenberger, O., Laqua, R., Muthig, D., Paech, B., Wst, J., Zettel, J.: Component-Based Product Line Engineering with Uml. Pearson Education, London (2002)
31. Ratner, D., Reiher, P., Popek, G.J., Kuenning, G.H.: Replication requirements in mobile environments. Mobile Netw. Appl. **6**(6), 525–533 (2001)
32. Barbará, D., Garcia-Molina, H.: Replicated data management in mobile environments: anything new under the sun? In: Proceedings of the IFIP WG10.3 Working Conference on Applications in Parallel and Distributed Computing, Amsterdam, The Netherlands. North-Holland Publishing Co., The Netherlands, pp. 237–246 (1994)
33. Gokkoca, E., Altinel, M., Cingil, R., Tatbul, E., Koksal, P., Dogac, A.: Design and implementation of a distributed workflow enactment service. In: Proceedings of the Second IFCIS International Conference on Cooperative Information Systems, COOPIS'97, pp. 89–98, June (1997)
34. Fortino, G., Garro, A., Russo, W.: Distributed workflow enactment: an Agent based Framework. In: Proceedings of WOA2006, pp. 110–117 (2006)
35. Yu, W., Yang, J.: Continuation-passing enactment of distributed recoverable workflows. In: Proceedings of the 2007 ACM Symposium on Applied Computing, SAC'07. ACM, New York, pp. 475–481 (2007)
36. Frincu, M.: D-OSyRIS: a self-healing distributed workflow engine. In: 2011 10th International Symposium on Parallel and Distributed Computing (ISPDC), pp. 215–222, July (2011)
37. VMware: Setup for failover clustering and microsoft cluster service (2011)
38. Atkinson, C., Bostan, P., Draheim, D.: A unified conceptual framework for service-oriented computing—aligning models of architecture and utilization. Trans. Large Scale Data Knowl. Centered Syst. **6** (2012) pp. 128–169

Part IX
Quality of ERP Systems

A Business View on Testing ERP Systems with Value-Based Requirements Coverage

Rudolf Ramler, Theodorich Kopetzky and Wolfgang Platz

Abstract Testing has been identified as a critical factor for a successful implementation of ERP systems. However, most testing activities are still value-neutral and do not utilize the information about the system's achievable business value, which is a particularly promising improvement for testing of business software and ERP systems. In this paper we therefore present an approach for value-based coverage measurement that can be used to align the testing effort to the value associated with requirements and typical usage scenarios. It has been implemented as part of the commercial test tool TOSCA Testsuite by Tricentis and was successfully applied in real-world projects. The results demonstrated its ability to adequately capture the distribution of the business value involved in different functional units. Furthermore, when compared with a value-neutral and a pure requirements-based approach for test case prioritization, it produced a higher benefit curve and an early positive ROI from testing.

1 Introduction

Successful ERP implementations increase the operational efficiency by automating an organization's business processes and create competitive advantages by supporting managerial control, rapid innovation as well as informed decision-making.

R. Ramler (✉) · T. Kopetzky
Software Competence Center Hagenberg, Hagenberg im Mühlkreis, Austria
e-mail: rudolf.ramler@scch.at

T. Kopetzky
e-mail: theodorich.kopetzky@scch.at

W. Platz
TRICENTIS Technology and Consulting GmbH, Vienna, Austria
e-mail: w.platz@tricentis.com

Due to the involved benefits and their pervasive nature, ERP systems have become an essential and also critical part of the infrastructure of many organizations [12]. As a consequence implementation failures are often disastrous and result in dramatic cost and schedule overruns [6].

System testing has been identified as a critical success factor for a successful implementation of an ERP project [1]: "The going live on the system without adequate and planned testing is a recipe for an organisational disaster... The testing and validation of an ERP system is important to ensure that the software works technically and that the business process configurations are practical. When business processes are up and running, an important test is of whether the processes described and represented in the application system actually match with the processes taking place in the organisation".

While testing is one of the most widely practiced quality assurance measures including a wide range of available methods and tools (e.g., [10]), it is also one of the most resource-intensive activities consuming up to 50 % of the total development costs [13]. The necessary effort for testing is therefore often in conflict with time and resource constraints implied by business considerations. Furthermore, this conflict is highly prevalent due to the typical organization of testing as last phase before the release. As a result, many organizations struggle with effectively completing the testing activities within given time and budget limits.

Empirical research has demonstrated that 80 % of the value comes from about 20 % of the features of a software system [3]. Moreover about 80 % of the defects come from 20 % of the modules, and about half the modules are defect free [4]. These findings are also reflected in the results presented by Kumar et al. [15] about a Pareto analysis of the implementation issues over six modules of an ERP system. The most erroneous module accounted for 40 % of the encountered issues, the top three erroneous modules together accumulated to 86 % of the error frequency [15].

Test management can make use of this knowledge by focusing the testing effort and scarce resources primarily on those parts of an ERP system which exhibit a high risk that the business value may be jeopardized due to implementation issues. Thus, from an economic perspective, the goal of test management is to bring the testing activities in alignment with the business risk associated to an ERP system's modules and requirements [21].

The objective of this paper is to provide an approach for determining the value contribution of individual test cases to support test management in taking a business perspective and setting the priorities in testing accordingly. The proposed approach goes beyond conventional requirements-based testing where the value of tests is primarily determined on the basis of the requirements' estimated business values or risks. This paper contributes an approach that includes the value of testing different usage scenarios within the implementation of a specific requirement.

The paper is structured as follows. Section 2 describes requirements-based testing and usage-based test design as foundation for the proposed value-based approach. In Sect. 3 the implementation of the proposed approach is outlined and explained using an illustrative example. In Sect. 4 the results from a real-world test project are used to evaluate the impact of the value-based approach on test case prioritization and the consequent ROI of testing. Section 5 summarizes and concludes the paper.

2 Approach

The approach we propose in this paper builds upon and extends the conventional best practice of requirements-based testing (see, e.g., [2]). In requirements-based testing the system under test is structured corresponding to (functional) requirements, i.e., functional units. The functional units are broken down into a tree structure with the actual requirements shown on the bottommost level. To cover the required functionalities, test cases are derived from the specification of the requirements. By tracing the test cases back to the requirements, the test execution results can be reported at the level of requirement (e.g., the passed or failed status of a test case can be used to indicate or enhance the requirements status).

In requirements engineering the expectations and value propositions of the stakeholders are elicited and reconciled. Thereby the defined requirements are linked to anticipated business value of the system [16]. Existing requirements engineering practices have been adopted and studied for ERP systems, e.g., by Daneva [7]. The anticipated business value associated to the requirements is inherited to test cases, typically in reciprocal form as risk value indicating the potential loss of the required functionality [21]. The resulting values enable setting priorities in requirements-based and risk-based approaches for system testing (e.g., [2] or [9]).

A test case exercises a requirement with a defined set of test input data. Several input data combinations may be necessary to cover a particular requirement. Each of these combinations forms an individual test case describing a specific usage scenario. However, from the perspective of testing, these input data combinations and corresponding usage scenarios (i.e., all test cases) are not equally important. Input data combinations that represent a standard usage scenario in the context of a requirement have a higher importance as they occur more frequently, affect a larger number of users and have a higher impact on the business value than, for example, boundary cases or invalid scenarios. Incorporating such information on usage scenarios has been suggested for testing software systems in general (e.g., [5]) as well as for testing ERP systems (e.g., [25]).

For determining the value contribution of individual test cases we combine both factors: (1) the requirements-based priority and (2) the usage-based impact. The requirements-based priority is derived from the business value of the associated requirements. The usage-based impact is calculated from weights assigned to the input data values combined to test cases. These two dimensions also reflect the *external perspective* and the *internal perspective* relevant for value-based testing [21]. Thereby, the external dimension is concerned with ensuring the value objectives of the external stakeholder. The internal dimension deals with organizing testing in order to optimally support the improvement of the software system's qualities. The implementation of the proposed approach reconciles these two dimensions and supports value-based testing by using weight factors representing the value impact in computing coverage measures for testing up to the level of requirements.

3 Implementation

Figure 1 shows how the involved entities of the implemented testing approach map to the external dimension based on the requirement business values that translate to risks and the internal dimension concerned with the combination of input data values.

In addition to depicting the involved entities, Fig. 1 provides an overview of the relationships between these entities:

- A *requirement* is derived to one or more *test cases* that cover a set of input *data values* provided for the data *attributes* relevant in the tested usage scenario.
- From the external view, *risks* threaten the realization of the business value of a *requirement*. The risks are therefore a key factor influencing the importance (value) of a test case assuring the requirement's quality. The risk's probability and potential damage determine the extent of the influence.

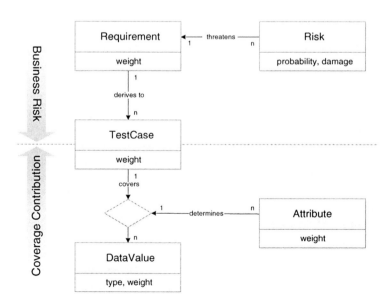

Fig. 1 Overview of entities relevant for coverage measurement

- From the internal view, the systematic coverage of the data *attributes* and their associated *data values* is a key factor influencing the importance (value) of a test case. The weight of the data values and attributes determine the extent of the influence.

Based on the outlined relationships the value of a test case V can be calculated by considering the influence factors coming from the external and internal dimension:

$$V = Risk(requirement) \cdot Coverage(datavalue_i, attribute_j) \quad (1)$$

where V is the value of a test case, *Risk* is the function determining the external influence based on the requirement and *Coverage* is the function determining the internal influence due to the covered attributes and data values. The functions representing the external and the internal view are described in further detail in the following.

3.1 External View: Business Risk

In requirements-based testing, the system under test is structured to the requirements (e.g., functional units), which are then associated with an expected *business value*. For testing, the requirement's business value is inverted to the business risk expressing to what extent the realization of this value is endangered by a defect impeding or decreasing the availability of the functionality. The corresponding risk weights are assigned to the requirements.

The risk weights are determined according to the general guidelines on risk assessment [19]

$$R = p \cdot D \quad (2)$$

where R is the business risk, p is the probability of occurrence and D is the potential damage. The probability factor p is the result of $p = p_{Usage} \cdot p_{Failure}$ that is based on the frequency of use p_{Usage} of the function and the probability $p_{Failure}$ that a failure will occur in usage.

The implemented approach supports risk estimation using risk and damage classes [19]. However, it does not dictate the use of a particular method for determining risk weights. Rather, the method appropriate for the needs of a specific project can be applied (e.g., multi-criteria methods as suggested by Li et al. [18] or the adapted risk assessment method proposed by Felderer et al. [9] considering time criteria).

Finally, the relative risk weight per requirement is computed as the share (percentage) of the total risk over all requirements. The relative risk weight is the first factor in determining the value of a test case.

3.2 Internal View: Coverage Contribution

In test design, a list of input data values is produced for each data attribute. The constructed test cases combine the data values associated to the different attributes (depicted as ternary association in Fig. 1). The resulting input data combinations constitute the different usage scenarios and sequences, as the different data values of an attribute trigger different processing and interaction flows. The number of required test cases to cover these usage scenarios and sequences depends on the underlying coverage criterion of the applied combinatorial technique.

In our previous work on investigating practical implications of combinatorial techniques [22], we identified the base choice approach of the *Linear Expansion* technique as a suitable technique for testing business software. The main reason is that in the majority of the cases some data values associated to an attribute are more common than others. Such data values are often set as predefined defaults or standard values in input fields and system configurations. By modeling the input data space accordingly (e.g., by defining the standard, normal, boundary, and invalid values of attributes), the base choice approach of the Linear Expansion technique produces test cases that represent the most common combinations (representing the standard usage scenarios) as well as frequently used variations (alternative usage courses) thereof.

Testing typical situations is more important than testing boundary cases [20], as a failure in a scenario uncommon in normal use will affect few users; a failure in typical use will affect many users. For considering the potential impact also in testing, the data values are augmented with weights that reflect the different practical importance of a data value due to their different usage frequency. The relative weight W_i of a data value is then calculated in relation (percentage) to all other data values of an attribute.

For attributes the use of weights is also supported. Attribute weights express the influence of the attribute on the interaction flow and the produced results. In that way, attributes that impact the flow of user interactions and data processing can be rated as more important for testing. The relative weight w_j of an attribute is calculated in relation (percentage) to all data attributes that are combined in constructing test cases.

Finally, the coverage contribution of a test case c_{ij} can be calculated as the product of the relative weights of attributes and input data values:

$$c_{ij} = W_i \cdot w_j \qquad (3)$$

where w_j is the relative weight of the attributes and W_i is the relative weight of the input data values of each attribute.

However, combinatorial testing approaches usually produce test cases that are partially redundant, i.e., where the same data values of an attribute are used in several tests. The proposed *Linear Expansion* technique, for example, produces one test for the standard scenario with the coverage contribution calculated as given above. Furthermore, it produces tests for each variations of the standard scenario by altering the data value for some of the attributes. Thus, these additional tests are partially redundant to the standard scenario. Therefore, for the additional tests only the weight of the new data values is counted in calculating the contribution. Thus, as for the test cases produced by *Linear Expansion*, the additional test cases covering variations of the standard scenario are exactly the contribution of the new data values that have not already been used in the standard scenario.

3.3 Tool Support

The approach has been implemented as part of the *TOSCA Testsuite*™ developed by *TRICENTIS*® (http://tricentis.com/en/tosca, *accessed on 20th Sept. 2012*). TOSCA is a comprehensive suite of tools for test management and test automation that provides a broad support for testing business software and ERP systems.

Figure 2 shows the computation of the value *Inner Value (%)* and its coverage contribution of the exemplary test case *TC3* for testing a *Vehicle premium calculation*. In this simplified example, test cases are defined by the attribute combination {*Age, Sex, Residence*}. The combination {*24.59, m, city*} specifies the input data values of test case *TC3*. Weights have been set for attributes as well as data values, e.g., weight 30 for attribute *Age* and weight 40 for the data value "*24 − 59*". The corresponding relative weights are $w_{Age} = 60\%$ and $W_{24-59} = 47.06\%$, which together result in the contribution $c_{Age * 24-59} = 28.24\%$.

The value of a test case is equal to the sum of the contributions of its associated data values. For test case *TC3* the contribution computes to the vale $28.24\% + 7.27\% + 21\% = 56.5\%$. Hence, if only *TC3* is executed, the

Name	Weight	Relative Weight (%)	Contribution (%)	Inner Value (%)		TC3
Vehicle premium calculation						TC3
Instances						
TC3	56508	100	100	56.51		
Age	30	60	60			24 - 59
Instances						
< 18	5	5.88	3.53			
18 - 23	15	17.65	10.59			
24 - 59	40	47.06	28.24			
> 59	25	29.41	17.65			
Sex	5	10	10			Male
Instances						
Male	8	72.73	7.27			
Female	3	27.27	2.73			
Residence	15	30	30			City
Instances						
City	7	70	21			
Country	3	30	9			

Fig. 2 Example computation of a test case value from attribute and data values weights

associated requirement would be covered to the extent of 56.5 % (see *Inner Value (%)* in Fig. 2).

Furthermore, TOSCA supports linking test cases to requirements and, thereby, the aggregation of the information associated to individual test case up to the level of requirements. For each requirement as well as the system as a whole the test progress can be assessed, for example, in terms of the specified test cases, their execution and the subsequent test results. Consequently, with this information the tool provides a comprehensive overview about the state of the entire project for stakeholders who understand and value the system from the viewpoint of the realized requirements.

Figure 3 shows an exemplary graphical representation of the aggregated information. The column *Coverage Specified (%)* provides an overview of the state of the test case development: Test cases have been specified and linked for 95 % of the requirement *Vehicle* (yellow bar), while one test cases is planned but has not yet been specified (white bar). The *Execution State (%)* provides an overview of the state of test case development and the state of test execution: 65 % of the requirement *Vehicle* have been tested with the result passed (green bar), 27 % show a failed test result (red bar), for 3 % tests are available but have not yet been executed (white bar) and for 5 % no tests have been specified (grey bar).

The aggregated information at the level of requirements also shows the major benefit of taking the value of the test cases into consideration. The test case values (*Relative Weight* in Fig. 3) supersede the generally reported value-neutral test cases counts (unweighted number of test cases). Since the test case values represent the importance of the test cases and their underlying combinations of attributes and input data, the aggregated information provides a more realistic picture of the project status indicating the true coverage of the requirements from a business perspective.

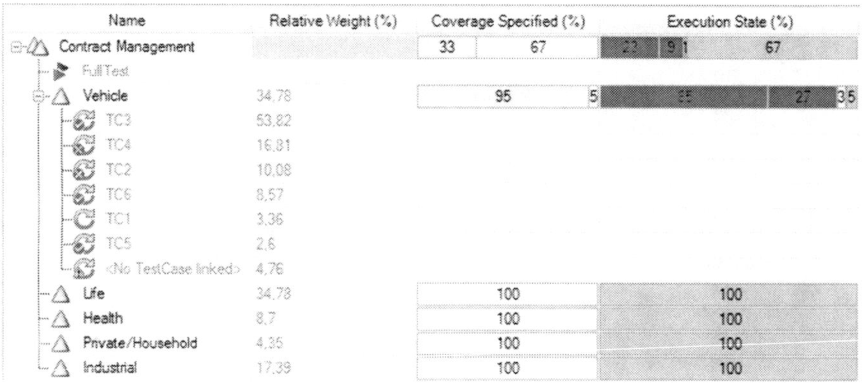

Fig. 3 Example computation of coverage and execution state at requirements level

4 Evaluation and Results

Based on this implementation, the approach has been evaluated in the context of testing a large real-world ERP software system. The test project serving as a study object encompasses about 1,600 test cases. These test cases are associated to 65 different requirements, which map to the functional areas of the software system. On average a test set associated to a requirement contains about 25 test cases, large test sets contain up to 40 test cases. In the project, weights were assigned for each of the requirements (external perspective) as well as for attributes and input data (internal perspective). These weights have been the basis for computing the corresponding values of test cases and the contribution per test case to the overall coverage.

First of all, the evaluation confirmed the high relative impact of the standard scenario in developing test cases. An analysis of test sets associated with the requirements showed that the standard case accounts for an average of 39.7 % of the requirement's business value; the values range from minimum 22 % to maximum 60 % (standard deviation s = 5.1, mean m = 39 %, $\frown$).

Furthermore, the computed values have been used for test case prioritization [24]. Prioritization allows ordering the test cases, e.g., for test execution. Thus, the more relevant test cases are executed first, making sure that defects in important requirements and/or usage scenarios are found earlier.

Barry Boehm illustrates the benefit of a value-based approach by investigating the Return on Investment (ROI) achievable with (a) test case prioritization considering the business value of the tested requirements in contrast to (b) automated but value-neutral test case generation [3]. Boehm's example demonstrates the advantage of focusing on the high value requirements first. Thereby the value-based testing produces an early positive ROI that is able to outperform automated test case generation for about 90 % of the test executions.

Following the example given by Boehm [3], we designed a study to compare the (ROI) for testing following three different approaches:

- A *value-neutral* prioritization strategy achieved by random ordering,
- a *requirements-based* prioritization strategy considering only the requirement values (external view) and
- an extended *value-based prioritization* strategy that combines the value from requirements and test cases (external view and internal view).

All strategies share the same cost function with an initial fixed share (50 %) and a linear increasing running share (50 %) of the total costs involved in testing.

Due to the size of the project and due to confidentiality restrictions a representative subset of 9 requirements associated with a total of 190 test cases has been selected for evaluation from the studied project. Table 1 shows the key characteristics of these requirements.

The requirements are sorted by their assigned weights (column *Requirements Weight*) indicating the potential loss regarding the associated business value if the

Table 1 Selected requirements of studied project

Requirement	Requirement weight	# Test cases	Test case share (%)	Standard test case weight (%)
A	171	19	5.26	35.30
B	85	26	3.85	38.17
C	85	12	8.33	49.41
D	43	42	2.38	30.47
E	21	17	5.88	41.96
F	11	28	3.57	45.23
G	11	15	6.67	44.56
H	5	18	5.56	42.12
I	5	13	7.69	40.91
Sum/average	–/49	190/21.11	–/5.47	–/40.90

requirement is not correctly or completely realized. The column *# Test Cases* shows the number of test cases that were developed to cover the requirements. In total there are 190 test cases including 9 tests covering the standard usage scenario of the requirements. The column *Test Case Share* shows the average weight of a test case per requirement when the test's individual coverage contribution is not accounted. For the studied project, the test case share is the risk weight of the requirement divided by the number of test cases. On average, the share is 5.47 %. In comparison, the column *Std. Test Case Weight* shows the weight of the test for the standard scenario calculated from the covered attributes and data values. The average coverage contribution of a standard test case is 40.90 %, which is more than seven times the average share of a not weighted test case.

We investigate the effect of value-based coverage measurement for test case prioritization by producing individually weighted test cases in contrast to an approach based on requirement values only and a value-neutral approach. The test cases are ordered according to the calculated coverage contribution or, respectively, their average share. In accordance with the example given by Boehm [3], we set the achievable benefit of testing (i.e., the software system's estimated business value) in relation to the effort consumed by testing, which is assumed to be half of the estimated business value. The effort is described by a simplified cost function. One half of this effort corresponds to fixed expenses that have to be invested upfront and the other half are running expenses that increase with every test. The resulting *Return on Investment* is computed as $ROI = (benefits - costs)/costs$.

Table 2 shows the relative levels of investment costs, achievable benefits and corresponding ROI numbers for the value-neutral, the requirements-based and the value-based prioritization approaches.

Column *% TC* in Table 2 shows the different relative levels of testing. The corresponding investment costs stated as percentage of the total costs are given in the column *Costs [%]*, the corresponding benefits achievable with a *neutral prioritization* approach, a *requirements-based prioritization* approach or a *value-based prioritization* approach are shown in the column *Value [%]*. All approaches start from

Table 2 Costs, benefit and ROI of a value-neutral versus a requirements-based versus a value-based test case prioritization approach; positive ROI values are printed in bold

% TC	Costs (%)	Value-neutral prioritization		Requirements-based prioritization		Value-based prioritization	
		Value (%)	ROI	Value (%)	ROI	Value (%)	ROI
0	25,0	0,0	−1,00	0,0	−1,00	0,0	−1,00
10	27,5	10,0	−0,64	39,0	**0,42**	62,8	**1,28**
20	30,0	20,0	−0,33	63,8	**1,13**	79,6	**1,65**
30	32,5	30,0	−0,08	78,0	**1,40**	87,1	**1,68**
40	35,0	40,0	**0,14**	83,4	**1,38**	91,4	**1,61**
50	37,5	50,0	**0,33**	87,8	**1,34**	94,5	**1,52**
60	40,0	60,0	**0,50**	92,2	**1,31**	96,6	**1,42**
70	42,5	70,0	**0,65**	95,3	**1,24**	98,1	**1,31**
80	45,0	80,0	**0,78**	97,0	**1,16**	99,1	**1,20**
90	47,5	90,0	**0,89**	98,7	**1,08**	99,7	**1,10**
100	50,0	100,0	**1,00**	100,0	**1,00**	100,0	**1,00**

0 % and yield a maximum benefit of 100 %. Figure 4 shows the corresponding benefit curves in comparison to the test cost curve. The value-based prioritization approach yields a slightly higher benefit than the requirements-based prioritization approach; both clearly outperform the neutral prioritization approach.

The intersection points of the benefit curves and the cost curve mark the break-even points where the investments in testing start to pay off. The effects are best observed in analyzing the ROI achieved with the different prioritization strategies;

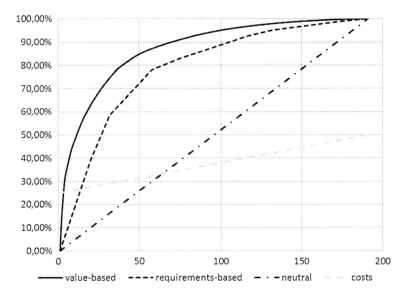

Fig. 4 Benefit of test case prioritization approaches in comparison to costs

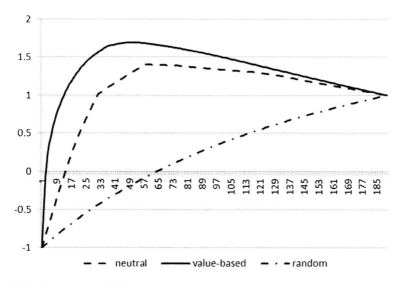

Fig. 5 ROI of test case prioritization approaches

see the columns *ROI* in Table 2 and Fig. 5. In Fig. 5 the break-even points are reached when the corresponding curves cross the zero-line.

Furthermore, it can be observed that the value-based prioritization of the test cases results in a much steeper increase of the ROI curve. As a result, the ROI of the value-based approach with weighted functional units will turn positive with only three tests (1.6 % of all test cases); these tests cover the standard scenarios of the three most important requirements. The requirements-based prioritization approach reaches the break-even point after 13 test cases (6.8 % of all test cases), all of them from the requirement with the highest weight. Although the test case for the standard usage scenario is included in the analyzed example, this is not guaranteed to be the case by this prioritization approach. In contrast, value-neutral prioritization treats all test cases equally important and will need 63 tests (33.2 % of all test cases) for a positive ROI.

Finally, it should be noted that the value-based approach will reach its peak ROI $max_{VBT\text{-}ROI} = 1.69$ after 45 tests, i.e., at only 23.7 % of all test cases. From that point onward the ROI starts to decrease again. The peak ROI for the requirements-based approach is $max_{RBT\text{-}ROI} = 1.40$, which is reached after 57 tests (30.0 % of all test cases). With the value-neutral or the random approach, the maximum ROI is only achieved when full testing is accomplished (100 %).

5 Related Work

In his agenda for a discipline of Value-Based Software Engineering [3], Boehm describes the challenge of value-based quality management as "the prioritization of desired quality factors with respect to stakeholders' value propositions".

Several approaches to extend quality management with value-based principle and practices have been proposed since then, e.g., by Li et al. [17].

These approaches address quality management in general. With respect to software testing, Ramler et al. [21] define the value-based objective of testing in producing information important to ensure the value objectives of the software system. In particular, testing should reveal defects or symptoms of risks that threaten the functionality of the software system or the associated quality characteristics. The information produced by testing helps mitigating these risks and, thus, testing helps realizing the expected stakeholder value propositions.

In support of these objectives, Ramler et al. [21] outlined a framework for value-based test management. In addition, Li et al. (see [17] and [18]) introduced a method for the prioritization in software testing based on business importance, quality risk and testing cost. Both, the proposed framework as well as Li's method, deal with the organizational level of testing. In contrast, the work of Zhang (see [26] and [27]) on value-based testing is concerned with applying artificial intelligence techniques (e.g., genetic algorithms) for test data generation. Value-based aspects are introduced by outlining a test data generation process that explicitly incorporates stakeholder value propositions and information about critical components and by considering these criteria in defining fitness functions. Furthermore, value-based principles have also been included by Farago [8] in developing key performance indicators (KPIs) from coverage metrics for model-based testing of nondeterministic systems.

Ramler et al. [21] also identified a number of practices that can be used to support and endorse the value contribution of testing, e.g., requirements-based testing, risk-based testing, iterative development and stakeholder involvement. The related works in these areas, such as by Bach [2], Srivastva et al. [24] and Srikanth and Williams [23], are often not linked to the concept of value-based testing.

Coverage measurement is a key practice in software testing. However, the primary focus of the work in this area is on white-box, code-based coverage measures. Related work regarding coverage measurement in combination with requirements-based testing contains: Gittens et al. [11] report on a prioritized coverage approach for setting priorities in testing, which is nevertheless still rooted in code-level coverage analysis. Krishnamoorthi and Mary [14] proposed a model for system level test case prioritization from software requirement specifications. The conceptual model is similar to our approach and considers six factors including customer priority and changes in requirements. Yet, business value and risks are only indirectly integrated.

Coverage measurement in our work follows the principles and practices of value-based software testing. It bridges the gap between incorporating high-level stakeholder value proposition and low-level test design measures. Moreover, the approach has been implemented in an industry-strength tool suite based on more than 15 years of experience in testing large software applications in domains such as banking, insurance, healthcare, the public sector, and industry. This foundation allowed us to focus specifically on business software and ERP systems, a context that is not well addressed by the related work.

6 Summary and Conclusions

Today, most of the available methods, techniques and tools in software testing as well as in quality assurance in general are still value-neutral and do not take the achievable business value of the tested software system into account. This shortcoming is particularly evident in testing business software and ERP systems, where the requirements and functional areas can be linked with their potential business value. Therefore, in this paper we introduced an approach for value-based coverage measurement that can be used to align the testing effort with the achievable benefit of testing, i.e., the detection and elimination of defects that threaten the business value associated with the tested system's requirements.

The proposed approach is based on the foundation of requirements-driven testing as well as combinatorial test techniques (e.g., Linear Expansion) that systematically produce test cases for important usage scenarios. In that way our approach extends conventional requirements-based approaches that derive the values only from the corresponding requirements. In contrast, we combine the external view and the internal view of value-based testing by connecting the business value of the tested requirements with the value of the individual test cases representing different usage scenarios. Weight factors are used to represent the impact of requirements, attributes and input data in computing the corresponding coverage values.

The proposed coverage measurement approach has been implemented as part of the *TOSCA Testsuite*^{TM}, making it applicable for testing large real-world systems. We evaluated the implemented approach in the context of a test project for an ERP system containing about 65 requirements and 1,600 test cases. The results confirmed that the value-based approach for coverage measurement is suitable to capture the distribution of the business value and risks across the test cases of the requirements. We found that the importance varies significantly across the tests for the various usage scenarios of a specific requirement. While the average share of a test case is 5.47 %, the average value of the test for the standard scenario calculated from the covered attributes and data values is 40.90 %. Consequently, differentiating test cases only on basis of the requirements cannot be considered sufficient.

When the value-based coverage measure has been applied for test case prioritization, it produced a steeply increasing benefit curve that reaches the break-even point already after a few (i.e., three) tests. Thus, we were able to demonstrate the advantage of the value-based prioritization approach by calculating the ROI of prioritized testing and comparing it to the results from, first, a requirements-based approach that only considers the value associated to the requirements and, second, a value-neutral prioritization approach resembling a random prioritization strategy. The value-based approach clearly outperforms a value-neutral approach and it also supersedes the conventional requirements-based approach. Furthermore, a higher ROI can be achieved by applying the value-based approach, especially without complete testing.

Refining the approach for value-based coverage measurement described in this paper and completing the implementation as part of the *TOSCA Testsuite*™ is an ongoing activity that inspires future work. Among these is the improved support for selective development of test portfolios. In many projects, test managers face hard decisions about what parts of a system to test and at what extent before even investing in test design and development. At that stage, no actual tests exist for prioritization and the available information about requirements and risks may still be incomplete. An approach for determining the coverage contribution can provide guidance in the early stages of testing by giving estimates of the number of required tests and their potential value contribution.

References

1. Al-Mashari, M., Al-Mudimigh, A., Zairi, M.: Enterprise resource planning: a taxonomy of critical factors. Eur. J. Oper. Res. **146**(2), 352–364 (2003)
2. Bach, J.: Risk and requirements-based testing. IEEE Comput. **32**(6), 113–114 (1999)
3. Boehm, B.: Value-based software engineering: overview and agenda. In: Biffl, S., et al. (eds.) Value-Based Software Engineering, pp. 3–14. Springer, Berlin (2006)
4. Boehm, B., Basili, V.R.: Software defect reduction top 10 list. Computer **34**(1), 135–137 (2001)
5. Brooks, P.A., Memon, A.M.: Automated GUI testing guided by usage profiles. In: Proceedings of the Twenty-Second IEEE/ACM International Conference on Automated Software Engineering. ASE'07, pp. 333–342. ACM, New York (2007)
6. Chen, C.C., Law, C., Yang, S.C.: Managing ERP implementation failure: a project management perspective. IEEE Trans. Eng. Manage. **56**(1), 157–170 (2009)
7. Daneva, M.: ERP requirements engineering practice: lessons learned. Softw. IEEE **21**(2), 26–33 (2004)
8. Farago, D.: Nondeterministic coverage metrics as key performance indicator for model- and value-based testing. 31. Treffen der GI-Fachgruppe Test, Analyse and Verifikation von Software (TAV) (2011)
9. Felderer, M., et al.: Integrating manual and automatic risk assessment for risk-based testing. In: Software Quality. Process Automation in Software Development. Software Quality Days 2012, pp. 159–180. Vienna (2012)
10. Gerrard, P.: Test methods and tools for ERP implementations. In: IEEE, pp. 40–46 (2007)
11. Gittens, M., Romanufa, K., Godwin, D., Racicot, J.: All code coverage is not created equal: a case study in prioritized code coverage. In: Proceedings of the 2006 Conference of the Center for Advanced Studies on Collaborative Research (CASCON '06) (2006)
12. Holland, C.R., Light, B.: A critical success factors model for ERP implementation. Softw. IEEE **16**(3), 30–36 (1999)
13. Huang, L., Boehm, B.: How much software quality investment is enough: a value-based approach. IEEE Softw. **23**(5), 88–95 (2006)
14. Krishnamoorthi, R., Mary, S.A.: Factor oriented requirement coverage based system test case prioritization of new and regression test cases. Inf. Softw. Technol. **51**(4), 799–808 (2009)

15. Kumar, M., Suresh, A.V., Prashanth, P.: Analyzing the quality issues in ERP implementation: a case study. In: Proceedings of the Second International Conference on Emerging Trends in Engineering and Technology, ICETET 2009, pp. 759–764 (2009)
16. Lehtola, L., Kauppinen, M., Kujala, S.: Linking the business view to requirements engineering: long-term product planning by roadmapping. In Proceedings of the 13th IEEE International Conference on Requirements Engineering. RE'05, pp. 439–446. IEEE Computer Society, Washington, DC (2005)
17. Li, Q., Li, M., Yang, Y., Wang, Q., Tan, T., Boehm, B., Hu, C.: Bridge the gap between software test process and business value: a case study. Proceedings of the International Conference on Software Process: Trustworthy Software Development Processes (ICSP '09) (2009)
18. Li, Q., Yang, Y., Li, M., Wang, Q., Boehm, B., Hu, C.: Improving software testing process: feature prioritization to make winners of success-critical stakeholders. J. Softw. Maint. Evol. Res. Pract. (2010). doi: 10.1002/smr.512
19. Pandian, C.P.: Applied Software Risk Management: A Guide for Software Project Managers. Auerbach Publications, Boston (2006)
20. Petschenik, N. H.: Practical priorities in system testing. IEEE Softw. 2(5), 18–23 1985
21. Ramler, R., Biffl, S. Grünbacher, P.: Value-based management of software testing. In: Biffl, S., et al. (eds.) Value-Based Software Engineering, pp. 225–244. Springer, Berlin (2006)
22. Ramler, R., Kopetzky, T., Platz, W.: Combinatorial test design in the TOSCA testsuite: lessons learned and practical implications. In: Proceedings of the 2012 Workshop on Combinatorial Testing, ICST 2012 (2012)
23. Srikanth, H., Williams, L.: On the economics of requirements-based test case prioritization. In: Proceedings of the Seventh International Workshop on Economics-Driven Software Engineering Research (EDSER '05) (2005)
24. Srivastva, P.R., Kumar, K., Raghurama, G.: Test case prioritization based on requirements and risk factors. SIGSOFT Softw. Eng. Notes 33(4), Article 7 (2008)
25. Urem, F., Mikulic, Z.: Developing operational profile for ERP software module reliability prediction. In: 2010 Proceedings of the 33rd International Convention MIPRO, pp. 409–413 (2010)
26. Zhang, D.: Machine learning in value-based software test data generation. In: Proceedings of the 18th IEEE International Conference on Tools with Artificial Intelligence (ICTAI '06) (2006)
27. Zhang, D.A.: Value-based framework for software evolutionary testing. Int J Softw Sci Comput Intell 3(2), 62–82 (2011)

A Quality Analysis Procedure for Request Data of ERP Systems

Michael Felderer, Emir Tanriverdi, Sarah Löw and Ruth Breu

Abstract Request data is a valuable source for the release planning and request management of Enterprise Resource Planning systems. As a prerequisite the request data has to be analyzed to check its quality and to identify correlations. In this paper we propose a quality analysis approach for ERP request data and apply it in an industrial case study.

1 Introduction

Managing the requests of various stakeholders, such as customers, sales partners or developers, is important for the continuous adaptation, maintenance, and development of modern Enterprise Resource Planning (ERP) systems. Therefore ERP vendors integrate their products with *request management systems*, which process various types of external and internal *requests*. Over time a huge amount of request data like bugs, extension wishes, planned features or questions is gathered that is valuable for defining requirements of future releases, and for improving the request management process. As a prerequisite the request data has to be analyzed to check the quality of the request data and to identify correlations.

M. Felderer (✉) · E. Tanriverdi · S. Löw · R. Breu
University of Innsbruck, Innsbruck, Austria
e-mail: michael.felderer@uibk.ac.at

E. Tanriverdi
e-mail: emir.tanriverdi@uibk.ac.at

S. Löw
e-mail: sarah.loew@uibk.ac.at

R. Breu
e-mail: ruth.beu@uibk.ac.at

Such a quality analysis of ERP request data has to be performed in a systematic way to guarantee the representativeness and validity of its results. It is essential to build the quality analysis on a quality model for request data defining quality criteria and related metrics. Additionally, guidelines are needed on how to explore the request data and on how to interpret the result.

In this paper we present a quality analysis procedure for request data of ERP systems. The procedure consists of the steps (1) preparation, (2) quality model definition, (3) implementation, (4) measurement, (5) exploration, (6) validation, and (7) definition of measures. The procedure is then systematically applied to analyze the quality of request data of an ERP system for small and medium-sized businesses. The request data is gathered over several years and enables statements about the underlying support request process and the definition of possible measures to adapt the process.

Request data analysis is especially important for ERP systems where tailoring and customization activities recur quite frequently [1] leading to numerous requests by various stakeholders like customers, sales partners, developers, project managers, process managers or testers. In this respect, the quality of the support request management process is essential for the acceptance and success of the overall ERP system. Thus, lots of request data are collected and can be used to improve the request management process. Additionally, ERP systems have to be adapted steadily. As requests are a valuable source to manage this evolution, release quality is important in this respect. We contribute to this problem by defining and applying a request data quality procedure applicable to ERP systems with several implementations. This problem has not been addressed before [2, 3] but is highly relevant for practice to control and optimize the product release and support request management. We provide concrete guidelines and an industrial case study how to perform such a request data quality analysis and how to interpret its results.

This paper is structured as follows. In Sect. 2 we present our quality analysis procedure. In Sect. 3, we then show how the quality analysis procedure is applied in an industrial context to analyze the request data of an ERP system for small and medium-sized businesses. Finally, in Sect. 4 we conclude and present future work.

2 Quality Analysis Procedure

ERP systems support companies and public organizations performing and monitoring business activities. During the development and adaptation of the ERP system lots of request data is gathered to be analyzed, mainly by the ERP System vendor. In this section we present the steps of our quality analysis procedure for request data. The procedure is based on best practices of the standards ISO/IEC 14598 (Information Technology-Software Product Evaluation) [4] and ISO/IEC 15939 (Systems and Software Engineering—Measurement Process) [5]. The quality analysis procedure is shown in Fig. 1. The process consists of the steps (1) *preparation*, (2) *quality model definition*, (3) *implementation*, (4) *measurement*, (5) *exploration*, (6) *validation*, and (7) *definition of measures*. The results of the validation may lead to changes in the analysis procedure, e.g., if abnormal values are identified the implementation or measurement may be adapted. In Fig. 1 this feedback cycle is denoted by an edge from step (6) to step (1). In the following paragraphs we explain the steps (1) to (7) in more detail.

(1) **Preparation.** In this phase the goals and the data sources of the quality analysis are defined. The goal may address specific aspects of the product release and support request management like the average processing time of a request. Related to the goal and as a basis for the data selection the types of requests relevant for the analysis, e.g., bugs, extension wishes, or questions for support have to be fixed. The underlying data can be extended to be collected from several sources but also restricted to criteria like a specific time period or specific types of requests. The goals may be refined to questions supporting the definition of quality criteria and data sources following the Goal Question Metric approach [6].

(2) **Quality Model Definition.** In this phase the relevant quality criteria are defined and operationalized by metrics. Additionally, evaluation criteria are defined for the interpretation of the metrics. As there exists no standardized quality model for requests, quality criteria and metrics can be defined from scratch or based on suitable standards like IEEE 830-1998 (Recommended Practice for Software Requirements Specification) [7] defining quality criteria for requirements or ISO/IEC 9126 (Software Engineering—Product Quality) [8] defining software product quality criteria.

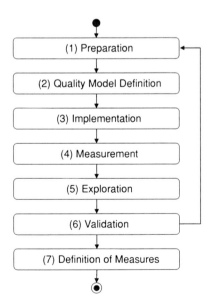

Fig. 1 Quality analysis procedure

(3) **Implementation.** In this phase the tool chain for performing the analysis is fixed. This comprises tools for the extraction, processing and reporting of data. This process may include the implementation of adapters necessary to integrate several tools and data sources as well as queries to compute the relevant metrics based on the data sources.
(4) **Measurement.** In this phase the actual measurement of metrics is performed. As a result the raw values like size measures are provided for further processing.
(5) **Exploration.** In this phase various analysis methods are applied to identify quality relevant relationships in the data. As a first step, the graphical representation of data is often very helpful as it provides a good overview, e.g., data clusters or trends can be identified. As a second step, various analysis methods like distribution, extreme value, correlation, time series or cluster analysis are applied to identify properties in the data which are interpreted with respect to the identified goals.
(6) **Validation.** In this phase the results of the previous phases are validated. The validation addresses the trustworthiness of the results and to what extent the results are biased by the investigators subjective point of view. For this purpose, classification schemes for various aspects of validity are useful. Yin [9] distinguishes between

- *construct validity* which reflects to what extent the studied operational measures represent what is investigated,
- *internal validity* which is of concern when causal relations are examined where one factor affects another factor and the influence of additional factors is not considered,
- *external validity* which is concerned with to what extent it is possible to generalize the findings, and
- *reliability* which is concerned with to what extent the data and the analysis are dependent on the specific analyst.

Several case studies have shown that this classification is suitable for evaluations in IT [10]. We also apply the classification of Yin, i.e., we consider construct validity, internal validity, external validity and reliability, to validate the results of the request quality analysis in our approach.

(7) **Definition of Measures.** The validated results may lead to measures improving the product release management, the request management or the quality analysis procedure itself.

3 Industrial Case Study

In this section we apply the request quality analysis procedure defined in the previous section to an industrial case study. In this case study we analyze the support system data of an ERP system for medium-sized businesses. We first present the industrial context of the case study and then its application based on the quality analysis procedure described in the previous section.

3.1 Industrial Context

In the industrial case study we analyze the quality of request in the support system of an ERP system for small and medium-sized enterprises. The ERP system provides comprehensive functionality in areas as purchase, sales, warehouse logistics, mobile work, accounting, production, management control, CRM, project management, and document management. The ERP system is web-based and implemented in Java. It has a software logistics system to deliver updates to various systems running for specific customers and purposes like testing or production. As the ERP producer has a sales network (so called partners) which adapt the ERP system to the needs of their customers or to solutions for specific branches of industry. Therefore the support system of the overall ERP system has to manage various types of requests from customers, partners, developers, testers and product managers.

The request management system called "Support System" has been used by more than 1,000 users and contains more than 10,000 requests enabling the derivation of representative quality measures and correlations in the request data of the investigated ERP system. The request management system has been implemented based on the ERP system itself. It is therefore accessible via a web interface with the same look and feel as the other applications (e.g., for managing sales orders) and its request data is stored in a database. The screenshot in Fig. 2 shows the application for managing requests called "Support Requests" and the main attributes for requests like number, request editor, end customer, description, priority, installation and other fields like source of origin, urgency or strategic relevance. Additionally, the ERP system has a cockpit application to query requests and to process sets of requests.

3.2 Application of Quality Analysis Procedure

In this section we describe the application of the quality analysis procedure for request data following the steps defined in Sect. 2, i.e., (1) Preparation, (2) Quality

Fig. 2 Support request application of the ERP system

Model Definition, (3) Implementation, (4) Measurement, (5) Exploration, (6) Validation, and (7) Definition of Measures.

(1) **Preparation**

The request management system of the ERP system is quite complex as it is online since 2003 and has many stakeholders. The main goals of the quality analysis are to get an overview of the size and complexity of the request management system, to control the processing time of requests, to restructure the request types managed in the system, and to investigate the suitability of the request management system to derive features for development. Over the years and due to several restructurings in the development organization, many requests of various types are managed in the support system. These requests are the natural data source for the quality analysis. Before starting the evaluation we selected all relevant types of requests together with developers, the quality manager and the product manager. We found that requests of meta-type *Problem Report* (PR), i.e., requests concerning detected bugs or unwanted behavior, and *Enhancement Request* (ER), i.e., requests by employees, partners or customers that are related to desired changes or extensions, are relevant to reach our goals of investigation. A problem report is implemented by several concrete request types abbreviated by BUG or SUP describing observed bugs or requests for support. An enhancement request is implemented by several concrete request types abbreviated by DEV or WSE reflecting planned development activities and external wishes.

Further types of requests have not been considered for the analysis because they are so manifold that no conclusions can be drawn. For instance, requests concerning on-going development are as well in this category as requests about documentation changes or simple requests for arranging a meeting between customers and employees. Additionally, we considered the states of the observed requests. The lifecycle of a support request is defined by a state machine and contains 12 different states, with ENTERED as the initial state and CLOSED as the final state.

The support request data from 01/2003 to 07/2011 is available in an XML dump of the online request database and forms the basis for further quality analyses. To sum up, the data source for the quality analyses are all problem reports and enhancement requests from January 2003 to July 2011.

(2) **Quality Model Definition**

Our quality model consists of quality criteria for requests and assigned metrics to measure them. We use the standard IEEE 830-1998 (Recommended Practice for Software Requirements Specification) [7] for requirements specification as a starting point to define quality criteria. Table 1 shows the quality criteria, i.e., completeness, comprehensibility, consistency, stability, traceability, and verifiability we selected from IEEE 830-1998 and the assigned metrics to define request quality.

The selection has been done according to our experience and has been agreed with the stakeholders. For each criterion we defined respective metrics. The metrics are defined for single requests but can be aggregated by functions like sum, average, maximum or minimum to statements about the overall request database. Additionally, we determine the overall number of requests, the distribution of each

Table 1 Selected request quality criteria and metrics

Quality criterion	Description	Metrics
Completeness	All necessary attributes of request are filled	Completeness (COMP) is measured by the ratio number of the number filled attributes (NFA) and all attributes (NA).
Comprehensibility	A request is phrased in a way that is understood by all involved stakeholders	Comprehensibility is measured by the number and the understandability of the texts describing the request. A basic metrics is the number of texts per request.
Consistency	A request is stated without contradictions	Consistency is measured by the number of violations of consistency checks identifying inconsistencies in the data.
Stability	The attributes of a request are not changed frequently	Stability can be measured by the number of changes of attributes of a request. As the priority is a key attribute of a request, the stability is basically measured as the number of priority changes.
Traceability	A request is linked to artifacts representing its cause and effect	Traceability can be measured by the number of references to development requests and tests.
Verifiability	For each request, there is a defined procedure to decide whether it is implemented or not	Verifiability can be measured by the number of texts between different stakeholders and the number of assigned tests.

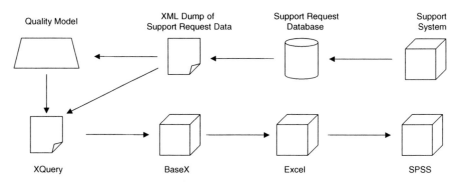

Fig. 3 Tool chain for quality analysis

metrics per creation year of the assigned request, which gives us the possibility to investigate the quality of requests over time, and the processing time of closed requests. Finally, evaluation criteria have to be defined to interpret the metrics with respect to the goals. In this case study we focus on the goals (i) overview of the size which is measured by the distribution of the number of requests, and (ii) control of the processing time of requests which is evaluated by correlating completeness and other metrics of closed requests to their processing time. The investigation of further goals is considered as future work.

(3) **Implementation**

After definition of the quality metrics, the tools and techniques for determining them have to be fixed and implemented. Figure 3 shows the tool chain for analyzing the request data.

The online Support System stores its data in a relational database management system (Support Request Database). Due to performance, integrity, security and data privacy, the quality analysis was not performed directly on the database, but on an XML dump containing all anonymized support requests from January 2003 to July 2011 (XML Dump of Support Request Data).

Based on the XML dump of the support request data and the Quality Model defined in the previous step, queries with XQuery [11] are defined to compute quality metrics and to prepare the data for further statistical analysis. XQuery uses the XPath [12] expression syntax to address specific parts of an XML document. It supplements this with a SQL-like FLWOR (For, Let, Where, Order By, Return) expression to query data and to perform joins. For instance, the XQuery expression in Listing 1 computes the maximum completeness of problem reports per year.

```
for $year in $creationYears
let $outputYear := concat(''&#10;'',$year, ''&#10;'')
return let $completeness :=
max (
for $x in $supportRequest
```

```
  where count($x/*:References) != 0 and local:problem($x)
and
        local:creationYear($x) = $year
  return sum(
    for $y in $x//*
    where string-length($y) != 0 (: NFA :)
    return 1)
    div
    count($x//*) (: NA :)
  )
  return ($outputYear, $completeness) (:Computation:)
```

Listing 1. XQuery Statement for Maximum Completeness in a Year

To evaluate the request data the following types of queries were implemented:

- number of problem reports (PR) and enhancement requests (ER)
- distribution of the number of PR and ER per year and state
- distribution of the number of closed problem reports (PR CLOSED) and closed enhancement requests ER CLOSED)
- number of all attributes (NA) and number of all filled attributes (NFA) of PR and ER
- processing time (PT) of closed PR and ER.

Additionally, we calculated the aggregation functions minimum, maximum and average for all query results to gain a statistical overview.

The queries performed on the XML dump are processed with BaseX [13], an open source, light-weight, high-performance and scalable XML database engine and XPath/XQuery processor. The results are post-processed, analyzed as well as visualized in tables and diagrams in the spreadsheet application Excel [14]. Finally, a statistical analysis of the data with SPSS [15] is performed.

(4) **Measurement**

In this step the actual measurement of the implemented metrics is performed. Representative for all metrics, we show the actual results for distribution of the number of problem reports and enhancement requests per year (Table 2), the number of closed problem reports and enhancement requests per year (Table 3) as well as the aggregated values of the processing time of closed problem reports (Table 4) and enhancement requests (Table 5).

Table 2 shows the distribution of problem reports (PR) and enhancement requests (ER) per year.

Table 2 Distribution of problem reports (PR) and enhancement requests (ER) per year

	2003	2004	2005	2006	2007	2008	2009	2010	2011	Sum
PR	308	494	1210	771	794	824	1075	934	522	6932
ER	94	157	326	310	388	436	532	407	230	2880

Table 3 Number of closed problem reports (PR CLOSED) and enhancement requests (ER CLOSED) per year

	2003	2004	2005	2006	2007	2008	2009	2010	2011	Sum
PR CLOSED	308	494	1139	580	552	366	389	300	105	4233
ER CLOSED	94	157	314	156	86	83	66	42	15	1013

Table 4 Aggregated values (average, maximum, minimum) for processing time (PT) of completed problem reports (PR)

PR	2003	2004	2005	2006	2007	2008	2009	2010	2011
AVG	50	86	101	143	134	86	73	99	42
MAX	349	364	364	364	364	357	363	364	185
MIN	0.085	0.76	0.017	0.019	0.061	0.056	0.018	0.017	0.051

Table 5 Aggregated values (average, maximum, minimum) for processing time (PT) of completed enhancement requests (ER)

ER	2003	2004	2005	2006	2007	2008	2009	2010	2011
AVG	60	97	104	83	112	62	96	94	29
MAX	357	363	303	360	352	337	319	342	134
MIN	0.05	0.03	0.006	0.003	0.004	0.038	0.011	0.008	0.049

According to Table 2, the overall number of problem reports is 6,932 and the overall number of enhancement requests is 2,880.

Table 3 shows the number of closed problem reports and enhancement requests per year. The overall number of problem reports in state CLOSED is 4,233, and the number of enhancement requests in state CLOSED is 1,013.

Tables 4 and 5 shows aggregated values, i.e., the average (AVG), maximum (MAX), and minimum (MIN) for the processing time of problem reports and enhancement requests.

The metrics gathered in this phase contribute to the goals. PR, ER, PR CLOSED and ER CLOSED provides a rough overview of the size of the system and contributes to goal (i), PT is the basis to reach goal (ii). Additional information to fulfill the goals is provided by exploring the data in the next phase.

(5) **Exploration**

In this step the static data measured in the previous step is explored to identify new relationships. The exploration depends on the experience of the investigator. We show two types of analysis, i.e., *time series analysis* and *correlations analysis* based on the static values measured before.

A time series is a sequence of data points measured typically at successive time instants spaced at uniform time intervals. Time series analysis [16] comprises methods for analyzing time series data in order to extract meaningful statistics and other characteristics of the data. Time series forecasting is the use of a model to predict future values based on previously observed values. In our context, we applied a specific time series analysis technique, namely regression analysis to model and predict the cumulated number of closed problem reports (CUM PR CLOSED) and enhancement requests (CUM ER CLOSED) over time. Figure 4 shows bars representing the temporal development of CUM PR CLOSED and CUM ER CLOSED and logarithmic regression functions predicting the cumulated sums.

The logarithmic approximation function suggests that the overall number of closed problem reports and enhancement requests grows logarithmically, i.e., slow. A reason for this behavior can be the growing maturity of the overall system which requires fewer requests to be closed relative to the growing functionality of the system. Thus, one can conclude that the size of the closed request data grows logarithmically which provides additional information contributing to goal (i).

Correlation refers to any of a broad class of statistical relationships involving dependence. Correlations are useful because they can indicate a predictive relationship that can be exploited in practice. We investigate the correlation between the completeness of (closed) problem reports (COMP PR) or the completeness of (closed) enhancement requests (COMP ER) and the processing time (PT) as one may suggest that a high completeness of attributes may correspond to a shorter processing time if all attributes of a request are used to pre-classify a request to reduce its processing time, i.e., there is a negative correlation between COMP and PT. We use Pearson's product-moment correlation coefficient [15] which fits for interval scaled data to show whether there is a correlation between COMP PR and PT as well as between COMP ER and PT. For COMP PR and PT, the Pearson correlation coefficient is -0.042 and for COMP ER and PT it is 0.103. This shows that there is hardly any negative correlation between completeness and processing time for PR. For ER there is even a weak positive correlation. Before computing the Pearson correlation coefficient, we removed anomalies in the data, i.e., requests with missing completeness or processing time values.

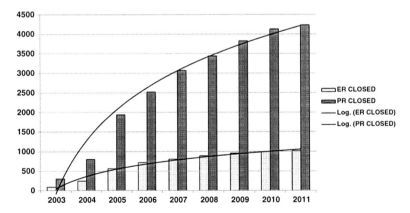

Fig. 4 Time series analysis for cumulated number of closed enhancement requests (CUM ER CLOSED) and problem reports (CUM PR CLOSED)

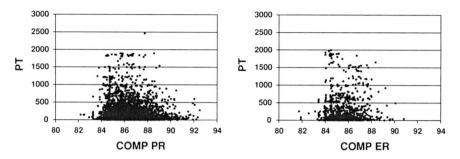

Fig. 5 Scatter plot of completeness and processing time

The missing negative correlation between the completeness of problem reports and enhancement requests is also reflected by the scatter plot in Fig. 5 where there is no significant trend line from top left to bottom right. The missing correlation may have several reasons. First, it may be the case that the requests have too many attributes with the consequence that processing them may be confusing. Second, it may be the case that there is no specific internal workflow based on the attribute values, e.g., by allocating it to a specific person automatically. Finally, it may be the case that the overall processing time of a request does not depend on its completeness as long as the mandatory attribute values are available.

The information that there is no correlation between completeness and processing time provides additional information contributing to goal (ii). As future work, the correlation between the processing time and other attributes like the priority or quality criteria like comprehensiveness may be investigated.

(6) **Validation**

As the performed quality analysis applies empirical methods, the validity of the results has to be guaranteed. We consider construct validity, internal validity, external validity, and reliability.

Construct validity. As many types of requests are defined in the support system, it may be the case that some requests have been classified in the wrong way which may influence the computed metrics. The involved stakeholders applied plausibility checks to minimize such effects as much as possible. For performing the correlation analysis, the Pearson correlation coefficient has been computed. Other correlations coefficients like the Spearman rank correlation coefficient [15] may lead to slightly different results. But in our respect, the qualitative results are similar, i.e., there is hardly any Spearman correlation between COMP PR and PT as the Spearman rank correlation coefficient is 0.013, and there is a weak positive correlation between COMP ER and PT as the Spearman rank correlation coefficient is 0.152.

Internal validity. We assumed a logarithmic growth of the cumulated number of closed problem reports and enhancement requests over time. On the one hand, the logarithmic growth is just an approximation and on the other hand unconsidered factors like new functionalities, a restructuring of the request management system or changes in the development organization can affect the logarithmic growth in future. The missing correlation between completeness and processing time may have been biased by modifications of the request management system, e.g., automatic state changes of requests. But according to the feedback of the involved stakeholders such modifications have not been applied.

External validity. The findings of the quality analysis are specific for the investigated data and it was not the aim of the procedure to generalize them to other types of data or organizations. Only the quality analysis procedure itself is generalizable to other cases.

Reliability. The performed quality analysis procedure is clearly defined and all results are documented. So the procedure is repeatable and can be performed by other investigators as well. The analysis was performed iteratively. First, the data was not classified into problem report and enhancement request data, there was no distribution over years, and the closed requests were not cumulated. The relevance of these types of analysis was discussed together with all stakeholders. So if other persons would be involved in the analysis perhaps other properties would be analyzed. But the results itself are reproducible.

(7) **Definition of Measures**

After the analysis has been performed concrete measures are derived. Already in the preparation phase we noticed that there are types of requests which do not have a clear meaning. Therefore the number of different request types was reduced and their meaning was defined more precisely. Additionally, we observed some anomalies which were reviewed and adapted manually. As we did not observe a correlation between the completeness of requests and their processing time, we discussed possible reasons for that with the stakeholders. As a result we concluded that the processing time does not depend on the completeness of requests. Therefore we plan additional correlation analyses to investigate other possible influence factors on the processing time. For instance, we will investigate the relationship between the priority of a request and its processing time.

4 Conclusion and Future Work

In this paper we defined a quality analysis procedure for ERP request data. The procedure consists of the steps (1) preparation, (2) quality model definition, (3) implementation, (4) measurement, (5) exploration, (6) validation, and (7) definition of measures. In an industrial case study we applied the procedure for analyzing the quality of the requests of an ERP system for small and medium-sized enterprises. Based on static quality metrics extracted with XQuery from an XML dump of the request data, we performed a regression and correlation analysis to analyze the size of the request database and the processing time of requests. We identified a logarithmic approximation function for the cumulated number of request and could not find a correlation between completeness and processing time of requests. Finally, we defined measures to interpret the results.

The main contribution of the paper is the quality analysis procedure for request data of ERP systems. The performed case study presents only initial results which will be refined in future case studies. Therein, we will for instance analyze the correlation between priority and processing time. We will also consider more complex quality metrics, e.g., advanced comprehensibility metrics will be defined based on language processing techniques [17], and further goals like improvement of the release planning based on request data. Additionally, we plan to refine the procedure by providing more guidelines how to apply our approach for the quality analysis of the request data of arbitrary ERP systems. Finally, we plan further case studies to compare how the procedure scales for different ERP systems.

Acknowledgments This work was partially funded by the research project "QE LaB—Living Models for Open Systems" (FFG 822740).

References

1. Nöbauer, M., Seyff, N., Dhungana, D., Stoiber, R.: Managing variability of ERP ecosystems: research issues and solution ideas from microsoft dynamics AX. In: Sixth International Workshop on Variability Modeling of Software-Intensive Systems, ACM (2012)
2. Haddara, M., Zach, O.: ERP systems in SMEs: a literature review. In: 44th Hawaii International Conference on System Sciences (HICSS 2011), IEEE (2011)
3. Moon, Y.B.: Enterprise resource planning (ERP): a review of the literature. Int. J. Manage. Enterp. Dev. **4**(3), 235–264 (2007)
4. ISO/IEC: ISO/IEC 14598: Information Technology—Software Product Evaluation (1999)
5. ISO/IEC: ISO/IEC 15939:2007. Systems and Software Engineering—Measurement Process. International Organization for Standardization (2007)
6. Basili, V.R., Rombach, H.D.: The TAME project: towards improvement-oriented software environments. IEEE Trans. Softw. Eng. **14**(6), 758–773 (1988)
7. IEEE: IEEE Standard 830-1998(1998). IEEE Recommended Practice for Software Requirements Specification (1998)
8. ISO/IEC: ISO/IEC 9126-1:2001 Software Engineering—Product Quality—Part 1: Quality Model. International Standardization Organization (2001)
9. Yin, R.K.: Applications of Case Study Research. Sage publications, Thousand Oaks (2011)
10. Runeson, P., Alexandersson, M., Nyholm, O.: Detection of duplicate defect reports using natural language processing. In: 29th International Conference on Software Engineering (ICSE 2007), IEEE (2007)
11. Simeon, J., Chamberlin, D., Florescu, D., Boag, S., Fernandez, M. F., Robie, J.: XQuery 1.0: An XML query language—W3C bibliography (2007)
12. Berglund, A., Boag, S., Chamberlin, D., Fernandez, M. F., Kay, M., Robie, J., Simeon, J.: XML path language (XPath) 2.0. W3C working draft 15 (2002)
13. Steinbeis: BaseX. The XML database. http://basex.org/. Accessed 30 April 2012
14. Microsoft: Excel 2010. http://office.microsoft.com/en-us/excel/. Accessed 17 Sept 2012
15. Argyrous, G.: Statistics for Research: With a Guide to SPSS, Sage publications, London (2011)

16. Hamilton, J.D.: Time Series Analysis. Cambridge University Press, Cambridge (1994)
17. Jurafsky, D., Martin, J.H., Kehler, A., Vander Linden, K., Ward, N.: Speech and Language Processing: An Introduction to Natural Language Processing, Computational Linguistics, and Speech Recognition, Prentice Hall New Jersey (2000)

Part X
Implementation of Innovative Business Concepts

How to Consider Supply Uncertainty of Renewable Resources in the Basic Data Structures of ERP-Systems

Stefan Friedemann and Matthias Schumann

Abstract Production planning in companies often assumes that resource flows are constant. This idealized assumption does not reflect the problem of uncertain procurements. Especially renewable resources are underlying natural influences which result in uncertainties of the quality and quantity of the resource as well as an uncertain time of harvest and delivery. In this paper we analyze how procurement uncertainties of renewable resources can be taken into account in the basic data structures of ERP-systems, namely bill of materials (BOM), work schedules and time schedules. Therefore we describe certain variations methods as general possibilities to handle uncertainty. As a result it can be stated that not every type of BOM can consider uncertainties well enough. The work and time schedules cannot represent every kind of variation which is needed. Overall, a combination of both structures is a good possibility to gain a more flexible and thus a more certain planning.

1 Introduction

There are many uncertainties in business planning: sales numbers on the client side cannot be predicted safely, production may be delayed or come to a standstill and resources may be hard to obtain due to unforeseeable events. The area of marketing and sales is well researched both with respect to practical and scientific aspects. There are many adequate forecasting methods and explanatory models.

S. Friedemann (✉) · M. Schumann
University of Göttingen, Göttingen, Germany
e-mail: stefan.friedemann@wiwi.uni-goettingen.de

M. Schumann
e-mail: matthias.schumann@wiwi.uni-goettingen.de

The same holds true for intra-corporate uncertainties, where concepts such as decentralized control centers enable adequate handling of problems.

With regard to procurement, however, one still assumes constant streams of resources, which is an idealized assumption. Examples, such as the impact of the earthquake and tsunami in Japan or the flooding in Thailand on the automobile and electronic industries, show that this is already the case with conventional commodities. This problem increases within the industrial use of renewable resources. Thus, it is not possible to accurately predict when goods will be ready for harvest or variations may occur regarding the quality and quantity, e.g. through humidity or droughts [1]. At the same time, the German Federal Government demands an increase of renewable resources in the industry in its national resource efficiency program [2]. Adequate planning is needed with regard to possible uncertainties when using these renewable resources and it is therefore necessary to model them in an easy and flexible way in ERP-systems. This problem will be discussed in the following by analyzing how these uncertainties in procurement can be taken into consideration in the basic data structure of the production planning, on which all further production steps are based on. Flexibility in this basic data and planning level can ensure that all functions and processes that build upon it will gain more flexibility, too. Corporations consider this flexibility in production and procurement to be very important [3]. The process of planning will be demonstrated in an exemplary use case of a company which uses renewable resources for the production of natural fiber reinforced plastics.

The specificity about renewable resources and their uncertainties will be described in Chap. 2. Chapter 3 deals with general IT-independent methods, which enable a consideration of the uncertainties in the planning process. In Chap. 4 is shown how procurement uncertainties can be considered in production planning and controlling systems (PPC). The article closes with a conclusion and an outlook on further possible areas of research.

2 Background Information

2.1 Uncertainties in the Procurement of Renewable Resources

Uncertainty is defined as the absence or incompleteness of information [4]. Uncertainties can be categorized according to different characteristics, which are presented in Table 1. Sourcing uncertainties include both uncertainties caused by direct suppliers, as well as sub-suppliers, and the logistics [3]. The focus in this paper lies on external uncertainties in the source process.

Many authors stress that it makes sense to clearly differentiate between the uncertainties according to cause and effect [5]. The *cause-related analysis* focuses on the uncertainty source, in order to prevent or eliminate it [5, 6]. The

Table 1 Ways of differentiating between uncertainties

Object of observation	Characteristics
Business	Internal, external
Cause	Operational, disruptions
Operational activity	Sourcing, production, sales, logistics, (IT, organization)
Process	Plan, source, make, deliver and return
Production process	Internal, external

effect-related analysis examines the uncertainty effects, in order to minimize these [7]. In order to measure an effect, ex-ante defined plans, goals and expected values have to exist, with the possibility of deviation due to the uncertainty [5, 8]. Thus, an effect can only exist if it can be objectively identified and/or measured. The effect in terms of this paper is an impact on production plans.

In the area of renewable resources there are some special uncertainties in comparison to conventional resources. Due to natural growth processes it is difficult to ensure exact times of harvests as well as the qualities and quantities of the resources [9–11]. Non-influenceable factors like precipitation, solar radiation or infestation by pests are not taken care of in actual production planning [12]. It is rare that complete harvests are lost through natural disasters, droughts or pests. But it is more likely that parts of the harvests are lost, have differences in size, material defects, divergences from defined requirements or damages. These factors can cause qualitative or quantitative uncertainties. A postponed harvest results in uncertainties of time. We do not regard cost uncertainties, which play an important role during procurement, but which only slightly affect production planning. We will demonstrate that it is possible to substitute a resource that is not delivered or to substitute an expensive resource with a cheaper one, so that cost uncertainties are equal to quantity uncertainties with regard to possible reactions. Furthermore location uncertainties are excluded from analysis, as they result in quantity uncertainties in two locations. In conclusion, we will only examine quantity, quality and time uncertainties.

In order to show the practical relevance, a reference to a study shall be made: This study among companies in German-speaking countries, which use renewable resources as an input, was conducted in 2010 [13]. Overall, 28 % of the companies perceive uncertainty in their supply chain. Most of the companies do not use advanced information technology like RFID to handle this uncertainty, but the demand for simple planning concepts which can be integrated easily into existing systems like Enterprise Resource Planning (ERP) is nevertheless present. Four qualitative interviews with companies which mainly use plant fibers are almost confirming these results: The companies typically use storage to hedge against uncertainty, as they obviously feel a lack of easy planning concepts. Only one participant said that information systems are not needed, as they know how to handle uncertainties due to their experience even without IT. We will use a company that uses fibers as an input for natural fiber reinforced plastics as an example in the following. The fibers can be used interchangeably in certain ratios [14], which means that for example hemp fibers can be substituted by flax fibers to produce flower pots.

2.2 Production Planning

In the following, the term PPC-system is understood as a software that supports and automates the production planning (and controlling) in line with the concepts of Material Requirements Planning (MRP I) and Manufacturing Resource Planning (MRP II). These concepts are an elementary component, as they led to the implementation of PPC-Systems over time. PPC-systems can also be modules within integrated standard software like ERP-Systems. Special emphasis lies on the focal production planning and control of an individual business. The areas of material planning, capacity planning and manufacturing controlling are also supported. Shop-Floor scheduling can be integrated.

3 General Possibilities of Considering Uncertainties in the Production Planning

In this chapter, different scenario planning methods and resource substitution will be evaluated in line with the uncertainties shown above. Scenario planning does not offer a direct decision on the production plans during the development of the scenarios. Instead, different alternatives are developed which are decided on later with the aid of a decision criterion. Thus, the decision on the alternative is made when information is complete, i.e. when the criteria becomes known, and is therefore postponed. This makes planning more flexible [15].

3.1 Quantity Variation

Quantity variation is a method that applies to quantity-related uncertainties. The production quantity is adapted to the actually delivered quantity, e.g. when shortfalls occur due to droughts or pests. It is also possible to split up the ordered quantity by increasing the number of suppliers, or to switch to alternative suppliers if uncertainties arise [3]. These suppliers should be distributed locally to avoid natural influences by the factors already mentioned in Sect. 2.1 and thus reduce the uncertainty of renewable resources. Scenarios can be developed prior to the adaptation of production plans, which include the actual delivery quantity as a decision criterion for choosing a scenario on delivery. Thus, one anticipates quantity variations and addresses these to a certain extent in the planning. The information can become known in the time of delivery or before when the supplier or carrier sends notifications during the transport.

3.2 Time Variation

It is also possible to develop scenarios on the time of delivery and in this way to consider time uncertainties. Changes are made to the order scheduling [3]. Planning occurs at a fixed point for a future delivery time. When the actual time of delivery becomes known, an alternative will be chosen with the point of time as the criterion. The delay of deliveries should become known when uncertainties arise; e.g. when a pest occurs and renewable resources are affected, which results in a later delivery. After harvesting the delivery time is announced by the carrier.

3.3 Quality Variation

A product is specified during its development and its characteristics are defined. Tolerance levels may also be set for these characteristics, in which the product can be developed with the desired quality. One refers to quality variation if these characteristics, which consist of primary and secondary characteristics, are changed [16]. Different levels of change are possible. Thus, a quality variation is a deviation from the original product specifications, resulting from a change in resource quality or other parts integrated into the product [17–19]. It is important to note that quality variation is not always deliberate, but can occur through unwanted characteristics or environmental impacts [17].

It is therefore possible to transfer the described variations onto quality-related uncertainties. Different scenarios for the values of one or more quality characteristics are determined during planning. A scenario can then be chosen at the time of delivery or, in the best case, when the delivery quality becomes known before that time. The decision criterion is a quality trait, which can for example be hardness, flexibility, viscosity, water content or something else in renewable resources [19]. Depending on the scenario, products with different qualities are produced, as one assumes that lower quality resources result in lower quality product characteristics and vice versa. In the extreme case, the choice of which product can be produced at all is made at the time of decision, depending solely on the quality criterion [19].

3.4 Renewable Resource Substitution

Besides the mentioned variations, it is also possible to vary the utilized renewable resource or their proportions [3]. This structural variation depends on the used resources, their substitutes and the production process. Examples are compound material that can be substituted by renewable resources and varying compositions [14]. For example, the wood fibres in Wood-Plastic-Components can be replaced by plant fibres to some degree. The same applies to the already mentioned natural fibre reinforced plastics, where plant fibres can be replaced by each other. The substitute resource has to be included in production planning in order to enable substitution. First, possible substitutes have to be determined and substitution options have to be analyzed with regard to time, amount, composition and material properties. The substitute resource should be deposited within the data structures of the production planning. One can chose between different alternatives when planning the amount of resources that are to be ordered:

- The substitute is always in stock and available for production during an emergency.
- Prior experience allows an estimate of a deficit in the primary resource and an adequate amount of the substitute can therefore be included in the order.
- The substitute can be obtained within a short time and no storage is needed.

It is important to consider that extra costs may arise through storage or prompt procurement. Summing up, the structural variation 'resource substitution' seems like a good option if the resources and production process allows it, which is often the case with compound material which includes renewable resources [14].

3.5 Summary

Flexible resources such as machines, equipment and personnel are needed for nearly all variations, because even though scenarios are planned in advance, the actual plan can only be chosen shortly before production begins. The variation methods are a good way to predefine potential alternatives and to delay deciding on a plan to a time when information is complete or better. Rolling planning enables updating scenarios and adaptation to changing external factors and environmental impacts [20]. These variation methods should therefore be updated regularly to improve planning. Forecasts are available for many characteristics of renewable resources: Beside the well-known weather forecast modern agricultural machinery or aerial observation can measure plant characteristics [21]. Farmers and forestry workers can also measure these data manually. When these data are made available, a rolling update of the production planning with actual (and thus more certain) data is possible to change or refine the plans. Related to our example, this means that the plans for the ratio of different fibers can be planned in advance and afterwards chosen regarding the quality, quantity and time points of the deliveries. The ratios of the fibers can be changed easily according to these plans. At the same time, early consideration of uncertainties is advantageous, as it forces planers to think about possible variations, their impacts and influences (e.g. the environmental factors mentioned above).

4 Consideration of Uncertainties in PPC-Systems

Basic data are the master data in PPC systems, i.e. those data that are independent of concrete orders or plans [22]. The basic data for PPCs include for example bill of materials (BOM), work plans, parts master data, operating materials and other data structures of the production process. Parts master data describe a certain part (i.e. a final or intermediary product, raw material or assembly groups) in more detail and include e.g. terms, descriptions or measurements [22]. As these data are merely descriptive and find entry into the planning of other structures, such as work plans, they are not discussed explicitly in this context. Instead, the focus lies on those product structures which are typically stored as BOMs and on work plans.

4.1 Variable Bill of Material

BOMs are at the core of all production planning processes, because they reflect all those structures that describe the composition of a product such as raw materials, other materials, assembly groups or intermediary products [20, 22–25]. There are several kinds of variable BOMs differing in the way they store and represent data. The *type parts list*, sometimes also called *identical parts list* or *variant parts list*, provides a comparison of parts and types of the final product [22, 23, 25, 26]. The total amounts of all parts contained in the product are entered into the rows. The variations of the product are entered into the columns. The cells of the intersections contain the amount of a part for a certain product. In order to avoid redundancy of data, a column of identical parts can be introduced, where the amount of parts is entered which is identical for all variations [22, 24, 27, 28]. Table 2 shows an example. The column of identical parts reduces the complexity of parts lists and increases the processing speed. If there are few variations, these parts lists are also easy to read as all variations can be shown in one list due to the single-step structure [22, 24, 28]. A disadvantage here is the increased work load if the amounts of the identical parts for different variations change [24]. Furthermore, it is not possible to assign the general parts lists to a certain order, so that individual order parts lists have to be produced for each variation [23]. It is possible to produce variations according to quantity or according to structure and thus to handle quantity and quantity variations as well as substitutions.

Table 2 Type parts list

	Identical parts	Variation A	Variation B	Variation C	Remark
Part 1	3				Identical parts
Part 2		1	2	3	Varying quantities
Part 3		1		1	Varying structures

The *complex parts list*, also called *selection parts list*, is quite similar to the type parts list, as all variations of a product are included [26, 27]. It is different because it contains all potentially required parts and leaves only the option to select whether or not a part is included in the configuration. Therefore the configuration may be changed (i.e. structural variations are possible), but not the quantities [25]. The discussion in Sect. 3.1 showed that variations of quantities are useful, so this type of list will be excluded from further discussion.

A *plus-minus parts list* differentiates between standard parts (identical parts) which are used for all variations and stored in an independent basis parts list and a specific parts list for each variation [22, 23, 26]. The specific parts list includes all changes against the basic parts list in negative or positive quantities [24, 25, 27, 28]. Table 3 shows an example. Geitner defines the plus-minus parts list only as variations of the variable parts - not of the identical parts - and introduces the additional term of identical parts list [25]. We do not follow this separation here, as it is possible to enter the identical parts directly into the plus-minus parts list which provides sufficient differentiation and avoids creating an additional type of parts list. This type of parts list has the advantage that the data of the parts list can be managed separately, meaning that for example in case of change of identical parts in the basis parts list, the specific variation parts list will not have to be changed [24]. Data redundancy, more precisely the repeated listing of identical parts in each variation, is avoided. This has the disadvantage that the relationship of basic configuration and different variations is not immediately visible and that data management is made more difficult by the duplication of listings. The representation of plus-and-minus quantities makes it possible to show quantity as well as structural variations, which means that also quality variations and substitutions can be handled.

The *complementary parts list*, where only additions to the basic parts list are entered into the specific parts list, is a sub-type of the plus-minus parts list. This kind of list only makes sense for products that require more of certain materials. It is therefore not suitable for products where less or different kinds of materials are required. Theoretically a negative change would be possible by adapting the basic

Table 3 Plus-minus-parts list

Basic parts list	Identical parts	Specific parts list	Variation A
Part 1	3	(Part 1)	
Part 2		Part 2	+1
Part 3		Part 3	+1

parts list (in this case the amount of a specific part would be reduced) and all variation parts list are also adapted (i.e. increasing the amount where applicable) [24]. However, the processing effort is so high that instead the plus-minus parts list should be used in these cases.

All variations include implicit opportunities to deal with uncertainties. Thus variations for possible scenarios can be formed well ahead as described in Chap. 3 and used when needed. If renewable resources are missing, it can be checked whether they may be substituted by other parts, which is a structural variation of the parts list and the resource substitution mentioned above. The complex parts list is an exception, where this substitution is only possible by using explicit and non-contradictory alternatives instead of a direct substitute as in the other parts list. This makes the representation of a substitution very difficult here. Therefore the question is whether there are parts lists for the same product assembled without the missing renewable resource. It would also be possible to search the order queue using the parts lists with varying quantities for possible products without the missing renewable resource. This is equivalent to the quantity variation mentioned above. Here the question is whether there are open production orders for a product which needs less or none of the actual missing renewable resource.

The same is true for the consideration of quality-related uncertainties. If parts lists are developed well ahead containing the renewable resources in varying qualities as variation, it is possible to decide flexibly which of the parts lists is actually to be used. This is equivalent to the quality variations described above. Thus it is possible to develop e.g. two type parts lists for the same product, of which one variation contains 'renewable resource 1 in good quality' and another one 'renewable resource 1 in bad quality'. Once the quality of the material delivered is known, the adequate parts list can be selected. This parts list may also include more amounts of the renewable resource to balance the quality, e.g. in compound materials [19]. This is equivalent to the structural variation of the parts list, which is possible with all variations described above. Table 4 shows an example. It is also possible that simply using higher quantities of material counterbalances bad quality. This can be taken care of by an adapted parts list with a variation for good quality and smaller quantities and a variation for bad quality and higher quantities [18, 19, 29]. This is equivalent to a quantity variation, an

Table 4 Structural variations of a parts list according to varying quality of material

	Identical parts	Variation A: bad quality additions[a]	Variation B: bad quality substitution[b]	Variation C: good quality
Part 1	3			
Part 2		2		1
Part 3: compensate bad quality		1		
Part 4: Substitute			1	

[a] In this case, the bad part is used anyway (2 pieces of part 2) and an additional part 3 is added
[b] The bad part is not used but substituted by another part 4

Table 5 Quantity variation of a part list according to varying quality of material

	Identical parts	Variation A: bad quality	Variation B: good quality
Part 1	3		
Part 2		2	1

example of which is shown in Table 5. The increase of part 2 shall counterbalance the bad quality.

Parts list cannot take account of time-related uncertainties. The early or late delivery of renewable resources does not change the composition of the product and postponement of delivery dates has no impact on the product structure. This issue is solved by variable work plans or processing plans, which will be discussed in the following chapter.

4.2 Configurators for Variable Bill of Materials

Parts lists variations have been used for some time to represent the variability of final products. Customers' increasing demand for individualisation is often quoted as a reason for this [23, 27, 30]. In production processes with many variations, such as automobile production, the sales departments or customers may use (product) configurators to check the feasibility with respect to technical and functional aspects and to select or, in the case of dynamic composition to develop, the appropriate parts list [20, 22, 31]. A configurator can also be used to take account of uncertainties in planning the production process. Instead of making the selection of the required parts lists dependent on customer request, the selection can be done according to the decision criterias described in Chap. 3. When these become known, in the best case before arrival at the place of production, in the worse case only at the point of delivery, information about quantities, quality and time of delivery are available. These data make it possible to let the configurator select a parts list which is feasible under the given restrictions. Flexible parts list selection makes it possible to postpone the production process if the delivery of a certain renewable resource is delayed and to push the orders for which the renewable resource is required to a period after the planned date of delivery. It is also possible to substitute the missing renewable resource or to use alternative materials. In this case all order parts lists have to be searched for the renewable resource in question and a variation of the parts list has to be selected. The same is true for uncertainties in quantities and qualities. As explained above, alternative part lists for different material qualities can be created, which can be selected according to the existing data on the quality of a material. Thus variable parts lists lead to flexible production processes. In our example the configurator could choose the ratios and substituting materials automatically according to predefined requirements, which were set by the production planner.

4.3 Variable Work Schedules/Time Schedules

Work schedules (task lists) are another structure of the basic data in production planning. They include instructions for the production process as well as processing steps of producing elements [22, 25]. Every produced element thus has its own work schedule. The work schedule is therefore a summary of all steps and needed resources. *Alternative work schedules* are one way of considering uncertainties. Different work schedules are developed which differ in the determinants of their usage. Unit based work schedules are a typical example, in which it is possible to integrate different process steps or times for some ranges of quantities. This corresponds to the variation in quantities. However, it is also possible that a work schedule is chosen according to the resource quality [22]. The condition characteristics and possible value (ranges) then have to be added to the work schedules. These characteristics have to be evaluated during planning, so that a plan can be chosen based on the conditions. This corresponds to the variation in quality.

Time schedules are the time plan for producing an element. They display the chronology of steps, including possible periods of waiting, setup and processing. During shop-floor scheduling, the final resources are assigned, e.g. machines and personal. The lead time scheduling of a production process is planned during the rough-cut scheduling, including the starting and ending time for every individual step as well as possible *buffer time in the work and time schedules*. The buffer time is the time by which the beginning or ending or a step can be delayed without postponing the project end [32]. This is a first possible reaction against uncertainties, at which buffers are only short periods that prevent idle times and thus enable full economic capacity utilization. It is therefore possible to bridge short time uncertainties, with quick decisions being made either during material planning or rather during production control. Buffer periods do not safeguard against longer delays of delivery dates of necessary renewable resources. However, prolonged processing times caused by low quality resources can be compensated, which addresses an internal area of process uncertainty with the external source of the uncertainty in bad resource procurement. In summary, work and time schedules can have buffer times to hedge against time uncertainties.

The time schedules, which are developed from the alternative work schedules, are another way of considering uncertainties. *Alternative operations* can exist within the time schedules [22]. Thus, it is possible to include steps for preprocessing or postprocessing when faced with quality variation. These steps are integrated into the standard work plan as optional steps, which possibly delay the process when they are used. An operation "preprocessing" could be included in the work plan, which is only carried out when a characteristic does not pass the quality control. Otherwise, this step is disregarded and the standard process is chosen, so that two alternative working sequences in the time schedule emerge. This case is illustrated in Fig. 1. The same applies to optional postprocessing steps. This shows that possible additional or alternative steps already have to be known during the development of work and time schedules, in order to include them. The actual decision is made during the shop-floor scheduling.

In addition to alternative work schedules, it is also possible to implement *different sequences* in work plans. Even though interdependencies will always exist, making a specific order of processing steps indispensable, specific operations may be changed [22]. Thus, time or quantity uncertainties can be counteracted by shifting operations either backwards or forwards either in the phase of material planning or shop-floor scheduling (depending on when it becomes known). This also influences the release of production steps in shop-floor scheduling: depending on the availability check, orders can either only be released prior to production (static availability check) if all resources are available or even when resources are (partly) unavailable (flexible availability check). A flexible availability check thus is necessary to adapt the sequence and to release production steps under the condition that not all resources are available (as it is the case in time and quantity uncertainties). Alternatively, availability can already be checked prior to individual steps (dynamic availability check). Thus, other steps can be processed first, while those for which resources are missing can be postponed. This approach is illustrated in Fig. 2.

When switching a sequence it makes sense to determine the earliest and latest points for the beginning and end of an operation within the time schedule, so that the planned delivery deadline is not exceeded. For example, if an operation cannot be carried out because the renewable resource is unavailable or being preprocessed to solve quality problems, the part to be produced can pass through other operations, which do not require this resource. If quality is low, it is also possible that an operation takes longer than usual, e.g. if the renewable resource is wet or hard to handle. Besides buffer periods, one could also do other operations concurrently. Operation time might also be shortened if fewer renewable resources are delivered than needed or planned for. Quantitative uncertainties can also be indirectly addressed by moving forward subsequent operations, because fewer units require less time than planned. All of these variations require a flexible way of postponing subsequent process steps and a flexible machinery setup in order to prevent undesirable downtimes.

It is also possible to reorganize operation sequences over several orders. If a time schedule is changed due to such a reorganization, resources that were originally reserved become available now. Operations from other orders could be

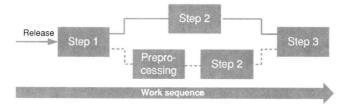

Fig. 1 Alternative operations in work and time schedules

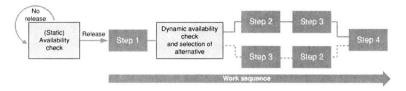

Fig. 2 Different sequences in work and time schedules

processed during this time. Thus, it is possible to develop alternative sequences and operations of several orders. This makes also sense when quantitative variations occur: Processing times are reduced if delivery shortfalls or degraded material occur because fewer resources have to be processed. Subsequent steps can therefore be carried out earlier than planned. This frees up resources which can be used by other orders. Otherwise it is possible that resources needed for the next step are not yet available because they are being blocked by another order. Idle periods then occur. This also shows that it is important to coordinate between alternative sequences across several orders and resources. If the mentioned delivery shortfall is taken into account at an early stage, it is easier to be flexible, as it is possible to define several alternative sequences for different orders and resources. This planning would be carried out within the material planning phase. The final scheduling of work plans and resource utilization can be carried out when the actual delivery shortfall becomes known. If problems suddenly occur or information becomes known too late, planning is carried out within the sequence or operations planning at the stage of shop-floor scheduling, which results in a weak planning result and system nervousness.

For the shown methods it is necessary to expand the conventional standard work plans in such a way that they are able to include the following data: earliest and latest points for individual operations, if–then conditions for sequences, if–then conditions for the choice of work plans, exchangeability of operations (sequence conditions), alternative operations, optional operations and finally simultaneous operations. One also has to consider that process-related time frames, steps and sequences are determined during the conversion into concrete order related schedules, which cannot be revised later on [22]. This excludes other flexible methods which are well suited. Kurbel refers to optional paths through the network of possible operations which are no longer available [22]. Nevertheless, there are these alternatives that were planned for individual operations beforehand and that can actually be carried out later on.

A long-term option for safeguarding against uncertainties is through variable capacities within the rough capacity planning. The actual planning of capacity changes would then be carried out in the requirement planning. Thus, it is not only possible to integrate time but also capacity buffers into work schedules. This enables a spontaneous increase in the workload, for example for the pre- or postprocessing of bad quality renewable resources (which means for example drying) or additional work, which would reduce this uncertainty. It is then necessary to *increase the offered capacity*, which can happen through overtime, additional shifts, adjustments in the intensity of machinery, quantitative staff adjustments or use of additional (reserve) machines [32]. It is also absolutely necessary to ensure flexibility in resource capacities [33]. Furthermore it is possible to provide certain resources as backups that can be used during emergencies. As we assume that not more renewable resources are delivered than ordered, we will not go into the impacts this will have on quantity uncertainties (increased quantities). Capacity adjustments however are a way of reacting to reduced quantities. If material delivery shortfalls result in a reduced production, then *the offered capacity is decreased* so that only the needed resources are used. A decrease can be achieved by reducing staff, adjusting machinery intensity or reducing machinery runtimes. The released capacities can then be used for other orders or to process the delivery of the missing quantities at a later time.

In general, the sooner uncertainties become known and are integrated into planning in the PPC, the better one is able to react. Thus, it is easier to integrate them during rough-cut scheduling to create absorbing buffers. The following steps and orders are postponed in order to make a realistic plan of resource allocations. It is harder to react if uncertainties become known too late during shop-floor scheduling. As this step focuses on target variables such as the delivery deadline or utilization rate and economic targets are neglected, postponement of the process steps would have a large impact [32]. In the worst case a new plan would be developed which cannot meet the deadline. One should therefore try to plan with information of supply chain partners like farmers, harvesters or forestry workers and companies as early as possible and to consider these data in the planning.

5 Conclusion and Further Research

In this paper we analyzed how procurement uncertainties can be considered in the basic data structures of ERP-systems. The general possibilities to consider uncertainties in planning were identified as methods for a variation of quantity, time and quality. Furthermore the substitution of renewable resources was described.

All of the methods are suitable to reduce the specific uncertainties of renewable resources. Finally we examined how the basic data structures can implement these variation methods and how suitable they are for doing so. The results are summarized in Table 6. It turns out that the type parts list or the plus-minus parts lists are well suited to implement the variation methods. The same is true for the complementary parts lists as a subtype of the plus-minus parts list. If these variable BOMs are supplemented with variable work schedules, all the mentioned variation methods can be implemented: While the BOMs cannot implement time variations, the time and work schedules can cover this aspect. Vice versa the time and work schedules cannot implement resource substitutions, but the BOMs can. Thus, a combination of both data structures can cover all the variation methods.

Table 6 Summary of the possibilities to consider uncertainties in the basic data structures

	Quantity variation	Quality variation	Time variation	Resource substitution
Bills of material				
Type parts list	Yes	Yes	No	Yes
Complex parts list	No	Yes	No	Limited[a]
Plus-minus parts list	Yes	Yes	No	Yes
Complementary parts list	Yes	Yes	No	Yes
Work schedules	Yes	Yes	Yes	No
Time schedules	Limited[b]	Yes	Yes	No

[a] By selecting the substituting renewable resources
[b] By order shifting

In our exemplary case, the production of natural fiber reinforced plastics, the production planner can use the mentioned parts lists to plan the substitution of the fibers in advance. For example a type parts list can be build up with two alternatives of a 50–50 %-mixing of two types of fibers or as an alternative a 60–40 %-mixing of these fibers. In this way the needed substitutes are planned, too. The used parts list with fitting ratios according to the deliveries is chosen when the true deliveries become known. This is an easy enhancement for existing ERP-systems and fits the needs of especially small and medium enterprises.

It was repeatedly pointed out that the exchange of information among the members of the supply chain is an important point. The early knowledge of the real values of scenarios' decision criteria is necessary to update and refine the plans and thus to get better and more realistic plans. In this context we recommend further researchers to focus on data collection and exchange in the supply chain of renewable resources. It has already been shown that, for example, Radio Frequency Identification (RFID) enables a more accurate and earlier data collection along the supply chain, resulting in a positive impact on reducing uncertainty in production planning and control [1]. The reaction of PPC systems to frequent changes of plans results in so called "system nervousness" [34–36], which has a negative impact on planning reliability and is itself a new intern source of uncertainty. Further research should examine the reactions of PPC systems and develop a model how the most valuable use of the data can be ensured. This includes the question which data are useful for the production planning with renewable resources.

References

1. Friedemann, S., Schumann, M.: Potentials and limitations of RFID to reduce uncertainty in production planning with renewable resources. J. Syst. Manage. Sci. **1**, 47–66 (2011)
2. Bundesministerium für Umwelt, Naturschutz und Reaktorsicherheit: Deutsches Ressourceneffizienzprogramm (ProgRess). Programm zur nachhaltigen Nutzung und zum Schutz der natürlichen Ressourcen. Berlin (2012)

3. Kersten, W., Singer, C.: Aufbau von Flexibilitätspotenzialen zur Beherrschung von Supply Chain-Risiken. Ind. Manage. **27**, 61–64 (2011)
4. Rowe, W.D.: Understanding uncertainty. Risk Anal. **14**, 743–750 (1994)
5. Reh, D.: Entwicklung einer Methodik zur logistischen Risikoanalyse in Produktions- und Zuliefernetzwerken. Fraunhofer-Verlag, Stuttgart (2009)
6. Thiemt, F.: Risikomanagement im Beschaffungsbereich. Cuvillier, Göttingen (2003)
7. Sinha, P.R., Whitman, L.E., Malzahn, D.: Methodology to mitigate supplier risk in an aerospace supply chain. Supply Chain Manage Int. J. **9**, 154–168 (2004)
8. Spille, J.: Typspezifisches Risikomanagement für die Beschaffung von Produktionsmaterialien in der Automobilzulieferindustrie. Shaker, Aachen (2009)
9. Narodoslawsky, M.: Renewable resources—new challenges for process integration and synthesis. Chem. Biochem. Eng. Q. **17**, 55–64 (2003)
10. McCarthy, M.A., Burgman, M.A.: Coping with uncertainty in forest wildlife planning. For. Ecol. Manage. **74**, 23–36 (1995)
11. Dennis, B., Brown, B.E., Stage, A.R., Burkhart, H.E., Clark, S.: Problems of modeling growth and yield of renewable resources. Am. Stat. **15**, 374–383 (1985)
12. Krupinsky, J.M., Bailey, K.L., McMullen, M.P., Gossen, B.D., Turkington, T.K.: Managing plant disease risk in diversified cropping systems. Agron. J. **94**, 198–209 (2002)
13. Friedemann, S., Dehler, C., Friedrich, T., Haack, A., Schumann, M.: Diffusion of IS in companies using renewable resources and its impact on uncertainty. In: AMCIS 2011 Proceedings—All Submissions, Paper 148 (2011)
14. Mediaville, V., Sell, J.: Marktchancen von Naturfasern im Kunststoffbereich. http://www.mediavilla.ch/wordpress/wp-content/uploads/2010/01/kunststoffbranche.pdf (2005)
15. Adam, D.: Planung und Entscheidung. Gabler, Wiesbaden (1996)
16. Bortis, H.: Produkttechnischer Fortschritt und Profite. Duncker & Humblot, Berlin (1971)
17. Thornton, A.C.: Variation Risk Management. Wiley, Hoboken (2004)
18. Rutten, W.G.M.M.: Hierarchical mathematical programming for operational planning in a process industry. Eur. J. Oper. Res. **64**, 363–369 (1993)
19. Fransoo, J.C., Rutten, W.G.M.M.: A typology of production control situations in process industries. Int. J. Oper. Prod. Manage **14**, 47–57 (1994)
20. Alicke, K.: Planung und Betrieb von Logistiknetzwerken. Springer, Berlin (2005)
21. Zhang, N., Wang, M., Wang, N.: Precision agriculture—a worldwide overview. Comput. Electron. Agric. **36**, 113–132 (2002)
22. Kurbel, K.: Enterprise Resource Planning und Supply Chain Management in der Industrie. Oldenbourg, München (2011)
23. Stonebraker, P.W.: Restructuring the bill of material for productivity: a strategic evaluation of product configuration. Int. J. Prod. Econ. **45**, 251–260 (1996)
24. Geiger, W.: Computergestützte Produktionsplanung und -steuerung im Mittelstand. Gabler, Wiesbaden (1992)
25. Geitner, U.W.: Methoden der Produktionsplanung und -steuerung. Hanser, München (1987)
26. Wiendahl, H.-P.: Betriebsorganisation für Ingenieure. Hanser, München (2008)
27. Steven, M.: Handbuch Produktion. Kohlhammer, Stuttgart (2007)
28. Grupp, B.: Materialwirtschaft mit EDV im Klein- und Mittelbetrieb. Expert Verlag, Renningen (2003)
29. Burt, J., Kraemer, B.: Integrating material and product control systems into a tightly regulated processing environment. APICS Conference Proceedings, pp. 32–34 (1979)
30. Olsen, K.A., Sætre, P., Thorstenson, A.: A procedure-oriented generic bill of materials. Comput. Ind. Eng. **32**, 29–45 (1997)
31. Baltes, G.H., Schäfer, T., Sticksel, P.: Steigerung der Vertriebseffizienz durch den Einsatz von Produktkonfigurationen: Vertriebskonfigurationen erfolgreich implementieren. Ind. Manage. **26**, 51–55 (2010)
32. Dyckhoff, H., Spengler, T.S.: Produktionswirtschaft. Springer, Berlin (2007)

33. Hartmann, H.: Produktion, Bereitstellung und Eigenschaften biogener Festbrennstoffe. In: FNR (ed.) Leitfaden Bioenergie: Planung, Betrieb und Wirtschaftlichkeit von Bioenergieanlagen. pp. 52–90, Fachagentur Nachwachsende Rohstoffe e.V., Gülzow (2007)
34. Ho, C.-J.: Evaluating the impact of operating environments on MRP system nervousness. Int. J. Prod. Res. **27**, 1115–1135 (1989)
35. Koh, L.S.C., Saad, S.: Modelling uncertainty under a multi-echelon ERP-controlled manufacturing system. J. Manuf. Technol. Manage. **15**, 239–253 (2004)
36. Koh, L.S.C., Simpson, M.: Change and uncertainty in SME manufacturing environments using ERP. J.Manuf. Technol. Manage. **16**, 629–653 (2005)

Towards Total Budgeting and the Interactive Budget Warehouse

Dirk Draheim

Abstract This paper aims at establishing a strictly information system science viewpoint onto management accounting and budgetary processes. This viewpoint is presented in terms of a strictly subject-oriented, time variant data model—the so-called interactive budget warehouse. The target is to overcome the ERP/ad-hoc planning divide that challenges budgetary planning as well as budgetary control in many of today's enterprises. With respect to technology we see the need to establish budgetary IT systems that potentially enable a total budget control across all levels down to the smallest cost units we deal with in daily operations. However, total budget control is not the target. We try to characterize a possible sweet spot between the obvious micro management of total budget control and today's budgeting practices, which we tentatively call total budgeting. Total budgeting is the organizational concept corresponding to a reasonable usage of the interactive budget warehouse. Total budgeting is about commitment to the power of financial flows, pervasive profit and cost awareness, overcoming the budget responsibility-accountability divide, and a tight integration of budgetary control with the overall management system of the enterprise.

1 Introduction

Still in today's budgeting processes, both in planning and during the budget period, we encounter cost drivers and budget misuse. Known problems are budgetary slack or padding. In many of today's enterprises we encounter frictions between support for budgetary processes in the ERP systems and a diversity of ad-hoc techniques and tools to plan and control budget. This problem can be succinctly characterized as the ERP spreadsheet border.

D. Draheim (✉)
University of Innsbruck, Innsbruck, Austria
e-mail: draheim@acm.org
URL: http://draheim.formcharts.org/

We strictly believe that with appropriate ERP support certain management practices that are widely accepted as ideal but not yet fully implemented in enterprises can eventually turned into reality. Therefore, we introduce the notion of interactive budget warehouse. The purpose of the interactive budget warehouse is to make clear that a total budget control is a possibility and not a fiction. However, a total budget control is not the target but a device. We are seeking to characterize a sweet spot between today's management accounting implementation and total budget control for which we use the term total budgeting in this paper—see Fig. 1.

We do not think that total budgeting is a panacea for all enterprises. But as [1] we think that currently emerging counter-programmes to established management accounting practice like Beyond Budgeting [2] are also no panacea. In my opinion beyond budgeting only fits organizations that succeed in scaling an entrepreneurial flavor in the sense of Mintzberg's entrepreneurial organization [3] to a kind of swarm intelligence of profit units. I doubt that such agile organizational structure does optimally fit all business models, though Beyond Budgeting [2] brings examples from a wide range from industries. So, our discussion rather follows the strand of work done in the ABB (activity based budgeting) realm. In a sense, from the viewpoint of today's actual management accounting practice we move into the opposite direction as Beyond Budgeting, however, with the same objective to overcome flaws and frictions encounter in today's management of financial flows—see Fig. 1

Data warehousing and OLAP are obvious tools for budgeting. None other than Edgar. F. Codd has used a budgeting example for explaining cross dimensional analysis in the paper in which he defines OLAP [4]. Also the data warehouse product that has been sponsored by Codd, i.e., Hyperion Essbase, have evolved to Hyperion System 9+ [5] now, and Hyperion System 9+, taken as a product line, is known to have a strict emphasis on financial management, i.e., it offers concrete modules for this domain. The aim of this paper is to explicitly establish subject orientation and time variance in the form of the interactive budget warehouse as the information system science viewpoint per se onto mature budgeting processes.

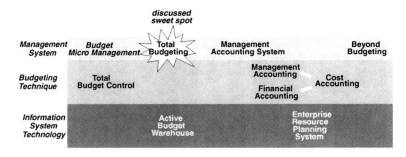

Fig. 1 Relationship between management systems and budgeting techniques

It translates and complements the organizational viewpoint of budgeting as recursive feedback control system.

In Sect. 2 we introduce and discuss the notion of interactive budget warehouse. In Sect. 3 we delve into the implementation facet of the interactive budget warehouse, i.e., total budget control. In Sect. 4 we discuss the organizational counterpart of the interactive budget warehouse, i.e., total budgeting. We outline further work in Sect. 5. We discuss related work throughout the paper. We finish the paper with a conclusion in Sect. 6.

2 The Interactive Budget Warehouse

We want to discuss the notion of total budget control in terms of a concrete data model. Such data model is shown in Fig. 2. The purpose of the data model is to set the stage for the total budgeting approach. The data model adheres to some important characteristics of OLAP (online-analytical processing) [4] data schemas:

- Star schema which embodies subject-orientation:
  - Multidimensional data points.
  - Hierarchical. Crucial dimensions are internally organized as hierarchies.

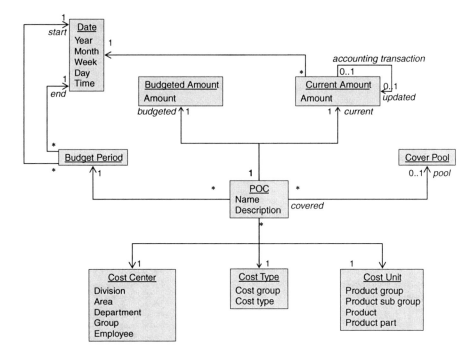

Fig. 2 Example basic data schema for total budget control

- Non-volatile, historical. Information is never deleted.
- Time-variant, time-based. Current values from the underlying ERP system or systems are part of the schema as well as the time of information creating events.

Because of these characteristics, the data schema is well-suited for treatment and exploration by today's online-analytical tools like Hyperion System 9 [5] or Cognos [6]. This also means that the domain of budgeting is particularly well suited for online-analytical processing. In the list above we have not mentioned a further typical ingredient of data warehousing, i.e., integration. Integration is an implementation issue and a high-level characteristic of how data warehouses usually arise in today's enterprises as integration technologies. We defer the discussion of implementation issues until Sect. 3. For the time being we take a conceptual implementation-independent viewpoint. Please also note, that it is not neither our intention to prescribe a concrete nor a complete data model with Fig. 2. We just want to grasp the most important issues of the budgeting process to outline basic ideas, in particular, the inherent OLAP nature of management accounting. Against the background of the many concepts that might play a role in a given enterprise's budgeting scenario, e.g., rolling budgets or flexible budgeting, it becomes clear that Fig. 2 shows a core example data model only.[1]

We are interested in complete master budgets consisting of a revenue facet and a cost facet. The basic aspects of the interactive budget warehouse can be discussed in terms of the cost facet and transport immediately to the revenue facet. Some crucial cost drivers show particularly in cost centers and non-profit organizations. They can be analyzed and addressed appropriately without a consideration of the revenue and profit facet of budgeting. A full discussion of budgeting and its role in enterprises needs both facets. Figure 2 shows the cost facet of the budget. The revenue facet can be developed similarly.

2.1 A Multidimensional Budget Information Model

Point of Cost. The concept of POC[2] (point of cost) forms the center of the data model. Basically, a POC is what is usually called a cost object, i.e., any item or issue, e.g., product or service, that one's cost we want to plan, measure and control. However, with POCs we want to consider the smallest of the cost objects

---

[1] Compare our single cost center entity to the number of different kinds of cost centers that exist in SAP merely in module RM (real-time cost accounting): primary cost center, cost center to be debited, node cost center, collective cost center, final cost center, overhead cost center.

[2] We have chosen the POC terminology in analogy with the POS (point of sale) terminology in the retail domain, which is still the role model domain for data warehousing [7]. The cost point class is the hub of the whole budget data schema. It is a point in a *multidimensional* information space. This is similar to the POS in the star schemas of the retail domain [7] where it plays exactly the same role.

in the enterprise's budgeting process, or, to say it in a different way, POCs reside at the level of finest granularity. In an enterprise we usually also want to deal with complex cost objects that are sums of other cost objects. Such complex cost objects arise naturally, e.g., in cost unit accounting as costs for products and services. Actually, in ERP systems the notion of cost object is sometimes used exclusively for the cost units in cost unit accounting or activity costing,[3] which further motivates the usage of POC instead of cost object in order to avoid confusion.

A major target of our viewpoint is to foster a unification of budgeting activities that appear at different levels of granularity in the enterprise. In that sense, it is fair to say that we also foster a higher level of detail for the modeling of costs in the central ERP systems of the enterprise. However, if we have said that POCs are about the finest level of cost objects, this by no means prescribes a certain level of granularity. The choice of the appropriate level of granularity is still done by those responsible for budgeting. For example, in an IT department you might not want to turn each of the expected hundred laptop purchases into a cost point. Rather you still budget all the laptop purchases as one cost point and mention the number of expected purchases in an auxiliary calculation in the description of the cost point.

Accounting Transactions. A cost point is planned for a budget period. A certain budgeted amount is fixed for each cost point as part of budget planning for the budget period. Each cost point has also a current amount. It stands for effective costs at each point in time. We use a simplified data model for instructional reasons—the current amount can be understood as the aggregate of actually made payments plus all purchase order commitments. The current value is continuously updated during the budget period by accounting transactions—orders and payments.

Budgeting ERP systems offer the possibility to establish constraints, in particular, constraints that must hold with respect to the amounts throughout the budget period. A typical constraint found in ERP systems is that the current amount of each cost point must not exceed its budgeted amount. Actually this constraint is usually relaxed by some notion of cover pool. It must hold only for those cost points that do not belong to such a cover pool. Cover pools are a standard device in budgeting ERP systems. They relax the control of expenditures during the budget period to groups of mutually compensable cost points. Our data model contains also the concept of cover pools. Each cost point can be part of at most one cover pool. The sum of all current amounts of cost points belonging to a cover pool must not exceed the sum of its budgeted amounts.

The discussed constraints on amounts safes persons accountable for budget from deviation from plan. It therefore disburdens them from obvious budget infringements by persons responsible for budget. It does prevent the misuse of budgeted amounts and does not free those accountable or responsible to control the most rational usage of the amounts. The control imposed by the constraints

---

[3] Cost object is the name for cost units in the SAP cost unit accounting module CO-PC (Controlling—Product Costing).

depends on the granularity of cost objects. Fine-grained constraint control, e.g., at the level of single shipped items, imposes a strict, inflexible budget discipline, whereas coarse-grained cost control at some higher level of budgetary topics, e.g., kinds of cost types or cost units, imposes an at minimum needed budget safety. This discussion leads us back to a further explanation of the concept of cover pool. Cover pools are motivated by the fact that you might want to plan the budget at a finer granularity than you want to control it formally. The responsible-minded budget planner wants to predict the expected budget as exact as possibly. In order to do so a fine granularity of estimation and argumentation is needed for budget planning. However, adopting this granularity as a level of control in the budget period might be too restrictive and therefore might discourage the usage of the appropriate granularity in budget planning. A distinction between granularity of planning and granularity of control is exactly what is realized by cover pools. Cover pools are a subtle form of what we call *potential savings declaration* as opposed to *hidden padding* in total budgeting.

Values of current amounts are never deleted by accounting transactions, i.e., current amounts are *non-volatile*. Furthermore the data model is *time-variant* with respect to accounting transactions, i.e., updated values are chained together with each concrete amount storing the time of its update. Given the importance of these time stamps in the analytical exploitation of the data, the schema is *time-based*.

Refining Means of Transactions. Obvious refinements of the data schema in Fig. 2 are means to update the budgeted amounts and the budget period, of course, in a non-volatile manner. Updating a budgeted amount stands for a plan adjustments during the budgeted period. A means to update the budget period would be necessary for realizing rolling budgets.

Strands of Accounting. In today's enterprises different strands of accounting practice may exist in parallel. They range from the basic *cost center accounting* over more elaborate *cost type accounting* to the challenging *cost unit accounting*. To put it simply, we would distinguish these accounting practices by the keywords 'Where?', 'Why?' and 'What?'. Cost type accounting is about understanding the costs in terms of the organizational units *where* they arise. Basically, cost type accounting is about understanding them in terms of selected crosscutting concerns, i.e., in terms of business functions, technical functions or infrastructural topics that are spread over more than one department. It is about making visible the reasons of costs, i.e., in a sense it is about the 'Why?' of costs. The quality of cost type accounting heavily depends on the quality of the selected crosscutting concerns. Eventually, cost unit accounting is about understanding *what* the sold products and services of enterprise cost. Different budgeting approaches combine and emphasize these accounting practices in a different manner. For example, the activity-based budgeting (ABB) [8] approach developed by CAM-I (Consortium for Advanced Manufacturing) heavily relies on elements of cost unit accounting.

The cost point carries information for the purposes all three kinds of cost accounting that we have mentioned represented by the classes cost center, cost type and cost unit. The cost centers, cost types and cost units form dimensions of the *star schema* and make it *hierarchically*. Each of the dimensions has an internal hierarchy and, as usual in data warehousing, the hierarchical structure is presented in a highly denormalized manner. As an example, Fig. 3 makes explicit the hierarchy of the cost center dimension by a normalized data model version.

Refining Responsibilities. Proper access right management is crucial for a budgeting ERP system. In particular, participatory budgeting approaches need sophisticated access right management. Note that the total budgeting viewpoint discussed in this paper heavily relies on arguments concerning participatory budgeting. Therefore the following discussion of total budgeting is also a high-level, yet sometimes hidden, discussion of access rights management.We have not modeled access rights management in Fig. 2. Modeling of concrete access right structures is straightforward can easily become too detailed for our purposes.We tried to model enough crucial aspects of a possible realizing data warehouse to have a solid basis for the discussion of total budgeting. For example, we included the notion of cover pool in the data model, which is implicitly strictly related to a notion of access rights management.

Point of Revenue. So far, we have discussed the budget in terms of cost facet as presented in Fig. 2. The discussion applies immediately to the revenue fact. The counterpart of the POC (point of cost) in the cost facet is the POR (point of revenue) in the revenue facet.

3 Total Budget Control

The interactive budget warehouse is oriented towards data warehousing. However, it is not necessarily realized by a data warehouse product. The interactive budget warehouse concept is technology independent. In particular, we do not impose integration, which is an important characteristics for data warehousing, as a key characteristics of the interactive budget warehouse.

3.1 Implementation Issues

In the context of data warehousing integration means the enterprise application integration aspect (EAI) of today's data warehouse architectures. In technical terms, integration stands for the ETL (extraction–transformation–load) layer of today's data warehousing products. The integration aspect of data warehousing reflects the history of how data warehouses emerged as tools that complement already existing ERP system landscapes with business intelligence.

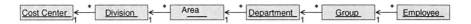

Fig. 3 Internal hierarchy of the cost center dimension

Even without this integration aspect, OLAP is a well-defined IT category worth considering. Furthermore, the borders between ERP and data warehousing continuously vanish – vertically and horizontally. Vertically, active data warehousing research [9] and products [10] has become mainstream in the meantime. The IIIB (industrial information integration backbone) or smart production architecture that we have discussed in [11, 12] is also an example for such vertical integration from scratch. Horizontally, database technology for OLAP and OLTP (online-transactional processing) grow more and more together with the ORACLE Exadata technology [13] as a recent example. Conceptually, there is no reason to view ERP and data warehousing as strictly separated and this is also and in particular so for data warehouses in the sector of accounting information systems.

The interactive budget warehouse stands for subject-orientation and time variance that we see as a key ingredients of each mature accounting information approach. However, the interactive budget warehouse is an implementation independent viewpoint. One natural implementation is by a classical data warehouse architecture consisting out of ETL layer and appropriate analytical data bases and tools. With the inter-activeness we want to stress that it should be possible to experience the budget warehouse as direct manipulatable—a data warehouse architecture that relies on overnight runs for updates would be hardly acceptable for this purpose. Therefore we argue in favor for the second possible implementation option, i.e., to integrate OLAP features and experience for budgeting into the ERP systems from scratch.

3.2 Total Budget Control: A Thought Experiment

Total budget control is a thought experiment that stands for the highest possible and yet arguable level of control of financial items throughout all levels of the organizational hierarchy. The interactive budget warehouse is the materialization of total budget control. Information about all the financial flows at each granularity is always at the fingertips of the management accountants. The notion of total budget control shows best in the level of detail we have chosen for the cost center dimension in our data model in Fig. 2: the single employee. Management accountant can, on suspicion of potential deviation from plan, follow traces down to single employees or single product items.

The power of total budget control lies in the capability of drilling down, rolling up, slicing and dicing investigations on cost aggregates during budget planning and the budget period via all hierarchical levels. To make this point clear, we give a few natural example questions that might be also particularly interesting in the total budgeting approach. During budget planning: comparison of budgeted amount of a cost aggregate to budgeted amount of previous periods, relative amount of costs in new cost types or new cost units. During the budget period: current amount of a cost aggregate compared to its last year's value at same date, current amount of a cost aggregate compared to the average of its last years' values at same dates, ratio of current amount of a cost aggregate to budgeted amount in comparison to average of this ratio of all cost points or last year's value of this ratio at same date, ratio of current amount to planned expenditure.

Total budget control is not an asset in its own right. It is neither a budgeting technique nor a budgeting approach. It merely stands for the best achievable pervasiveness and completeness of an enterprise's accounting information systems. Total budget control must be appropriately exploited by the budgeting process and this means also, that it should not be over-exploited ending in micro management.

4 Total Budgeting

The notion of total budgeting is a vehicle to discuss the tight integration of budgetary planning, management accounting and budgetary control by means of organizational means and technological support. It is about acknowledging this triad the role it always plays in enterprises—a key factor for excellence. Total budgeting is about establishing this triad as a leading organizational function beyond a crucial, but nevertheless mere administrative device—a center pillar of the organization's management system. This means we follow the point of view of the CIMA (Chartered Institute of Management Accountants) [14] which understands management accounting as crucial and necessarily tightly integrated with the other management systems.

From an information system scientist's viewpoint the technological support for mature budgeting processes is particularly important. We prefer a more conceptual discussion of this technological support than a low level discussion of concrete implementing technologies, although such low-level discussion is instructive from time to time. In any case, we consider organizational issues as equally or even more important for the establishment of a mature budgeting process, in particular, total budgeting must not be confused with total budget control as we already mentioned in Sect. 3.2.

The notion of total budgeting does not outdate other elaborate and established budgeting techniques and approaches [15] like rolling budgets, flexible budgeting or activity-based budgeting but is meant to be combined with them to the full benefit of the organization.

4.1 Commitment to the Power of Financial Flows

In organizations you find many different, sometimes mutual-dependent factors of power, formal and informal, direct and indirect: right of direction, permission to draw, length of service, natural authority, networks, committee work, intellectual properties, know-how in general [16, 17], process know-how in particular, functional supervision, project direction, project management responsibility, and, last but not least, budget accountability and budget responsibility. Amongst these factors budget accountability and responsibility, i.e., the formal or informal capabilities to plan, propose and approve budgets and to eventually steer and control expenditures, are particularly powerful. This should not be underestimated. And the reason is immediately identified: with money you steer suppliers and external service provider. Also, expenditures can be used to impact work environments and work relationships.

Many indicators exist that financial flows in enterprises are particularly powerful. In PMI (post-merger integration) endeavors, a special emphasize is put on the financial management. The CFO (chief financial officer) is often the most powerful executive board member in an enterprise. In particular, this becomes obvious in crisis and corporate restructuring.

4.2 Pervasive Profit and Cost Awareness

Profit and cost awareness should be established as a major crosscutting concern in the enterprise, i.e., as an everywhere issue for everybody in the organization. We want to draw the parallel with quality in TQM (total quality management) here [18]. TQM is not a tool for some superficial improvement of quality, but a business philosophy. It considers quality as a critical success factor for today's enterprises and calls for an integration of quality orientation into all endeavors and activities of the enterprise. Orientation towards quality in the sense of TQM is not in conflict to cost awareness. It's a basic opinion of TQM that the improvement of quality decreases costs [18], arguments that are given in favor of this opinion are that better quality stands for fewer mistakes, delays, amount of rework etc. I think it is not the question, whether quality always decreases costs. But, we follow [18] in that the opposite opinion is actually not valid. In general, there is no tradeoff between quality and cost and it is not acceptable if such tradeoff is used as argument against quality initiatives in an enterprise. Furthermore, even if an improvement of quality increases costs in a given scenario, this might be not usable as a counter-argument, because despite increased costs, the profit might also increase and eventually we are interested in profit.

The comprehensive discussion of how to foster profit and cost awareness in an organization is way beyond the scope of this paper. However, we want to give some important remarks with respect to this. Profit and cost awareness is usually differently developed in different groups of the enterprise. Those responsible for profit have a high profit and cost awareness. For these persons such awareness arises naturally. It can be explicitly fostered by pecuniary incentives, but even without those, non-pecuniary motivation usually exists naturally: job description, self-conception, status, improved career opportunities. This is so, at least with respect to profit awareness. Profit awareness is amenable to foster cost awareness. In the group that are not responsible for profit there are still those that are responsible for costs, i.e., heads of cost centers or front-line managers that directly handle expenditures. Even if these people are formally required, i.e., by their job descriptions, to look after costs, there cost awareness might be under-developed or even absent. At all levels of management there is a conflict of interest between cost awareness and the immediate power of financial capabilities. Even for those staff that is neither responsible for profit nor responsible for costs, profit and cost awareness is an important issue. Many of those people are consulted in budgetary planning and control processes.

If staff is directly consulted by managers in the budgetary processes the advantages of an overall profit and cost awareness is obvious. However, there are also indirect forms of consultancy, e.g., the claim for better payment or the claim for the improvement of the work environment or conditions.

4.3 Responsibility-Accountability Transcendence

Budget proposal and approval necessarily form a negotiation scenario between those responsible and those accountable. We believe in more formal accountability for persons responsible for budget in order to prevent gaming and perversion like budget padding and budget misuse.

It is useful to distinguish the between those accountable and those responsible in the budgetary processes. Formally, those accountable are those that have the permission to draw. Those accountable for budget are also proportionally accountable for the profit and success of the organization. In first place, the top management is amongst those accountable. The provision of financial resources to persons responsible for budget may occur at all levels of the organization, i.e., not only between those accountable and those responsible but also between those responsible, however, the provision of financial resources—sponsorship—is considered the domain of those accountable here. Persons responsible for budget are those that are, by their job descriptions, involved in expenditure and budgetary control.

Unfortunately, the question of who is actually in control of budgetary planning and budget development, i.e., expenditures, is independent of the question of accountability and responsibility. Similarly, the question of who causes bad planning and budget misuse and who is actually called to account for those, i.e., who is blamed for those. Transcendence of responsibility and accountability is about a focus shift from questions of formal accountability to a sound and systematic balance between control, causing and means to penalize budgetrelated misbehavior. In each concrete organization, a first step in this direction is an analysis of the actually existing control over budgetary processes and the identification of hidden influences onto expenditures and budget development.

The responsibility-accountability transcendence goes hand in hand with the objective of pervasive profit and cost awareness that we have discussed before. It is achieved by strengthening the control of those that are actually called to account. Eventually, it is all about raising the monitoring expenditures [19] and establishing panels for misbehavior. As an illustration, you could try to overcome the responsibility-accountability friction by giving the permission to draw to substantially more employees in your organization. However, this would only help, if the permission to draw is then truly connected to the question of who is called to account.

A comprehensive discussion of how to overcome a misbalance between causing and penalization in budgetary processes is beyond this paper. Figure 4 serves as an illustration of responsibility-accountability transcendence. We use strictly hierarchical organizations in the examples (i) through (iv) in Fig. 4, because makes things simpler to explain. We do not want to express the opinion that only strictly hierarchical organizations are amenable for sound budgetary processes or a total budgeting approach. In examples (i) through (iii) a black trapezoid stands for accountability, a grey trapezoid for responsibility and a light grey trapezoid for consultancy. The size of a trapezoid indicates the amount of actual control [20] embodied by the corresponding group of employees.

Diagram (i) shows an example sound budgetary scenario. Top management is accountable, middle management is responsible and the rest of the employees is consulted. The control of top management over all budgetary processes, both planning and expenditures during the budget period, dominates control capabilities of all other groups in the enterprise. The control of middle management is at least more than the control of group managers and the workforces.

Diagrams (ii) and (iii) show a budgeting scenario in example dysfunctional organization. In budget planning work forces including work force managers, i.e., group managers, form a powerful interest group that heavily influences the resulting budget plan. Consultancy takes the form of pressure on middle and top management in this example. Budget planning takes the form of sheer negotiations. Middle management serves only as link and cushion between workforces and top management in these negotiations. Control between top management and work forces is almost equally balanced, the top management's control is only slightly higher enforced by its formal authority. Then during the budget period in (iii) budgetary control of top and middle management vanishes. Group managers

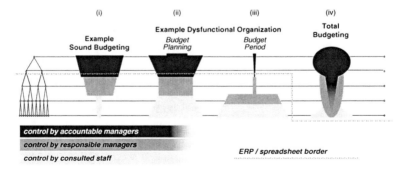

Fig. 4 Distribution and control of budgeting roles

gain formal responsibility. The control is taken over by the workforce. Front-line workers might effectively more control than the group managers.

An organization that follows the described pattern as described for (ii) and (iii) is not necessarily a dysfunctional organization. A professional organization as described by Mintzberg [3] can be perfectly work after this pattern and may be excellent. A problem can arise, if an intrinsic machine organization [3], i.e., an organization that can be managed successfully only as a machine organization, mimics the behavior of a professional organization. This can easily result into a dysfunctional organization and it is exactly what we want to express by our example. Little management culture, missing management structure and almost zero governance are characteristics of such a situation. Typical phenomena of budget misuse in such a situation are: overpriced orders to relatives and friends as suppliers or external service-providers, hidden payment improvements, expenditures on useless technical gadgets and hobbies, non-functional expenditures into work environments, explosion of travel expenses, explosion of raining costs, unreasonable expenditures on team building activities.

Diagram (iv) visualizes targets of total budgeting in contrast to the problems described by example (ii) and (iii). Control by those accountable becomes pervasive in the enterprise and the frictions between accountability and responsibility are resolved.

4.4 Potential Savings Declaration

We still face two inter-related problems in budgetary processes that are both cost drivers, i.e., budgetary padding and hiding of savings. Budgetary padding is about intentionally overestimating costs to make it easier to achieve budgetary targets. It is usually impossible to exactly forecast costs. If admitting an underestimation is penalized harder than admitting an overestimation during the budget period, those who plan will tend to padding. If it is easier to obfuscate an overestimation than to obfuscate an underestimation, once more those who plan will tend to padding.

Hiding of savings is about the obfuscation of overestimation. It may be the result of padding or not. If admitting an overestimation is penalized, persons responsible for budget will tend to hide savings. A concrete problem may be that admitting savings may result in a decrease of budget for the next budget period. You will find this as an explicitly, i.e., admitted rule only in old-fashioned styles of budgeting in the area of fiscal or governmental accounting. Even in these areas such cameralistic approach to budgeting is considered out-dated and zerobased budgeting [21] techniques apply. However, you will still find such rules, even if not officially admitted, in budgetary planning and control system. The reason for this then might be unresolved frictions between the needs of financial accounting and management accounting in the enterprise. If savings are not the result of padding they still provoke the suspicion of padding and might be hidden for this reason.

It is very important not to mix this discussion with carryforward of unused budgets. The discussion is not about this issue. If carryforward of unused budgets are not possible in an organization, this must be simply considered a flaw.

The solution to these problems is making hidden budget padding explicit. Implicit slacks become declared potential savings. As easy as it sound it requires a rethinking of those accountable or responsible. Mechanisms must be defined how savings that are realized during the budget period are used. Rolling budgets combined with project-related flexible budgeting provide the correct technique for this purpose. We use the word project-related flexible budgeting to distinguish it from flexible budgeting in the narrow sense. Flexible budgeting which makes explicit the difference between fix costs and production-dependent variable costs is not sufficient for this purpose. Rather, a kind of over-budgeting with nice-to-have projects and expenditures as a counter-part to declared potential savings might be the correct answer.

4.5 Budgeting as a Recursive Feedback Control System

Total budgeting is about using the same techniques and tools consistently at all levels of the enterprise's hierarchy. It is about establishing budgeting as a recursive feedback control system and its tight integration with other management systems. Here is where total budgeting meets the interactive budget warehouse most obviously. Budgeting is not merely an administrative service process. It is heavily intertwined with all other management instruments. The plethora of relationships should be made subject to explicit holistic design.

5 Further Work

The appropriate approach to systematically evaluate the hypotheses of the paper, i.e., the problem statements, e.g., concerning the accountability-responsibility divide or the ERP-spreadsheet border, is to conduct surveys among persons accountable or responsible for budgeting in enterprises as well as accountants and also persons responsible for the necessary IT infrastructure.

With respect to the proposed solution we currently design a CSCW tool that combines the lightweight proven CSCW features of social software tools with spreadsheet features. In this emerging tool we will define templates that realize an interactive budget warehouse.

As theoretical further work we will review budgetary feedback control systems against the background of Stafford Beer's viable system theory [22, 23]. This way, we hope to carve out further justification, for the hypotheses stated in this paper.

6 Conclusion

We have discussed the total budgeting approach that views established management accounting approaches as crucial success factor for many organizations. As key ingredients of a total budgeting approach we would like to summarize the following:

- Commitment to the power of financial flows.
- Pervasive profit and cost awareness.
- Responsibility-accountability transcendence.
- Potential savings declaration.
- Budgeting and Accounting as recursive feedback control system.
- Tight integration with all other management systems.

We have introduced and discussed the concept of interactive budget warehousing. Interactive budget warehousing explains the aspects of establishing budgeting as a recursive feedback control system and its tight integration with other management systems. It also served as the background against which we discussed possible implementations of IT support for improved budgetary processes.

References

1. Otley, D.: Trends in budgetary control and responsibility accounting. In: Bhimani, A. (ed.) Contemporary Issues in Management Accounting, pp. 291–307. Oxford University Press, Oxford (2006)
2. Hope, J., Fraser, R.: Beyond Budgeting—How Managers Can Break Free from the Annual Performance Trap. Harvard Business Review Press, Boston (2003)
3. Mintzberg, H.: Mintzberg on Management—Inside our Strange World of Organizations. The Free Press, New York (1989)
4. Codd, E.F., Codd, S.B., Salley, C.T.: Providing OLAP to user-analysts: an IT mandate. Technical report. E.F. Codd and Associates (1993)
5. Hyperion: Hyperion System 9 BI + Interactive Reporting, release 9.0—User's Guide. Hyperion Solutions Corporation (2005)
6. Browne, D., et.al.: IBM Cognos Business Intelligence V10.1 Handbook. International Business Machines Corporation IBM, Armonk (2010)
7. Westerman, P.: DataWarehousing—Using theWal-Mart Model. Morgan Kaufmann Publishers, San Francisco (2001)
8. Hansen, S.C., Torok, R.: The Closed Loop: Implementing Activity-Based Planning and Budgeting. Bedford (2003)
9. Thalhammer, T., Schrefl, M., Mohania, M.: Active Data Warehouses: Complementing OLAP with Analysis Rules. Data Knowl. Eng. **39**, 241–269 (2001)
10. Hahn, B., Ballinger, C.: Tpump in Continuous Environment—Assembling the Teradata Active Data Warehouse Series. Active Data Warehouse Center of Expertise, NCR, Duluth (2001)
11. Draheim, D.: Business Process Technology—A Unified View on Business Processes Workflows and Enterprise Applications. Springer, Berlin (2010)

12. Draheim, D.: Smart business process management. In: Fischer, L. (ed.) BPM and Workflow Handbook, Digital Edition 2011. Future Strategies, Workflow Management Coalition, Future Strategies, Lighthouse Point (2012)
13. Weiss, R.: A Technical Overview of the Oracle Exadata Database Machine and Exadata Storage Server. Oracle White Paper. Oracle Corporation, Redwood Shores (2012)
14. Chartered Institute of Management Accountants: http://www.cimaglobal.com/ (2013)
15. Bhimani, A.: Contemporary Issues in Management Accounting, pp. 291–307. Oxford University Press, Oxford (2006)
16. Maier, R., Hdrich, T., Peinl, R.: Enterprise Knowledge Infrastructure. Springer, Heidelberg (2005)
17. Nonaka, I., Takeuch, H.: The Knowledge-Creating Company—how Japanese Companies Create the Dynamics of Innovation. Oxford University Press, Oxford (1995)
18. Deming, W.E.: Out of the Crisis. MIT, Center for Advanced Educational Services, Cambridge (1982)
19. Jensen, M.C., Meckling, W.H.: Theory of the Firm—Managerial Behavior, Agency Costs and Ownership Structure. J. Financ. Econ. **3**(4), 305–360 (1976)
20. Ashby, W.R.: Requisite variety and its implications for the control of complex systems. Cybernetica **1**(2), 83–91 (1958)
21. Nevada Legislative Counsel Bureau: Zero-Base Budgeting. Nevada Legislative Counsel Bureau Office of Research Background Paper, no. 2 (1997)
22. Beer, S.: The Heart of Enterprise: Companion Volume to—The Brain of the Firm. Wiley, London (1994)
23. Beer, S.: The Brain of the Firm: Companion Volume to—The Heart of Enterprise. Wiley, Chichester (1994)

Part XI
Selection and Customization

Customization of On-Demand ERP Software Using SAP Business ByDesign as an Example

Karl Kurbel and Dawid Nowak

Abstract This paper examines customization features of on-demand ERP systems. Special attention is given to SAP Business ByDesign, as an example of an on-demand ERP system. Customization requirements in general and options available for this system are discussed. Business ByDesign supports four major approaches to customization, namely parameterization, adaptation and personalization, functional extensions and enterprise application integration. The tools supporting these approaches are outlined. Our discussion shows that customizing features for on-demand ERP are more limited than the features available for on-premise systems, but on the other hand, innovative approaches not available for conventional systems are provided.

1 Importance of Customizing ERP Software

Customizing an ERP system means adapting the software to the needs of the enterprise that plans to use it. Nowadays, customizing is an inherent element of ERP implementation. However, the need to adapt and extend the ERP system does not end with the end of the implementation project, but continues throughout the entire lifecycle.

With on-demand ERP solutions becoming available on the market, customization has changed. While in the past, customizing meant adapting a system that is installed on-premise, today's on-demand systems are typically installed outside the company's borders and increasingly, "in the cloud". This has consequences for what can and what cannot be customized.

K. Kurbel (✉) · D. Nowak
European University Viadrina Frankfurt, Frankfurt (Oder), Germany
e-mail: wi-sek@europa-uni.de

This paper investigates the customization of current on-demand ERP systems and evaluates how extensively customization tasks can be performed within the given software architecture. The presented analysis should contribute to systemizing current customization methods and to developing novel, more flexible customization approaches.

This paper is organized as follows. In the next section, the different approaches to customizing an on-demand ERP system and customizing an on-premise ERP system are outlined. Section 3 focuses on general customization tasks and gives an overview of the approaches supported by SAP Business ByDesign, an on-demand ERP system offered by SAP AG and targeting the SME market. In Sect. 3, we investigate in more detail the features available to customize Business ByDesign. Section 4 concludes the paper with a summary and outlook to future research.

2 Customizing ERP-as-a-Service

2.1 Integrating Customization into ERP-as-a-Service

On-demand ERP is today considered a type of software-as-a-service (SaaS). In this context, *ERP-as-a-service* (*ERPaaS*) means a type of ERP software provided as a collection of services to the ERP vendor's customers. In contrast to on-premise ERP systems, the users of ERPaaS share a common software and hardware infrastructure, which is managed by the service provider [1].

The downside to ERP-as-a-service is that it is difficult to customize to the individual company's needs. Because a single ERP instance is shared, every change made to this instance, in particular to the application's source code, would affect all tenants simultaneously.

To overcome this problem, developers of ERPaaS systems are moving from customization based on code changes to extending the system's configurability with the help of metadata [2]. In this way, customers can set the look and feel of the application according to their individual requirements.

In the case of *SAP Business ByDesign*, certain customization tools were embedded directly in the software. By doing so, SAP has made adaptations easier for the user.

2.2 Common Customization Tasks

There are many different definitions of the term customization. In this paper, customization means tailoring a standard software system to a company's individual requirements [3, p. 2]. Customizing includes adjusting, extending and modifying the software [4].

Customization of an ERP system can be divided into a series of fundamental activities. These activities have to take place so that the system will meet the organization's needs.

Common techniques for the customization of conventional on-premise systems include parameterization, user exits, application programming interfaces (APIs), changing the installed program code and developing extensions inside and outside the ERP system [5].

The preferred technique is *parameterization*, because it does not require the company to deal with the system's program code. Parameters refer to the selection of modules or business functions to be included, industry-specific and country-specific settings (e.g. currency, time zone), the organizational structure, business rules and many more aspects [5].

Adaptation and *personalization* features, beyond parameter settings, also play an important role, both in the initial installation and when the system is in use.[6, p. 30] The ability to adjust system components visually (personalization of application screen layouts) and functionally (tailoring functionality, facilitating access to often used functions) greatly influences how effectively users interact with the software.

Functional extensions—i.e. extending the system's pre-prepared functionality—include developing additional functions as well as creating company-specific reports, generating custom information structures, and modeling custom business workflows and procedures [7].

Although an ERP system covers all major business areas, it usually needs to cooperate with other application systems the company has in place. Therefore, enabling *enterprise application integration* (*EAI*) [5] is another crucial customization task. The goal is here to allow different systems to smoothly work together—especially when it comes to internal data exchange, but also in the collaboration with customers and suppliers.

On-demand software requires a different customization approach than methods used by conventional on-premise systems, since on-demand software is shared by many companies.

2.3 Customizing SAP Business ByDesign

In order to allow for continuous adaptation, SAP Business ByDesign offers a wide spectrum of solutions based on the idea of "continuous system engineering" [6, p. 201]. These solutions are intended to make customizing more systematic, thereby maintaining system integrity and flexibility in the face of prospective upgrades.

One such solution is adding built-in customization tools, which are available as a part of the so-called *Key User Tools*. A key user is an expert who specializes in ERP solutions and has more access rights than a typical ERP end user. He or she can implement predefined solutions in the production environment by selecting certain options from a "business adaptation catalog" (e.g. industry-specific functions, features). Customization tasks as distinguished by SAP and tools supporting these tasks will be discussed in more detail in the next section.

3 Customization Tasks Supported by SAP Business ByDesign

3.1 Parameterization

To simplify the configuration task, Business ByDesign provides an automated parameterization process with integrated customer decision support, guiding a key user through the process steps [8].

The process is supported by *configuration tools*. Solution capabilities based on industry experience and knowledge have been integrated into these tools.

Since every enterprise has different requirements, the user must answer a series of questions so that the system can be adapted to the needs of the business. This series of decisions determines the elements and content of a system to be customized to a particular business.

To be able to keep the system up-to-date with current business needs, a key user may change the initial business configuration at any time, even in the post-implementation phase. This includes changes to the business adaptation catalog that the SDK is applied to [6, pp. 222–226, 8].

Changes in the company's organization and/or procedures that stimulate customization activities may lead to changes involving data structures. Adaptive tools performing these tasks are also available as part of the Key User Tools.

3.2 Adaptation and Personalization

Built-in *personalization tools* (a part of the Key User Tools) are used to make standard alterations to the system, including system settings, navigation settings and changes to the layout of individual screens and functional areas [9]. Key users have administrative rights within the system, allowing them to make advanced adaptations for the entire company, based on their expertise.

Personalization tools are available not only during the initial implementation phase, but also throughout the entire software lifecycle. They allow screen layout modifications, resituating screen elements, and activation/deactivation and relabeling of fields and screen sections [9]. Experts using Key User Tools can also define the order of fields and adapt the way in which tables are displayed.

Customization of On-Demand ERP Software Using SAP Business ByDesign   293

Fig. 1 Adaptation of start screen layout

An example of a personalized screen layout is presented in Fig. 1. The screenshot in the background shows the default Business ByDesign start screen. This screen was customized by setting a different background image and adding two reports and a clock. Whenever the system is started, the reports and the clock will be displayed based on current data.

More adaption options provided by the Key User Tools include creating additional functional areas (called "work centers") in the Business ByDesign environment, adjusting the naming conventions to the terminology used by the enterprise [7], and managing business tasks (i.e. defining new tasks, clarifying requests, managing alerts and notifications) without interrupting business workflows [10]. Furthermore, Key User Tools can be applied to create additional fields on the user interface and to include pre-configured third-party applications to allow users to access external data and services [6, p. 205].

Personalized screen components that are not predefined in the standard system can be created by a key user with the help of the SDK.

3.3 Functional Extensions

In addition to the adaptation options outlined in the previous section, Business ByDesign allows key users to expand the software's functionality. This can be done using three different approaches: extension tools, SAP Business ByDesign Studio and SAP Store.

The *first option* is to use built-in *extension tools* to adopt application elements according to the customer's needs. Key users can employ these tools, for example, to define standardized form templates using the company's corporate design. The templates can then be applied to create PDF documents or standard e-mails [11]. The extension tools also allow customers to create their own reports, data sources and key performance indicators [12].

Key User Tools also allow the creation of company-specific content, which can be used as learning material in the Learning Center, or as instructions in the Help Center. This content is available for all end users [13].

The *second option*, targeting extensions of the main application backend, involves the use of *Business ByDesign Studio*. This is an integrated development environment (IDE) based on Microsoft Visual Studio. It allows the user to create company-specific objects and object screens, and to implement any business logic according to the company's requirements [7].

The *third option* is to buy extensions from the *SAP Store* [14]. This is an electronic marketplace where customers can find and purchase solutions complementary to the core Business ByDesign application. While the built-in tools allow custom-ization only within certain limits, solutions from the SAP Store can add any kind of functionality.

The store allows users to search for add-ons developed by SAP or by SAP partners, and also to test whether the extensions are compatible with their system before purchasing [6, p. 212, 15].

Because the add-ons provided through the SAP Store use built-in expansion points and do not alter the Business ByDesign source code, future upgrades to the system core are less likely to violate the integrity of an individual user's software configuration.

3.4 Enterprise Application Integration

Internet-based business-process and data integration between business partners (business-to-business) is a core element of Business ByDesign [6, pp. 84–85]. This integration also simplifies the collaboration between subsidiaries and company headquarters using SAP ERP [16].

There are two ways that businesses can collaborate with each other through Business ByDesign: through interactive forms and through messages in XML format [17]. Both communication methods can be adapted using Business

ByDesign Studio to meet the requirements of a collaborative business process. A key user may, for example, develop company-specific interactive forms and define custom input scenarios to import third-party data into SAP business objects [18].

Additional integration mechanisms can be developed using Business ByDesign Studio or purchased from the SAP Store [6, p. 211]. The software environment Business ByDesign is embedded in allows for flexibility as to including additional services and applications needed for the company's business processes. It allows key users to compose highly customized interfaces, including individual interface elements and composition themes, with the help of built-in tools and the SDK [9].

Today, many users require access to external, web-based data sources and programs for their work. Key users can integrate these data and programs into Business ByDesign through composition. SAP enables web services (e.g. Twitter, Google Maps etc.) to be embedded directly into the system environment [16] and data sources on the Internet to be accessed through mashups [6, p. 304, 9].

As mobile devices are playing an increasingly important role for business users, an objective in the development of Business ByDesign was to support a wide variety of devices and platforms. By applying solutions based on design patterns [3, pp. 291–297], Business ByDesign Studio allows key users to freely create user interfaces, reports and forms that can be adapted to most output devices [6, pp. 57–60].

4 Summary and Outlook

This paper discussed customizing needs and options offered by on-demand ERP systems. As an example, the features available to customize SAP Business ByDesign were examined.

Our discussion showed that, on the one hand, the possibilities for customizing an on-demand system are less comprehensive than the possibilities available for a conventional on-premise system. Limitations include, for example, the creation of new business processes and simultaneous data exchange with other business applications. On the other hand, there is a variety of modern con-figuration and composition options, going beyond the current state-of-the-art of ERP customization. Examples include web services and mashups on the user's interface, a simpler configuration mechanism using a business adaptation catalog, and enhancing the system by external solutions from the SAP Store.

Many fine-tuning tasks can be solved ad-hoc, with the help of built-in tools. More sophisticated changes require the use of the SDK (Business ByDesign Studio). These changes also do not interfere with the main source code, thereby minimizing the risk of integrity problems in future upgrades.

Most customization limitations are connected with the software architecture, and therefore affect all on-demand solutions. Because on-demand ERP systems are installed outside the company, advanced modifications can be performed only within certain limits and using dedicated software. The multitenant architecture of the on-demand solution also raises data privacy and data security issues.

An innovative option to extend the standard ERP functionality is the SAP Store. By introducing this platform and making the SDK available to customers, SAP involves not only their partners, but also their customers in Business ByDesign customization and expansion. This marks a significant change in the way how customizing business software is approached.

The shift of focus in customization, as it shows in Business ByDesign, leads to more flexibility, less need for additional programming and thus lower customization cost.

Business ByDesign is only one of the on-demand solutions on the market. The analysis of customization possibilities offered by other on-demand ERP system vendors will be a subject of future research. This and future analyses are important contributions to the development of a more flexible approach to ERP customization.

References

1. Chong, F., Carraro, G.: Architecture strategies for catching the long tail. http://msdn.microsoft.com/en-us/library/aa479069.aspx
2. Sun, W., Zhang, C., Guo, C.J., Su, H.: Software as a service: configuration and customization perspectives. In: 2008 IEEE Congress on Services Part II, pp. 18–25. IEEE Press (2008)
3. Kurbel, K.E.: The Making of Information Systems—Software Engineering and Management in a Globalized World. Springer, Berlin (2008)
4. Haines, M.N.: Understanding enterprise system customization: an exploration of implementation realities and the key influence factors. Inf. Syst. Manag. **2**, 182–198 (2009)
5. Kurbel, K.E.: Enterprise Resource Planning and Supply Chain Management—Functions, Business Processes and Software for Manufacturing Companies. Springer, Berlin (2013)
6. Hufgard, A., Krüger, S.: SAP Business ByDesign Geschäftsprozesse, Technologie und Implementierung anschaulich erklärt. SAP Press, Bonn (2012)
7. Zinow, R.: SAP on the cloud—SAP Business ByDesign: flexibility & extensibility. http://blogs.sap.com/cloud/2012/03/22/sap-business-bydesign-flexibility-extensibility/
8. SAP AG.: SAP Business ByDesign business configuration. http://help.sap.com/saphelp_byd30/en/KTP/Software-Components/01200615320100003379/SAP_BBD/Print_Files/PDF_FILES/BusinessConfiguration_BA_en.pdf
9. SAP AG.: Personalization quick guide. http://help.sap.com/saphelp_byd35/en/KTP/Software-Components/01200615320100003379/WEKTRA_for_Work_Centers/CROSS_TOPICS/PERSONALIZATION/EndUser_Personalization/VQG_Personalization.html
10. SAP AG.: Business task management. http://help.sap.com/saphelp_byd35/en/KTP/Software-Components/01200615320100003379/WEKTRA_for_Work_Centers/CROSS_TOPICS/BTM_CONTENT/Essentials/Ess_Con_BTM.html
11. SAP AG.: Forms. http://help.sap.com/saphelp_byd35/en/KTP/Software-Components/01200615320100003379/WEKTRA_for_Work_Centers/CROSS_TOPICS/OUTPUT/forms/ESS_CON_Forms.html
12. SAP AG.: Analytics. http://help.sap.com/saphelp_byd40/en/KTP/Software-Components/01200615320100003379/SAP_BBD/SAP_BBD.html

13. SAP AG.: Company-specific learning and help content quick guide. http://help.sap.com/saphelp_byd40/en/KTP/Software-Components/01200615320100003379/SAP_BBD/SAP_BBD.html
14. Faisst, W.: Die nächste Generation der Unternehmens-Software am Beispiel von SAP Business ByDesign. Wirtschaftsinformatik & Management **4**, 24–30 (2011)
15. Wenzel, S., Faisst, W., Burkard, C., Buxmann, P.: New sales and buying models in the internet: app store model for enterprise application software. In: Mattfeld, D.C., Robra-Bissantz, S. (eds.) Multikonferenz Wirtschaftsinformatik 2012—Tagungsband der MKWI 2012, pp. 639–651. Braunschweig, GITO Verlag (2012)
16. SAP AG.: SAP Business ByDesign for subsidiaries. http://www.sapbydesign.com/_resources/SAP_Business_ByDesign_for_Subsidiaries.pdf
17. Hufgard, A., Legner, C., Winkelmann, A.: B2B-Geschäftsszenarien mit der Cloud-Lösung SAP. In: Hofmann, G.R., Alm, W. (Hrsg.) Beratungskonzepte für Cloud Computing—Trends im Software- und Servicemarkt, Tagungsband zum Fachgespräch im Rahmen der MKWI 2012, pp. 23–39. Aschaffenburg (2012)
18. Schneider, T.: External integration of custom solutions in SAP Business ByDesign/SAP Sales OnDemand. http://scn.sap.com/docs/DOC-27476

Index

A
Analysis patterns, 138
ASAP methodology, 107, 110–112

B
Best of breed, 11
Beyond budgeting, 272
Bill of material, 253
Browser-based clients, 2
Business intelligence, 2
Business management, 1
Business processes, 1, 2
Business process management, 202, 209

C
Capacity planning, 32, 40, 42, 48
Challenges, 20, 22, 24, 26
Cloud computing, 171, 202, 205, 206, 209
Cloud services, 134, 136
CogNIAM, 53, 58, 60, 64, 66
Cost-benefit analysis, 2, 144, 145
Cross-functional team collaboration, 116
Customers, 9, 10
Customizing, 289–291, 295

D
Data quality, 236
Data synchronization, 212
Decision making, 272, 274, 277
Decision support systems, 154
Dedicated clients, 2, 14, 13, 23
Desktop virtualization, 205, 210

Distributed object computing, 205, 212

E
E-learning, 87–90, 92, 98
End user training (EUT), 87, 88, 98
Enterprise content management, 19, 20
Enterprise resource planning (ERP), 1, 2, 9–11, 31–36, 43, 44, 103–105, 107, 153–155, 158, 160, 166, 167, 183–187, 190–195, 235, 236, 239, 240, 247, 248
Enterprise resource planning systems, 143
ERP^{III}, 11
ERP-as-a-service, 290
ERP benefit, 116
ERP implementation, 171, 172, 174, 178
ERP landscape management
ERP system, 2, 4, 7, 12–16, 18, 54, 57

F
Fact-based modelling, 58, 59, 62, 64

G
Government, 183–185, 187, 190, 191, 194
GUI, 144, 147

I
Implementation, 103, 105, 107, 183, 184, 186, 187, 189–191, 193–195
Information systems, 1, 20
Information system success, 87, 92
Integration project, 116–118, 125, 126

L
Lean ERP, 16
Lean management, 13–16, 18
Lot sizing, 42, 47, 48

M
Management accounting, 271, 272, 279, 285
Manufacturing, 32–36, 39, 41, 42, 44, 47–49
Master plan, 39, 40, 43
Material planning, 256, 265
Material requirements scheduling, 40
Mobile computing, 203
MRP, 32, 41
MRP II, 31–34, 39, 43, 49

N
NASA's task load index, 1

O
Object-relation mapping, 204
On-demand ERP, 289, 290, 295, 296

P
Post-implementation change, 126
Potential, 20–22, 24–26
Production planning, 254–256, 258, 259, 263, 267
Project success, 183–185, 187, 194

R
RDP, 45, 50
Real-time data warehousing, 272, 277–278
Renewable resources, 254–258, 261, 265, 267
Requirements-based testing, 220, 221, 223, 231
Requirements determination, 53–57, 65
Requirements elicitation, 56
Requirements engineering, 221
Rolling detail planning, 31, 45, 49, 50

S
SaaS, 131, 133, 134, 136, 173
SaaS implementation, 172, 174–176, 180
SAP business bydesign, 290–292, 294, 295
Semantic verification, 56–58, 62, 65
Service oriented architecture, 205
Social content management, 20
Software engineering, 211, 236
Software metrics, 236, 241
Software quality, 145, 148, 149
State owned company, 110, 112
System dynamics, 154
System testing, 220, 221

T
Team interdependence, 117, 124–126
Test automation tool, 147, 148, 150
Test case prioritization, 221, 227, 228, 231, 232
TLX, 1, 4, 14
Total Planning System (TPS), 46
Toyota Production System (TPS), 13

U
Uncertainty, 254–256, 263, 265, 267

V
Value-based testing, 221, 222, 227, 231, 232
Vendors, 9–11

W
Work schedule, 263–266
Workflow management, 201, 202, 212, 213